THINKING CRITICALLY ABOUT ETHICAL ISSUES

EIGHTH EDITION

VINCENT RYAN RUGGIERO

Professor Emeritus
State University of New York, Delhi

Mc Graw Hill

Connect
Learn
Succeed™

THINKING CRITICALLY ABOUT ETHICAL ISSUES, EIGHTH EDITION

Published by McGraw-Hill, a business unit of The McGraw-Hill Companies, Inc.,
1221 Avenue of the Americas, New York, NY 10020. Copyright © 2012 by The McGraw-Hill
Companies, Inc. All rights reserved. Previous editions © 2008, 2006 and 2005. No part of this
publication may be reproduced or distributed in any form or by any means, or stored in a
database or retrieval system, without the prior written consent of The McGraw-Hill Companies,
Inc., including, but not limited to, in any network or other electronic storage or transmission, or
broadcast for distance learning.

Some ancillaries, including electronic and print components, may not be available to customers
outside the United States.

This book is printed on acid-free paper.

1 2 3 4 5 6 7 8 9 0 DOC/DOC 1 0 9 8 7 6 5 4 3 2 1

ISBN: 978-0-07-353590-6
MHID: 0-07-353590-7

Vice President & Editor-in-Chief: *Michael Ryan*
Vice President EDP/Central Publishing Services: *Kimberly Meriwether David*
Editorial Director: *Beth Mejia*
Sponsoring Editor: *Mark Georgiev*
Executive Marketing Manager: *Pamela S. Cooper*
Managing Editor: *Meghan Campbell*
Senior Project Manager: *Joyce Watters*
Design Coordinator: *Margarite Reynolds*
Buyer: *Nicole Baumgartner*
Media Project Manager: *Sridevi Palani*
Compositor: *Glyph International*
Typeface: *10/13 Palatino*
Printer: *R.R. Donnelley*

All credits appearing on page or at the end of the book are considered to be an extension of the
copyright page.

Library of Congress Cataloging-in-Publication Data

Ruggiero, Vincent Ryan.
Thinking critically about ethical issues / Vincent Ryan
   Ruggiero. —8th ed.
     p.   cm.
     Includes index.
     ISBN 978-0-07-353590-6 (alk. paper)
     1. Ethics. I. Title.
BJ1012.R82 2011
170—dc22   2010039685

www.mhhe.com

To the memory of Vincent V. Ruggiero, my father,
Filomena Ruggiero, my grandmother, Francis and
Michael Ruggiero, my uncles, and Edith and Bernhard
Theisselmann, my "extra parents," whose quiet
lessons and example first introduced
me to the subject of this book.

⌐ PREFACE ⌐

No introductory textbook can do complete justice to the subject of ethics. The best it can do is to help students develop a basic competency in ethical analysis and acquire a measure of confidence in their judgment; it should also stimulate enough interest in the subject that they will want to continue learning about it, formally or informally, when the final chapter is completed and the course is over. Even that relatively modest aim is difficult to achieve. The author must strike the right balance between the theoretical and the practical, between breadth and depth of treatment, and between rigor and relevance, so that students are challenged but not daunted.

This book is based on several specific ideas about how that crucial balance is best achieved:

> *The emphasis should be on DOING ethics rather than on studying the history of ethics.* This does not mean that students should not become familiar with historical developments and the contributions of great ethicists. It means that more attention should be given to applying ethical principles to specific cases; that is, to conducting ethical analysis. This approach, which Alfred North Whitehead termed an emphasis on principles rather than details (and which he proposed as the standard for all education), is the same approach that many educators are recommending to promote the development of critical thinking skills in philosophy, the social sciences, and the humanities.

> *Careful attention should be given to overcoming students' intellectual impediments to ethical analysis.* Today's students have been exposed to numerous misconceptions about ethical analysis—indeed, about thinking in general. For example, it is fashionable today to regard all value judgments as undemocratic. This fashion has led many students to the belief that whatever one *feels* is right is by that very fact right. Even when they manage to avoid that notion, many students adopt other erroneous notions—for instance, that the majority view is necessarily the best view or that morality is a religious matter only, without any secular dimension. Unless students get beyond such crippling notions, their efforts at ethical analysis are unlikely to be effective and meaningful.

The fundamental concerns in ethical analysis should be presented first, and more complex concerns reserved, wherever possible, until later. This may seem too obvious to state. Yet it is a consideration that many textbooks in ethics ignore. Such textbooks present a concept in detail, with all the conflicting interpretations of it that have been advanced by various ethical schools. This conflicting information can paralyze students' efforts. Instead of applying the concept in their work, as the authors intend, students often think, "If the experts disagree, how can I be expected to make sense of this?" The time for identifying complexities is after students have been introduced to the basic concepts and have become comfortable applying them in their analyses.

SPECIAL FEATURES OF THIS BOOK

The influence of the foregoing ideas accounts for certain features that distinguish this book from other texts. The most significant of these features are the following.

ORGANIZATION

The history of ethics and the contributions of great ethicists are presented at the end of the book (in Chapter 12) rather than at the beginning or throughout. This arrangement reflects the author's experience that most introductory students learn ethical analysis better when they are not burdened with names and dates and details of ethical systems. Showing students how Plato, Kant, and Mill approached an ethical issue and then asking them to analyze an issue themselves is very much like showing them a professional athlete performing and then saying, "Now, let's see how you perform." Both situations are intimidating; students are put in a competitive situation in which they cannot compete. In ethics, as in sports, it is better to postpone introducing students to "the professionals" until they have gained a little experience and confidence.

This format does not diminish the importance of ethical history. On the contrary, students are better able to appreciate and remember historical contributions after they have grappled with problems themselves and pondered the question of how to judge them. (In cases where course syllabi require that historical material be presented first, instructors can begin with Chapter 12 and then proceed with Chapters 1, 2, and so on.)

CHAPTER LENGTH

Short chapters allow students to spend less time reading and underlining and more time analyzing ethical issues. More conscientious students gain an additional benefit from the brevity of the chapters. These students are able to read each chapter more than once and thereby master the material better than they would with a long chapter.

APPENDIX ON WRITING

Today's students often arrive at college without the English proficiency that instructors expect them to have. The guide to writing included in this text can save instructors time and effort. Instead of trying to teach rhetorical skills during class or in conferences with students, instructors need only direct students to the Appendix. Students, too, benefit by being able to break the common cycle of submitting poor papers, getting poor grades, becoming frustrated, losing interest, and blaming the instructor. By knowing what is expected in their analyses of issues and, more important, how to provide it, they can devote more attention to the mastery and application of ethical principles.

The correction symbols noted in the Appendix can be used to make the evaluation of papers faster and more effective. If a paper is lacking in both coherence and development, the instructor need write nothing more than the appropriate abbreviation. Students will be able to turn to the appropriate sections of the Appendix, see what errors they have committed, and note how to avoid those errors in the future.

CHANGES IN THE EIGHTH EDITION

In preparing the eighth edition, I have been guided by the suggestions of instructors who have used previous editions. The changes in this edition are as follows:

> In Chapter 1, a section on "Evaluating Your Internet Sources" has been added.

> Timely inquiries have been added throughout the book. The subjects include open borders, the "redistribution of wealth," the replacement of unions' secret balloting with "card check," the rationing of health care, free trade versus fair trade, and organ transplantation.

> In Chapter 7, a new case has been added to illustrate the basic moral criteria. The case concerns the events leading to the U.S. financial crisis of 2007 and thereafter.

STANDARD FORMAT VERSUS ALTERNATIVES

The standard format is based on the author's experience that investing sufficient time to overcome misconceptions and build a sound philosophical perspective pays dividends in student learning. This format entails following the chapter order at a fairly leisurely pace, with more time devoted to examining the inquiries and forming/sharing judgments than to reading. Accordingly, in a fifteen-week semester course, approximately one week would be spent on each chapter, perhaps slightly more than that on Chapters 6–10. In this format enough time would remain for students to do an extended analysis of one or maybe two issues from "Contemporary Ethical Controversies."

For any one of several good reasons, of course, an instructor may wish to adjust this format. The following adaptations can be made with relative ease.

ALTERNATIVE 1

Situation: Students have already had some training in critical thinking and, in the instructor's view, will be able to master the material in Section I relatively quickly.

Approach: Devote one class period and one homework assignment to each chapter in Section I—that is, to each of Chapters 1–5. Allocate the remaining thirteen weeks to Chapters 6–12 and "Contemporary Ethical Controversies."

ALTERNATIVE 2

Situation: Students have already had *considerable* training in critical thinking or have otherwise achieved an unusual level of intellectual sophistication.

Approach: Make Chapters 1–5 *a single reading assignment,* with either no inquiries or only a few selected ones. Devote the remainder of the course to Chapters 6–12 and "Contemporary Ethical Controversies," focusing on individual and/or group analysis and discussion of the inquiries, perhaps involving the preparation of a term paper and/or formal debates toward the end of the course.

ALTERNATIVE 3

Situation: In the instructor's judgment, giving students a historical perspective at the outset of the course will enhance the learning experience.

Approach: Have students read Chapter 12, "A Perspective on History," and address its inquiry at the very beginning of the course. Then proceed with the other chapters, following either the standard format or one of the other alternatives.

A NOTE ON STUDENT FRUSTRATION

The approach used in the early chapters of this book will be frustrating to some students. They will ask, "If it's not feelings and not majority opinion that decide the morality of an action, then what is it? Why doesn't the author tell us?" This reaction is a reflection of students' prior classroom conditioning. They expect textbooks to provide neat answers that can be swallowed and then regurgitated on a test. When asked to think, to reason out for themselves the best answers to moral problems, they naturally become anxious for a time because the activity is unfamiliar.

Whenever your students ask, "What *does* decide the morality of an action?" you will know that their minds have become engaged in the subject, that they are seeing the need for a standard (other than feelings, for example) and are struggling to define it. By the time the book suggests the criteria of judgment (Chapter 7), students will be ready to learn and apply those criteria. Many, in fact, will already have anticipated the criteria in their own analyses of problems. Without realizing it, they will have been *doing* ethics.

ACKNOWLEDGMENTS

I am grateful to all who had a part in the making of this book. We would like to extend special thanks to those who reviewed the manuscript for this edition:

Sarah Whedon, *Newbury College*
Rebecca Neagle, *Wake Technical Community College*
Christine Hollermann, *Alexandria Technical College*
Ira Breskin, *U.S. Merchant Marine Academy at Kings Point, NY*
Robert Friedenbach, *Colorado Technical University, Sioux Falls*
Matthew Mangum, *St. Mary's University*
Gail Joralemon, *Central New Mexico Community College*
Tom Riley, *Wake Technical Community College*

Thanks also go to James Brooks, *Bethune-Cookman College;* Ernie Collamati, *Regis College;* Elizabeth M. Hodge, *Gavilan College;* Steve Madagaria, *California State University, Fresno;* Ryan Rhodes, *University of Oklahoma;* Donald Riggs, *Wake Technical Community College;* Dan Campana, University of LaVerne; Anna Halligan, Broome Community College; Elizabeth Knight, Portland Community College; John Paige, St. Edwards University; Roselyn Schmitt, College of Saint Benedict; James A. Valovick, Northwestern Michigan College; and David F. White Jr., John Tyler Community College.

Vincent Ryan Ruggiero

Important Questions About Ethics

Why do we need ethics if we have laws to govern our behavior?

Does the majority view determine what is ethical and what is not?

Are feelings, desires, and preferences reliable ethical guides?

Can a person ever go wrong by following his or her conscience?

Is it ever appropriate to criticize another individual's ethical judgment? Another culture's?

By what criteria, if any, should the ethical quality of an action be judged?

Are the principles and rules of logic applicable to ethical reasoning?

Are people always responsible for their actions? Are there degrees of responsibility?

Do human beings have a natural tendency to good, a natural tendency to evil, both, or neither?

What is the relationship, if any, between ethics and happiness?

Is there a single moral code that is binding on all people, at all times, and in all places?

⌐ Contents ⌐

I / The Context

Chapter 1
The Need for Ethics   2

Why do we need ethics? We have laws to protect people's rights. If the laws are enforced, what need have we of further rules?

Chapter 2
The Role of the Majority View   24

Is the basis for deciding moral values the majority view? In other words, if the majority of the citizens of our country should decide that a particular action is right, would that very decision make the action right?

Chapter 3
The Role of Feelings   31

If the majority view does not determine the rightness of an action, should each person decide on the basis of her or his own feelings, desires, preferences?

Chapter 4
The Role of Conscience   40

If feelings are no better a guide than the majority view, is the basis of morality each person's own conscience? How trustworthy is conscience?

CHAPTER 10

CONSIDERING CONSEQUENCES   **122**

How do we deal with cases in which the consequences are not neatly separable into good and bad, but are mixed?

CHAPTER 11

DETERMINING MORAL RESPONSIBILITY   **134**

How do we determine whether a person is responsible for her or his immoral actions? Are there degrees of responsibility?

III / THE TRADITION

CHAPTER 12

A PERSPECTIVE ON HISTORY   **144**

When did the study of ethics begin? Who were the great thinkers in the history of ethics? What contributions did they make?

IV / CONTEMPORARY ETHICAL CONTROVERSIES

THE SAME MORAL ISSUES that men and women have grappled with throughout history have grown ever more complex in a society whose structures and forms are changing. And the impressive advances of science and technology have created a host of new issues.

Yet precisely at this time, when we most need a firm intellectual foundation to guide our judgment, we are confused by countless challenges to old and familiar faiths and standards.

The outlines of our very humanity are blurred by conflicting theories.

This, then, is the moral imperative of our time— to break the bonds of indecision, move beyond fad and foolishness, and address the dilemmas of modern living sensitively and sensibly, with regard for their complexity.

I

THE CONTEXT

CHAPTER ONE

THE NEED FOR ETHICS

Why do we need ethics? We have laws to
protect people's rights. If the laws are enforced,
what need have we of further rules?

Ethics is the study of the choices people make regarding right and wrong. Each of us makes dozens of moral choices daily. Will we go to work or call in sick? Follow the research protocol or violate it? Put quotes around borrowed phrasing or pretend the words are our own? Answer a colleague's question truthfully or lie? Obey the speed laws or drive as fast as our vehicles will go? Pay our bills or spend our money on entertainment? Keep our marriage vows or break them? Meet our children's emotional needs or ignore them? Pet the cat or kick it?

In most times and places, people have acknowledged the existence of an objective moral standard binding on all people regardless of their personal desires and preferences. (Of course, there was not always complete agreement on what that standard was.) Over the past several decades, however, that need for a standard has been called into question. It is fashionable today to believe that decisions about right and wrong are purely personal and subjective. This belief is known as *moral relativism.* According to it, whatever anyone claims to be morally acceptable *is* morally acceptable, at least for that person. Supposedly, there is only one exception to this rule: Judging other people's conduct is considered intolerant. (To this author's knowledge, no moral relativist has ever explained why, if *any* view of honesty, faithfulness, fairness, and justice is considered valid, only *one* view of tolerance is permitted.)

In the 1960s moral relativists challenged the traditional view that fornication and adultery are immoral. "Only the individual can decide what sexual behavior is right for him or her," they said, "and the individual's decision should be respected." Given the mood of the time (and the strength of the sex drive), it was not surprising that many people were disposed to accept this view. Critics raised serious objections, of course. They argued that even the wisest among us are capable of error and self-deception, especially where the emotions are involved. They predicted that the idea that everyone creates his or her own sexual morality would spill over into other areas of morality and provide an excuse for everything from petty pilfering, plagiarism, and perjury to child molesting, rape, spouse abuse, and murder.

More important for our purposes, the critics of relativism warned that "anything goes" thinking would undermine the subject of ethics. "If morality is merely a matter of preference, and no one view is better than any other," they reasoned, "then there is no way to distinguish good from evil or civilized behavior from uncivilized, and any attempt at meaningful discussion of moral issues is futile." Centuries earlier, Dr. Samuel Johnson saw the more personal implications in relativism and remarked, "If he does really think that there is no distinction between virtue and vice, why, sir, when he leaves our houses let us count our spoons."

At the time, relativists dismissed the predictions of the critics as irresponsible. Now, however, four decades later, we can see that those predictions were at least in part accurate. Evidence that civility has declined and human life has become cheapened can be found any day in the news. (To what extent relativism is responsible for this development is, of course, debatable.) Equally significant, many people are so possessed by the "Who can say?" mentality that they find it difficult to pass moral judgment on even the most heinous deeds.

One professor of philosophy estimates that between 10 and 20 percent of his students can't bring themselves to say that the killing of millions of people in the Holocaust was wrong. He calls this phenomenon "absolutophobia," the fear of saying unequivocally that certain behavior is unethical. Another professor reports that her students are reluctant to judge even so obvious a moral issue as *human sacrifice*! Speaking of one student who refused to say such sacrifice was wrong, the professor writes, "I was stunned. This was the [same] woman who wrote so passionately of saving the whales, of concern for the rain forests, of her rescue and tender care of a stray dog."[1]

As almost any ethics instructor will confirm, when it comes to more subtle issues—such as unauthorized copying of computer programs or plagiarism—the number of people who cannot bring themselves to make a moral judgment increases significantly. Such individuals may regard ethics as intrusive.

Why Do We Need Ethics If We Have Laws?

Many people reason that we don't need ethics because our system of laws, when consistently enforced, provides sufficient protection of our rights. In order to assess this idea we must understand who makes laws and how they make them. Who makes them is easy to answer: local, state, and national legislators. How they are made is somewhat more difficult. We know that legislators must get together to talk about a particular behavior and then vote on whether they want to criminalize it. But what do they say to one another? On what basis do they conclude that one act deserves to be classified criminal and another one doesn't? What kinds of reasons do they offer to support their views? How can they be sure those reasons are good ones?

What, for example, did legislators say before they decided that sexual harassment is illegal? Certainly something more than "I wouldn't commit such an act." The fact that two or ten or five hundred legislators expressed that personal view would not be sufficient reason to conclude that a law should be passed preventing *other people* from committing the act. Remember that according to relativism no one has any business criticizing other people's moral decisions. If that principle is valid, then the sexual harasser should be free to follow his or her preference. The only rational basis for a law against sexual harassment is that the act is *wrong*, not just for those who think so but for *everyone*. The proper focus for lawmakers is not on their subjective preferences but on the nature of the actions in question.

Why do we need ethics if we have laws? Because law is not possible without ethics. The only way for a law to be enacted or repealed is for one or more people to make a decision about right and wrong. That has always been true, whether the lawmaker was the chieftain of a nomadic band or tribe, a king or queen, or a group of elected officials.

If human beings were wise enough to create one set of laws that would last for all time, we might say that ethical judgment was once important but no longer is. Alas, humans are not that wise. New circumstances arise and laws must be revised to fit them. In addition, new insights sometimes reveal that a law punishes behavior that does not deserve punishment or makes unreasonable demands on people. The Eighteenth Amendment to the U.S. Constitution made Prohibition the law of the land—until the Twenty-first Amendment repealed it in the name of justice. Members of the Amish religious community, whose way of life called for less formal schooling than the law prescribed, were judged criminals for withdrawing their children from school—until the U.S. Supreme Court declared the application of the law to them unjust. In New York State, rape victims were required to prove they had given "earnest resistance" to the rapist—until the state legislature removed that unreasonable provision from the law.

ETHICS DEFINED

Ethics, as we noted, is the study of right and wrong conduct. Let us expand on that definition. In the scientific sense, ethics is a descriptive discipline, involving the collection and interpretation of data on what people from various cultures believe, without any consideration for the appropriateness or reasonableness of those beliefs. In the philosophical sense, the sense that concerns us, ethics is a two-sided discipline. One side, *normative ethics,* answers specific moral questions, determining what is reasonable and therefore what people should believe. (The term *normative* means setting norms, or guidelines.) The other side of philosophical ethics, *metaethics,* examines ethical systems to appraise their logical foundations and internal consistency.

The focus of ethics is moral situations—that is, *those situations in which there is a choice of behavior involving human values* (those qualities that are regarded as good and desirable). Thus, whether we watch TV at a friend's house or at our own is not a moral issue. But whether we watch TV at a friend's house without his or her knowledge and approval is a moral issue. Similarly, filling out an application for a job is a morally neutral act. But deciding whether to tell the truth on the application is a moral issue. An ethicist observes the choices people make in various moral situations and draws conclusions about those choices. An ethical system is a set of coherent ideas that result from those conclusions and form an overall moral perspective.

Ethicists are not lawmakers. They are neither elected nor appointed. Their only authority is the force of reasonableness in their judgments. Their words, unlike those of lawmakers, do not prescribe what must or must not be done. They merely suggest what *ought* to be done. If people violate their own or their society's moral code, no ethics enforcement officer will try to apprehend them—though if their action also violates a law, a law enforcement agency may do so.

Law enforcement, of course, extends beyond apprehension of alleged criminals. It includes the formal trial and judgment of guilt or innocence. There are, as well, degrees of guilt. A person who carries out a carefully planned murder is charged with a more serious crime than is a person who strikes and kills another in spontaneous, blind rage. In fact, if the individual in the latter case is judged to have been insane, he or she may go entirely unpunished.

The idea of varying degrees of responsibility for one's actions is applied in ethics, too. Although there are no courts of ethics as there are courts of law, and no formal pronouncements of guilt or innocence in moral matters, the ethicist nevertheless is interested in the question "Under what circumstances is a person to be considered culpable?" The conclusions ethicists reach in these matters provide guidance to lawmakers and law enforcers.

ETHICS AND RELIGIOUS BELIEF

Somehow the idea has arisen that ethics and religion are unrelated and incompatible. Thus, when religious thinkers discuss ethical issues—especially in the context of political policy—they are thought to be exceeding their reach and perhaps even committing an offense against the principle of separation of church and state. This notion is without historical basis. In fact, an interesting case can be made for ethics having *originated* in religion. G. K. Chesterton, for example, argued as follows:

> Morality did not begin by one man saying to another, "I will not hit you if you do not hit me"; there is no trace of such a transaction. There is a trace of both men having said, "We must not hit each other in the holy place." They gained their morality by guarding their religion. They did not cultivate courage. They fought for the shrine, and found they had become courageous. They did not cultivate cleanliness. They purified themselves for the altar, and found that they were clean.[2]

Throughout our civilization's history, religious thinkers have spoken to the larger society on moral issues, and society has generally profited from their guidance. Problems arise only when religious leaders go beyond speaking *to* society and begin speaking *for* it on the basis of their particular doctrines. To be productive, ethical discourse must take place on common ground, that is, using understandings and intellectual procedures and judgment criteria that all participants—Christians, Jews, Muslims, atheists, and others—affirm. Because theological doctrine depends to a great extent on faith, it does not provide that common ground. To say this is not to disparage theology but merely to acknowledge that it is not the tool for the job in question.

A focus on faith rather than reason can also prevent us from presenting the most persuasive ethical argument. A case in point is the controversy that arose some years ago over a National Endowment for the Arts (NEA) grant. It was awarded to artist Andres Serrano, who produced a work titled "Piss Christ," which consisted of a crucifix in a bucket of urine. Christians, believing that Jesus Christ is the Son of God, would understandably think Serrano guilty of blasphemy and the NEA guilty of supporting and approving the offense. But that charge would be ineffective as a *moral* argument offered to the general public. No matter how tasteless Jews, Muslims, atheists, and agnostics may have found

Serrano's work, they are not likely to be persuaded that ridiculing a religious belief constitutes an ethical violation. A more persuasive argument is that the use of *tax dollars* for such work is immoral because it requires Christian citizens to contribute to the blatant disparagement of their religion.

Similarly, when speaking with those who do not share our religious views, it is not very helpful to judge actions by the criterion of whether they "please or offend God." The question that naturally arises is "How do you know whether they do or not?" And the two most common answers serve more to close off ethical inquiry than to promote it: One is "Because the Bible (or Koran, and so forth) says so." The other is "This is my religious belief." If we wish to pursue the matter further, we are placed in the position of having to challenge the Bible or to invade the very private domain of the other person's religious belief.

In addition, both answers are based on erroneous notions. Saying "the Bible says so" suggests that the Bible is a simple book that has a single interpretation. Yet biblical scholarship clearly demonstrates that it is complex and open to numerous interpretations. Saying "this is my religious belief" implies that no aspect of a person's belief can be shallow or mistaken, that in religious matters there is no room for growth and development. The lives of the saints and holy men and women of the world's religions disprove any such notion.

Some ethical questions cannot be adequately answered by reference to religious beliefs alone. Take, for example, the case of a person's wrestling with this question: "Since I no longer accept some of the major teachings of the church I was raised in, is it morally right for me to remain a member? What should I do?" The question is by no means an easy one. Whatever approach the individual might use in answering it, the teachings of his or her religion would hardly be the definitive measure, for they are an integral part of the question. *Using those teachings would be equivalent to affirming them and closing the issue.*

Most religious thinkers recognize the error of judging moral issues merely by religious belief. They realize the importance of discussing such issues in a way that is meaningful and appealing to all people of goodwill and honest concern. For this reason, they distinguish carefully between religious belief and religious ethics. Religious ethics is the examination of moral situations from a particular religious perspective. In it, the religious doctrine is not a substitute for inquiry. It is a starting point, a guide to inquiry and to organizing the findings of inquiry. Fortunately, there is an easy, practical way to avoid confusion about the relationship between religion and ethics:

> When you are evaluating someone else's ethical judgment, focus on the reasonableness of the person's argument and the quality and

weight of the evidence that supports it, rather than on the religious perspective that might underlie it. If the argument is reasonable and the evidence is persuasive, affirm the judgment. (Note that doing so in no way constitutes affirming the religious belief of the person making the argument.)

When you are expressing your own ethical judgment to a mixed audience, including people who do not share your religious perspective, make your appeal to reason rather than to faith or, at the very least, in addition to faith. (Note that appealing to reason in no way compromises your religious belief—it merely presents your judgment in a manner that is meaningful to your audience.)

THE NEED FOR ETHICS

To summarize, some people believe that we don't need ethics because we have laws and religious beliefs. In reality, it is because of ethics (moral reasoning) that we have laws in the first place, and we continue to need ethics to refine and perfect our legal system. We also need ethics in order to discuss the practical implications of our religious beliefs with others who do not share those beliefs. In addition, in situations where the reasonableness of a particular belief is at issue, we need ethics to help us reach a sound decision. Three actual cases will further document the need for ethics.

The religion known as Voodoo, which originated thousands of years ago in Africa, is still practiced in some parts of the world by as many as 275 million people. It has a number of adherents in the United States, mainly in New York City, Miami, and New Orleans. Most of these adherents are black and Hispanic; some are white. Religious practices of Voodoo, known as Santeria in the United States, no longer include human sacrifice, but they do include animal sacrifice and the casting of spells with the aid of dolls or figurines. Some years ago, a farmer's field in upstate New York was the site of such a ritual. Four Voodoo dolls were found mutilated, and the area was littered with the bloody remains of a number of chickens, pigeons, lambs, and goats. Some of the animals and birds appeared to have had their heads bitten off.[3] Because the ritual was religious, it cannot effectively be objected to on religious grounds (except by saying, "My religious views make me deplore that religious practice"). And it may have broken no law, so the only legal objection may be "There *ought to be* a law." But on what basis ought there to be (or not be) a law? On the basis of moral judgment. Ethics.

The second case occurred in Minden, Louisiana. Because of their religious belief that God heals illness, a couple sought no medical help for their infant granddaughter, who was suffering from meningitis. When she died, they were arrested and charged with negligent homicide. A jury found them guilty.[4] In this case, the law and religious belief directly clash. If the law were the final arbiter of right and wrong, it would be impossible (or at least pointless) to discuss the case further. Yet we can discuss it further, can dispute whether the law is defensible and whether the decision in this case served justice. Whatever our position may be, it will be a product of ethical judgment.

The third case concerns a Santa Cruz, California, street clown known as Mr. Twister, who got into trouble with the law. As he walked about the downtown area in his clown costume, complete with painted face, a brightly colored wig, and a bulbous red nose, he would look for parking meters with time expired. When he found one, he would insert a quarter, often just before the meter maid arrived to issue a citation. Alas, his "random acts of kindness" violated a city ordinance against putting coins in the meter for another person. When the case was publicized, however, not only was the charge dismissed, but the city council also decided that the ordinance criminalized the virtue of kindness and so repealed it. Ethical judgment changed the law.

Ethics fills a basic intellectual need in helping us interpret everyday human actions and decide what actions we approve in others and want to emulate ourselves. It is a guide for living honorably.

PRELIMINARY GUIDELINES

Later chapters will develop the guidelines necessary to reach thorough, thoughtful ethical judgments. But you may find it useful to have a preliminary approach to use in the meantime. The basic problem you will encounter is the tendency to judge issues on the basis of preconception and bias rather than careful analysis. Few people are completely free from the inclination to prejudgment on at least some issues. Some people may have their answer ready for any question concerning war; others, for questions concerning private property; still others, for issues involving alcohol or drugs. And many will have answers ready for questions of sexual morality. The reasons for prejudging will vary— from traumatic experience to personal preference to simple opinion. The underlying attitudes may range from distrust of all regulations, all laws, or even all *thoughts* to an uncritical endorsement of all traditions. But in each case the effect is the same: to avoid thinking about the particular case at all and merely to call forth a prefabricated, all-purpose answer.

The alternative to the closed mind is not the empty mind, however. Even if we wished to set aside completely all our prior conclusions about human behavior and right and wrong, we could not do so. The mind cannot be manhandled that way. Nor should it be. We can expect, then, that a flood of impressions and reactions will rush in on our thoughts when we consider a moral issue. It is not the fact of that flood that matters, nor its force. It is what we do to avoid having our judgment swept away by it. Here are some guidelines:

1. *Be aware of your first impressions. Note them carefully.* Knowing the way your thinking inclines is the first step toward balancing it (if it needs balancing).

2. *Check to be sure you have all the relevant facts.* If you do not have them, get them. An encyclopedia is usually a good place to start. Almanacs also provide a wealth of information. For books and articles on the issue in question, check your library's online catalog. Also, ask your librarian what indexes, abstracts, and computer databases would be appropriate to consult. (A section on using the Internet follows these guidelines.) Occasionally, you may be unsure whether a particular statement is a fact or an opinion. In such cases, ask whether the statement is generally accepted by knowledgeable people. If it is, consider it a fact; if knowledgeable people disagree about it, consider it an opinion. By checking several sources, you can get a good idea of whether agreement exists.

3. *Consider the various opinions on the issue and the arguments that have been (or could be) used to support them.* The position that directly opposes your first impression is often the most helpful one to consider. If your impression is wrong, this step will help you find out. If it is not, then you can return to it with confidence and present it more effectively for having considered alternatives to it. Do not make the mistake, common today, of ignoring what religious thinkers have to say about moral issues. As long as they are presenting the reasoning of their ethical tradition (as opposed to simply stating their theological doctrines), their contributions to moral discussion are entirely relevant and should be welcomed. If you refuse to consider those contributions, you will be denying yourself the insights that historically enriched the subject of ethics and helped form the foundation of our system of laws.

4. *Keep your thinking flexible.* Do not feel obligated to your early ideas. The process of ethical thinking entails entertaining many ideas, some of which you will accept, some of which you will discard as inferior. No judgment is your official judgment until you endorse it publicly in speaking or writing, and even then you may choose to revise it. So change your mind as often as you like as you analyze an issue. The more fully and unprejudicially you explore the issue, the better your judgment is likely to be.

5. *Express your judgment precisely and explain the reasoning that underlies it.* It is all too easy to say something you don't quite mean, especially when the issue is both complex and controversial. The best way to avoid this problem is to experiment with several different ways of

expressing your judgment instead of accepting the first version you produce. If your judgment is not a simple "yes" or "no" but a form of "it depends," be sure to specify what it depends on and exactly how your judgment would vary in different circumstances. Finally, no statement of your judgment is sufficient by itself. Be sure to explain, in as much detail as necessary for understanding, *what line of reasoning led you to that conclusion rather than to some other one.*

Doing Research on the Internet

The Internet has become the research tool of choice. It provides access to a variety of sites. The general categories are designated in suffixes attached to the web addresses: commercial sites, by "com"; organizational sites, by "org"; government sites, by "gov"; and educational sites, by "edu." If you have a topic in mind but don't know which site to consult, you can use a search engine. One of the best is Google—the address is http://www.google.com. Once connected to the Internet, just type in that address and Google's main page will appear. The subject box is provided for you to enter the topic you wish to research. (*Note:* For information on Google's various features, just click on one of the departments presented in blue.)

Suppose you wanted to research the ethical aspects of human cloning. You would type *ethics human cloning* in the subject box and click on "Google Search." Google would respond with a page that lists the results. Then you could scan the results and click on the titles that seem most relevant to your search. When you have finished checking the results on that page, you would click on the number 2 at the bottom to proceed to the next page.

Use Google when you don't know which website is likely to provide the information you are seeking or when you wish to expand your search. On the other hand, if you do know the most likely website, start your search there. Here are some websites that may be helpful in researching issues in ethics.

For the Subject of Ethics

http://www.ethicsweb.ca/resources/
Sponsored by the Centre for Applied Ethics, this site provides an overview of Internet resources for applied ethics in numerous fields.

http://ethics.sandiego.edu/
This site is useful to both teachers and students of ethics.

For Finding Hoaxes

http://www.snopes.com/
This is an excellent general-purpose site.

www.cdc.gov/hoaxes_rumors.html
This site is run by the Center for Disease Control (CDC).

http://www.fraud.org/
This is the National Fraud Information Center site.

http://www.truthorfiction.com

http://urbanlegends.about.com/od/internet/a/current_netlore.htm

http://www.scambusters.org/legends.html

For Informed Opinion on Ethical and General Issues

Conservative

http://www.townhall.com/
Click on "Columnists" and then click on any of the featured columns or on any name in the list of contributors.

http://www.jewishworldreview.com/
Click on any of the names in the "Insight" column on the home page.

Liberal

http://www.prospect.org/
Click first on "Columnists" and then on "Find other authors."

http://www.thenation.com

Varied

http://www.blueagle.com/index.html
This site lists 700 columnists, many cartoonists, and links to political websites.

For News

http://www.foxnews.com/ (the Fox News Channel site)

http://www.ap.org/ (the Associated Press site)

http://www.cnn.com/ (the CNN site)

For Reference Materials (including encyclopedias; thesauruses; dictionaries; collections of quotations; guides to English usage, religion, and literary history)

http://www.bartleby.com/reference/

http://www.infoplease.com (the Information Please site)

For Quotations

http://www.toinspire.com/

EVALUATING YOUR INFORMATION SOURCES

The task of evaluating information sources, always important, has become increasingly so as use of the Internet has grown. No information source should be presumed error-free. Print and broadcast journalists can make honest mistakes in reporting. Commentators can let their biases color their thought and expression. Individuals with personal agendas can deliberately mislead their audiences. It is up to the reader/listener to remain alert and, where possible, to test the source's reliability, especially that of Internet sources because there are no editors checking what is "published" there. Anyone can set up a website and say anything.

False information typically takes the form of an excited e-mail from a seemingly credible source, often a trusted but incautious friend. One such message said that Bill Gates was giving away money and explained how to get some. Another warned against eating bananas from Costa Rica because they contain a flesh-eating virus. Yet another claimed that asparagus cures cancer. Then there was the one that instructed recipients to check their computers for a file with a teddy bear icon, and if they found such a file to delete it at once before it destroyed their computer. All these were hoaxes. The last one was especially harmful because it caused people to delete an essential file.

To evaluate the reliability of your information sources, answer the following questions. (Some apply to print or broadcast sources, some to Internet sources, most to both.)

What is the purpose of the publication or website? Is it to entertain, inform, persuade, sell products or services? In the case of a publication, the purpose will often be stated in the front matter (for example, in the preface of a book). In the case of an Internet source, it will be expressed in a "mission statement" on the home page. Identifying a source's purpose will help you decide its potential for bias.

What is the source's point of view? Determine where the source stands on the subject under discussion; in other words, is he or she endorsing or opposing a particular viewpoint or policy? Although there is nothing necessarily wrong with either perspective, knowing where the source stands on the subject will make you more aware of where the person might fall short of fairness and objectivity.

Does the source engage in personal attacks? When a problem or controversial issue is being discussed, the focus should be on supporting or challenging particular solutions or points of view, not on the personal characteristics of the person proposing them. The only exception to this rule is if someone's personal failings are *directly relevant* to the matter under discussion—in such cases, it is appropriate to mention them. However, it is never appropriate to engage in personal attacks gratuitously, or as a *substitute* for addressing the problem or issue. Sources that behave this way should be considered unreliable.

Does the source make extravagant assertions? Consider the assertion that astronauts never really landed on the moon but, instead, the entire story was manufactured by NASA. Also, the assertion that the people responsible for the loss of several thousand lives on 9/11 were not foreign terrorists, as reported, but that George W. Bush and members of his administration planned and executed the horrible events. Both examples qualify as extravagant—that is, beyond credibility—because they are inconsistent with voluminous photographic evidence and analytical data. Although we cannot rule out the possibility that these or other conspiracy theories are valid, that possibility is *so remote* that anyone who traffics in such theories should be considered unreliable.

Does the source present evidence for his/her assertions? Asserting is far easier than demonstrating or documenting: that is why many people settle for asserting. Entire articles and even books have been constructed almost entirely of assertions, one piled on another. When assembled by an articulate, engaging person, these works can give the impression that a formidable case has been made when, in fact, there is no case at all—only unsupported claims. That is why the question of what evidence is offered for assertions is among the most important to ask of any source. The kinds of evidence that responsible writers offer include personal experience, factual reports in reputable publications, eyewitness testimony, expert opinion, experimental data, statistics, and research studies. Be sure to check the amount and kind of evidence that the source offers for each important assertion.

What criticisms have been made, or could be made, of the source's assertions and evidence? How worthy are those criticisms? Unless you happen to be well versed in the subject under discussion, you will have to consult other sources to answer these questions. In some cases, you will find criticisms that have sufficient merit to affect your judgment. Consider the so-called "Birthers" assertion that Barack Obama was born in a foreign country and is therefore not qualified to be president of the United States. One particularly interesting fact offered by critics of this assertion and supported by photographic evidence is that an announcement of Obama's birth appeared in a Hawaiian newspaper at that time. In order for Obama's parents to have faked the announcement, they would have had to *foresee the possibility of his candidacy forty-seven years later!* Because that is impossible to imagine, the birth announcement poses a strong argument against the "Birther" assertion.

As you review your answers to these questions and decide on the reliability of your information sources, keep in mind that even honest, conscientious people can make mistakes. Distinguish carefully between sources that happen to be mistaken on an issue and those whose mistakes are so numerous and/or egregious that they suggest dishonesty or the habit of carelessness.

For an excellent slide presentation on evaluating websites, created by Jane Alexander and Marsha Ann Tate, go to: http://muse.widener.edu/ ~tltr/How_to_Evaluate_9.htm. Also see "Bibliography on Evaluating

Web Information" at http://eagle.lib.vt.edu/help/instruct/evaluate/evalbiblio.html.

MAKING DISCUSSION MEANINGFUL[5]

At its best, discussion deepens understanding and promotes problem solving and decision making. At its worst, it frays nerves, creates animosity, and leaves important issues unresolved. Unfortunately, the most prominent models for discussion in contemporary culture—radio and TV talk shows—often produce the latter effects.

Many hosts demand that their guests answer complex questions with simple yes or no answers. If the guests respond that way, they are attacked for oversimplifying. If, instead, they try to offer a balanced answer, the host shouts, "You're not answering the question," and proceeds to answer it himself. Guests who agree with the host are treated warmly; others are dismissed as ignorant or dishonest. Often as not, when two guests are debating, each takes a turn interrupting while the other shouts, "Let me finish." Neither shows any desire to learn from the other. Typically, as the show draws to a close, the host thanks the participants for a "vigorous debate" and promises the audience more of the same next time.

Here are some simple guidelines for ensuring that the discussions you engage in—in the classroom, on the job, or at home—are more civil, meaningful, and productive than those you see on TV. By following these guidelines, you will set a good example for the people around you.

WHENEVER POSSIBLE, PREPARE IN ADVANCE

Not every discussion can be prepared for in advance, but many can. An agenda is usually circulated several days before a business or committee meeting. And in college courses, the assignment schedule provides a reliable indication of what will be discussed in class on a given day. Use this advance information to prepare for discussion. Begin by reflecting on what you already know about the topic. Then decide how you can expand your knowledge and devote some time to doing so. (Fifteen or twenty minutes of focused searching on the Internet can produce a significant amount of information on almost any subject.) Finally, try to anticipate the different points of view that might be expressed in the discussion and consider the relative merits of each. Keep your conclusions tentative at this point, so that you will be open to the facts and interpretations others will present.

SET REASONABLE EXPECTATIONS

Have you ever left a discussion disappointed that others hadn't abandoned their views and embraced yours? Have you ever felt offended when someone disagreed with you or asked you what evidence you had to support your opinion? If the answer to either question is yes, you probably expect too much of others. People seldom change their minds easily or quickly, particularly in the case of long-held convictions. And when they encounter ideas that differ from their own, they naturally want to know what evidence supports those ideas. Expect to have your ideas questioned, and be cheerful and gracious in responding.

LEAVE EGOTISM AND PERSONAL AGENDAS AT THE DOOR

To be productive, discussion requires an atmosphere of mutual respect and civility. Egotism produces disrespectful attitudes toward others— notably, "I'm more important than other people," "My ideas are better than anyone else's," and "Rules don't apply to me." Personal agendas, such as dislike for another participant or excessive zeal for a point of view, can lead to personal attacks and unwillingness to listen to others' views.

CONTRIBUTE BUT DON'T DOMINATE

If you are the kind of person who loves to talk and has a lot to say, you probably contribute more to discussions than other participants. On the other hand, if you are more reserved, you may seldom say anything. There is nothing wrong with being either kind of person. However, discussions tend to be most productive when everyone contributes ideas. For this to happen, loquacious people need to exercise a little restraint, and more reserved people need to accept responsibility for sharing their thoughts.

AVOID DISTRACTING SPEECH MANNERISMS

Distracting mannerisms include starting one sentence and then abruptly switching to another, mumbling or slurring your words, and punctuating every phrase or clause with audible pauses ("um," "ah") or meaningless expressions ("like," "you know," "man"). These annoying mannerisms distract people from your message. To overcome them, listen to yourself when you speak. Even better, tape your conversations with friends and family (with their permission), then play the tape back and listen to yourself. And whenever you are engaged in a discussion, aim for clarity, directness, and economy of expression.

LISTEN ACTIVELY

When the participants don't listen to one another, discussion becomes little more than serial monologue—each person taking a turn at speaking while the rest ignore what is being said. This can happen quite unintentionally because the mind can process ideas faster than the fastest speaker can deliver them. Your mind may get tired of waiting and wander about aimlessly like a dog off its leash. In such cases, instead of listening to the speaker's words, you may think about her clothing or hairstyle or look outside the window and observe what is happening there. Even when you are making a serious effort to listen, it is easy to lose focus. If the speaker's words trigger an unrelated memory, you may slip away to that earlier time and place. If the speaker says something you disagree with, you may begin framing a reply. The best way to maintain your attention is to be alert for such distractions and to resist them. Strive to enter the speaker's frame of mind, understanding each sentence as it is spoken and connecting it with previous sentences. Whenever you realize your mind is wandering, drag it back to the task.

JUDGE IDEAS RESPONSIBLY

Ideas range in quality from profound to ridiculous, helpful to harmful, ennobling to degrading. It is therefore appropriate to pass judgment on them. However, fairness demands that you base your judgment on thoughtful consideration of the overall strengths and weaknesses of the ideas, not on your initial impressions or feelings. Be especially careful with ideas that are unfamiliar or different from your own because those are the ones you will be most inclined to deny a fair hearing.

RESIST THE URGE TO SHOUT OR INTERRUPT

No doubt you understand that shouting and interrupting are rude and disrespectful behaviors, but do you realize that in many cases they are also a sign of intellectual insecurity? It's true. If you really believe your ideas are sound, you will have no need to raise your voice or to silence the other person. Even if the other person resorts to such behavior, the best way to demonstrate confidence and character is by refusing to reciprocate. Make it your rule to disagree without being disagreeable.

AVOIDING PLAGIARISM[6]

Once ideas are put into words and published, they become *intellectual property,* and the author has the same rights over them as he or she has over material property such as a house or a car. The only real difference is that intellectual property is purchased with mental effort rather than money. Anyone who has ever wracked his or her brain trying to solve a problem or trying to put an idea into clear and meaningful words can appreciate how difficult mental effort can be.

Plagiarism is passing off other people's ideas or words as one's own. It is doubly offensive in that it both steals and deceives. In the academic world, plagiarism is considered an ethical violation and is punished by a failing grade for a paper or a course or even by dismissal from the institution. Outside the academy, it is a crime that can be prosecuted if the person to whom the ideas and words belong wishes to bring charges. Either way, the offender suffers dishonor and disgrace, as the following examples illustrate:

- When a university in South Africa learned that Professor Mark Chabel had plagiarized most of his doctoral dissertation from Kimberly Lanegran of the University of Florida, the university fired Chabel. Moreover, the university that had awarded him his Ph.D. revoked it.

- In 1988, when then U.S. Senator Joseph Biden was seeking the Democratic presidential nomination, it was revealed that he had plagiarized passages from speeches by British politician Neil Kinnock and by Robert Kennedy. It was also learned that, while in law school, he had plagiarized a number of pages from a legal article. The ensuing scandal led Biden to withdraw his candidacy.

- The reputation of historian Stephen Ambrose was tarnished by allegations that over the years he had plagiarized the work of several authors. Doris Kearns Goodwin, historian and advisor to President Lyndon Johnson, suffered a similar embarrassment when she was discovered to have plagiarized from more than one source in one of her books.

- When James A. Mackay, a Scottish historian, published a biography of Alexander Graham Bell in 1998, Robert Bruce presented evidence that the book was largely plagiarized from his own 1973 biography, which had won a Pulitzer Prize. Mackay was forced to withdraw his book from the market. (Incredibly, he did not learn from the experience because he then published a biography of John Paul Jones, which was plagiarized from a 1942 book by Samuel Eliot Morison.)

- When *New York Times* reporter Jason Blair was discovered to have plagiarized stories from other reporters and fabricated quotations and details in his own stories, he resigned his position in disgrace. Soon afterward, the two senior editors who had been his closest mentors also resigned, reportedly because of their irresponsible handling of Blair's reportage and the subsequent scandal.

Some cases of plagiarism are attributable to intentional dishonesty, others to carelessness. But many—perhaps most—are due to misunderstanding. The instructions "Base your paper on research rather than on your own unfounded opinions" and "Don't present other people's ideas as your own" seem contradictory and may confuse students, especially if no clarification is offered. Fortunately, there is a way to honor both instructions and, in the process, to avoid plagiarism.

Step 1: When you are researching a topic, keep your sources' ideas separate from your own. Begin by keeping a record of each source of information you consult. For an Internet source, record the website address, the author and title of the item, and the date you visited the site. For a book, record the author, title, place of publication, publisher, and date of publication. For a magazine or journal article, record the author, title, the name of the publication, and its date of issue. For a TV or radio broadcast, record the program title, station, and date of transmission.

Step 2: As you read each source, note the ideas you want to refer to in your writing. If the author's words are unusually clear and concise, copy them *exactly* and put quotation marks around them. Otherwise, *paraphrase*—that is, restate the author's ideas in your own words. Write down the number(s) of the page(s) on which the author's passage appears.

If the author's idea triggers a response in your mind—such as a question, a connection between this idea and something else you've read, or an experience of your own that supports or challenges what the author says—write it down and put brackets (not parentheses) around it so that you will be able to identify it as your own when you review your notes. Here is a sample research record illustrating these two steps:

> Adler, Mortimer J. *The Great Ideas: A Lexicon of Western Thought* (New York: Macmillan, 1992) Says that throughout the ages, from ancient Greece, philosophers have argued about whether various ideas are true. Says it's remarkable that most renowned thinkers have agreed about what truth is—"a correspondence between thought and reality." 867 Also says that Freud saw this as the *scientific* view of truth. Quotes Freud: "This correspondence with the real external world we call truth. It is the aim of scientific work, even when the practical value of that work does not interest us." 869 [I say true statements fit the facts; false statements do not.]

Whenever you look back on this record, even a year from now, you will be able to tell at a glance which ideas and words are the author's and which are yours. The first three sentences are, with the exception of the directly quoted part, paraphrases of the author's ideas. The next is a direct quotation. The final sentence, in brackets, is your own idea.

Step 3: When you compose your paper, work borrowed ideas and words into your writing by judicious use of quoting and paraphrasing. In addition, give credit to the various authors. Your goal here is to eliminate all doubt about which ideas and words belong to whom. In formal presentations, this crediting is done in footnotes; in informal ones, it is done simply by mentioning the author's name.

Here is an example of how the material from Mortimer Adler might be worked into a composition. (Note where the footnote is placed and the form that is used for it.) The second paragraph illustrates how your own idea might be expanded:

> Mortimer J. Adler explains that throughout the ages, from the time of the ancient Greeks, philosophers have argued about whether various ideas are true. But to Adler the remarkable thing is that, even as they argued, most renowned thinkers have agreed about what truth is. They saw it as "a correspondence between thought and reality." Adler points out that Sigmund Freud believed this was also the *scientific* view of truth. He quotes Freud as follows: "This correspondence with the real external world we call truth. It is the aim of scientific work, even when the practical value of that work does not interest us."*
>
> This correspondence view of truth is consistent with the common-sense rule that a statement is true if it fits the facts and false if it does not. For example, the statement "The twin towers of New York's World Trade Center were destroyed on September 11, 2002" is false because they were destroyed the previous year. I may sincerely believe that it is true, but my believing in no way affects the truth of the matter. In much the same way, if an innocent man is convicted of a crime, neither the court's decision nor the world's acceptance of it will make him any less innocent. We may be free to think what we wish, but our thinking can't alter reality.

*Mortimer J. Adler, *The Great Ideas: A Lexicon of Western Thought* (New York: Macmillan, 1992), 867, 869.

▦ SAMPLE RESPONSES TO INQUIRIES

Here are two sample responses to help you understand the kind of analysis and the form of response appropriate for the inquiries that follow. (You need not agree with the particular viewpoints expressed.) Note that the responses express not just the writers' moral judgments but also the reasoning that underlies those judgments.

Inquiry: A Vestal, New York, resident unwittingly paid sewer bills for more than $1,300 over an eighteen-year period and then discovered there was no sewer line connected to his home. Since the statute of limitations on civil suits of this kind is six years, the town attorney suggested that the man be reimbursed for six years of payments only.[7] Was this suggestion ethical?

Sample Response: *Having a time limit for filing may be reasonable in disputes about the quality or punctuality of a service. In such cases, the passing of time could make the merits of the claim difficult to determine. A time limit might also make sense where each side was partly at fault. But this case is different. No service* *was provided, and the town was completely at fault for the improper billing. The man should have received full reimbursement.*

Inquiry: Some coaches of nationally ranked college athletic teams are paid large sums of money by athletic shoe manufacturers for having their teams wear a particular brand of shoe. Is this practice ethical? Why or why not?

Sample Response: *It is my understanding that coaches of nationally ranked teams receive generous salaries from their institutions, so they can't be accepting the money because of economic need. They're using their positions to make a quick buck in the form of a bribe. Given that fact, it is likely that the shoe contract will go to the highest bidder, regardless of the quality of that company's shoes. I believe it is unethical for payment to be offered or accepted in this case.*

▣ INQUIRIES

If you need assistance composing your response, read "Writing About Moral Issues" in the Appendix.

1. Over the past few decades, a sizable industry has arisen to serve the demand for ready-made and even customized compositions and term papers. Many students presumably believe there is nothing morally wrong with the practice of buying one of these papers and turning it in to fulfill a course requirement. Review what you read about plagiarism in this chapter. Then write a several-paragraph explanation of its message for a friend who doesn't get it. (Be sure to follow the approach explained in that section so you avoid committing plagiarism yourself.)

2. The Fifth Amendment to the U.S. Constitution states that private property shall not be "taken for public use, without just compensation." Up until fairly recently, the words "public use" generally have been interpreted narrowly to mean that the state could take someone's private residence or place of business so that a highway could be expanded or a public park constructed but not so that a shopping mall, a condominium, or a golf course could be built. Then, in a 2005 case (*Kelo* v. *City of New London*), the U.S. Supreme Court decided by a vote of 5 to 4 that the redevelopment of a blighted inner-city area by building new upscale housing and shops qualifies as public use. Does what you read in this chapter have any application to this case? Explain. (You might want to do a Google search and explore the case more fully before answering.)

3. Canada's government proposed that color photographs of diseased hearts and cancerous lungs and lips be printed on the front and back panels of every pack of cigarettes sold in that country. Canada's tobacco industry claimed the practice would be illegal.[8] Is there an ethical issue in this case? If you believe there is, explain why. If not, explain why not.

4. When a Michigan man was arrested for soliciting a prostitute, the car he was driving was confiscated by the police in accordance with a local ordinance. His wife, who was co-owner of the vehicle, took the matter to court, claiming that the government's action was improper because it punished not only her husband but also her, even though she had no part in, or knowledge of, the crime he committed.[9] Was her argument morally sound? Explain.

5. The National Collegiate Athletic Association (NCAA) has no rule against colleges and universities making hundreds of thousands of dollars from the sale of tickets and television rights to games. Yet the NCAA does not permit colleges and universities to pay student athletes. Is the NCAA's position morally justifiable? Explain.

6. Although Maude is not physically handicapped, whenever she is in a hurry she parks her car in spaces reserved for the handicapped. Is she behaving unethically?

7. A village on the seacoast places restrictions on the use of its beaches. Residents of the village are issued beach passes for themselves and their guests. All others are barred. Is such a restriction a moral issue? That is, is it debatable in terms of right and wrong? Explain.

8. There is no legal obligation for an eligible voter to vote in an election in the United States. Is the decision to vote or not to vote a moral decision? Explain.

9. Certain people have spoken out against the American government's foreign and domestic policies. They have broken no laws. Their protests have been fully within the guarantees of free speech. Yet the FBI is directed to investigate each individual thoroughly. The FBI conducts background studies, including interviews with relatives, friends, and acquaintances. Are these investigations ethically justifiable? Explain.

10. A married couple, both addicted to drugs, are unable to care for their infant daughter. She is taken from them by court order and placed in a foster home. The years pass. She comes to regard her foster parents as her real parents. They love her as they would their own daughter. When the child is 9 years old, her natural parents, rehabilitated from drugs, begin court action to regain custody. The case is decided in their favor. The child is returned to them, against her will. Does ethics support the law in this case? Discuss.

11. A sociology professor spots a magazine article that will fit in well with the textbook chapter he has assigned his students. However, copyright law forbids his making copies of it without obtaining the publisher's or author's permission (usually given for a small fee). Because he cannot use college funds for this purpose, and because there isn't sufficient time to go through the process of obtaining permission, he decides to break the law and make the copies. Does he act rightly? Explain.

12. Zoo officials in Eureka, California, could not afford to house two healthy adult bears while a new bear grotto was being built, and the only zoo that would take the bears was in South Dakota. Because the zoo could not afford the $500 it would have cost to transport the bears, officials decided to destroy them. As their two 3-month-old cubs looked on, the bears were given lethal shots of sodium phenobarbital.[10] Was the bears' destruction a moral issue? If so, was the action morally wrong?

13. Lawrence Steubig stole six candy bars in 1941. He was judged incompetent to stand trial and was sent to a mental institution. He was freed in 1975, *thirty-four years* later, whereupon he sued officials at the institution for "loss of liberty and loss of enjoyment of life." The institution could produce no records to show that he had ever received therapy or a chance to prove his competency. The judge ruled that Steubig's Fourteenth Amendment rights had been violated, but that he was not entitled to collect damages because the officials of the institution had acted in good faith.[11] Was this verdict defensible on moral grounds?

14. A Milpitas, California, boy raped and then killed his girlfriend and dumped her body in a lovers' lane gully. Over the next few days, the killer boasted to his high school friends and the word quickly spread that the girl was dead and that her body was in the gully. Carload after carload of high school students visited the gully to see the body. Some students prodded it with sticks or kicked it; one girl ripped a decal from the dead girl's jeans. Only one boy reported the murder to the high school principal, and even after the police investigation was well under way, only two students would identify the killer or volunteer any information. Because failure to report a body or to volunteer to testify is not a crime, the students could not be charged legally. But was the behavior of any of the students morally objectionable?

CHAPTER TWO

THE ROLE OF THE MAJORITY VIEW

*Is the basis for deciding moral values the
majority view? In other words, if the majority
of the citizens of our country should decide that
a particular action is right, would that very
decision make the action right?*

We live in an age when statistics confront us at every turn. From the moment we arise, authoritative voices bombard us with percentages. "Sixty-seven point two percent of the American public support the President's tax program." "Seven out of ten doctors recommend No-Ouch tablets." "My group had 90 percent less underarm odor."

In addition, tabloid television shows solicit our opinion on the issues of the day. "To vote YES, dial 1-900-555-2345. To vote NO, dial 1-900-555-5678." Should patients be able to sue their health maintenance organizations? Is the estate tax unfair? Do rich nations have an obligation to assist poor nations? Tomorrow we'll learn how many people voted, and the official tally of their votes will be presented in the manner of sports scores—and we'll be tempted to believe that whichever side got the higher percentage won the contest.

Given a steady diet of such data, we may begin to believe that the majority view is the wisest, most informed view. But what, after all, is the "majority"? Nothing more than 51 percent or more of the *individuals* in a group. Although the conversion of a bunch of individual views into a statistic can create the impression of authoritativeness and wisdom, those qualities do not always result. *There is no magic in majorities.*

If we were to examine a particular majority and compare their individual thinking on a particular issue, what would we find? First, we would find that actual knowledge of the issue varied widely among the individuals. Some would be well informed about all details. Others would be completely uninformed yet unaware of their ignorance. Between these extremes would be the largest group of individuals: those partly informed and partly ignorant, in some ways perceptive but in other ways confused or mistaken.

Second, we would find significant variations in the degree and quality of consideration given the facts. Some individuals would have read or listened to the views of authorities, sorted out irrelevancies, appraised each authority's position in light of available evidence, and weighed all possible interpretations of the facts. Others would have taken the ultimate shortcut and forgone all inquiry on the assumption that their intuition is infallible. A large middle group would have made some inquiry, but it would have been less than exhaustive and sometimes less than adequate.

Finally, we would find wide differences in the quality of judgment of the issue. Some would have judged quite objectively, avoiding preconceived notions and prejudices and being critical of all views, including those to which they were naturally disposed. Others would have been ruled by emotion untempered by reason, their judgment little more than a conditioned reflex. Again, most would have achieved some middle position in which thought and gut reaction intermingled to produce more or less objective conclusions.

A SAMPLE SITUATION

To see how all these differences might work in an actual moral issue, let's take the question "Is it wrong to kill enemy civilians in time of war?" Imagine that we have asked this question of a representative sampling of the general public and that a majority have answered in the negative. What variations in knowledge, inquiry, and judgment would the statistical report cover? What actual lines of thought might have occurred to the individuals in the majority? Here are some probabilities:

> Mr. A: "If they started the war, then the blame would be on them and they'd deserve no mercy. They'd all be responsible for their government's actions; so all of them, civilians and soldiers alike, would be regarded as enemies. If they get hurt, that's the breaks."
>
> Mr. B: "I fought in Vietnam and, believe me, in that war you couldn't tell a friend from an enemy. I've seen children waving and shouting greetings as they approached with explosives attached to their backs. I've seen peasants who'd shoot you in the back or direct you into a minefield after you'd given them candy. It can't be wrong to kill civilians in war because it's necessary for survival."
>
> Ms. C: "No, it's not wrong if it helps to shorten the war. In World War II we avoided more deaths and injuries to our armed forces and brought them home sooner by dropping atom bombs on two Japanese cities. Many civilians were in those cities. But our main intention was not to kill civilians; it was to end the war. Therefore the bombing was justified."

Ms. D: "It's a complex question. It really depends on the circumstances. The bombings of Dresden, Hiroshima, and Nagasaki during World War II were very wrong in my view. Those targets were selected because they were population centers and their destruction would demoralize the enemy. In other words, civilians were deliberately singled out for elimination. No goal, however worthy, justifies such slaughter. On the other hand, in a guerrilla war, the distinction between combatant and noncombatant is somewhat blurred. Soldiers disguise themselves as civilians. And civilians are enlisted, sometimes against their will, to perform military acts. In such a war I can conceive of situations where the killing of civilians is justified; say, where a soldier is in doubt whether the civilian approaching him is armed and must choose to shoot or jeopardize his own life. Is it wrong to kill civilians? I'd have to say no, not necessarily."

Perhaps none of these views is the best one possible, but the last one is much more penetrating than the others. It shows a willingness to consider the differences, as well as the similarities, between particular acts of war. It reveals sensitivity to important distinctions—specifically, to the distinction between the circumstances of the World War II bombings and the conditions of a guerrilla war. Finally, it demonstrates an awareness of the dilemma faced by particular people who must make a moral decision in actual war situations, the kill-or-be-killed choice that must be made instantly, without time for careful reflection.

Although Ms. D's view is a much wiser, more informed response than the others, in a statistical report its excellence would be ignored. It would merely be lumped with the others, including the utterly shallow and morally insensitive view of Mr. A. In statistical computation, the depth or shallowness of the thought that supports the answer counts for nothing. (It is possible, of course, for statistical reports to include the full answers, but even when a report is set up to provide for such answers, which it seldom is, the need for brevity often forces their omission.)

THE MAJORITY CAN ERR

In short, the majority view is less than perfect. To assume that it is necessarily enlightened is a serious mistake. If 1 percent or 49 percent of the population can be shallow or prejudiced in their view of an issue, so can 51 or 99 percent. Majority ignorance is as common as majority wisdom.

At various times in history, the majority have supported outrageous deeds. In some ancient societies, the majority believed in and practiced murdering female babies, abandoning handicapped infants to die, murdering young men and women as sacrifices to the gods or to serve a deceased monarch in the afterlife. The majority have supported religious wars, child labor, even child prostitution. In Hitler's Germany the majority gave at least silent assent to a program of genocide against the Jews. For centuries the standard treatment of the mentally ill, universally accepted, bordered on torture. Until recently in the southern United States, racial intermarriage was not only morally condemned but legally prohibited as well.

If the majority view determines right and wrong, then slavery was not wrong when it was practiced in America. It was right as long as the majority accepted it and became wrong only when more than 50 percent of the people rejected it. If the majority's moral perspective cannot err, then the religious persecutions that drove the early colonists to this continent were not vices but virtues. Such a view, of course, is nonsense. Slavery and religious persecution would be no less immoral if every country in the world approved them. There must be more to right and wrong than a showing of hands.

To be sure, the majority view may be the only one a democratic society can follow in its procedures of representative government. Even in lawmaking, the majority view will rightly exert considerable influence on legislators (though an honest legislator will not hesitate to oppose the majority view when the common good is served in doing so). But we cannot afford to pretend that the majority counsel is necessarily the counsel of wisdom—there is too much room in it for irrationality and self-deception. We do well to remember that, just as we view certain practices of past centuries as morally indefensible, later generations may judge some of our practices similarly. Every age has its blindness, perhaps even its barbarism.

What then should be our reaction to the views of majorities? We should give them careful consideration but resist the temptation to accept them uncritically. Instead, we should examine each issue for ourselves and embrace the most reasonable view. In some cases, that will be the majority view; in others, it will not.

⊞ Sample Response to Inquiries

Here is a sample response to help you understand the kind of analysis and the form of response that are appropriate for the inquiries that follow. (You need not agree with the particular viewpoint expressed.)

Inquiry: At the beginning of the twentieth century, a majority of lawmakers considered it morally right to deny women the right to vote. Was the majority morally correct in this instance?

Sample Response: *The majority was wrong in this case. The lawmakers, of course, had reasons for believing women shouldn't be allowed to vote—for example, that women lacked the necessary level of intelligence and that involvement in politics would rob women of their femininity. But such reasons were not valid then and are* *laughable today. No* legitimate *reason ever existed for depriving women of their rights of citizenship.*

🔲 INQUIRIES

If you need assistance in composing your responses, read "Writing About Moral Issues" in the Appendix.

1. According to the Gallup polling organization, in 2001, 45 percent of Americans believed abortion is morally wrong, but by 2009, the percentage had risen to 56 percent. During the same period, the percentage of people who believe that it is morally acceptable to have a baby outside of marriage rose from 45 to 51 percent. However, the percentage who believe gay and lesbian relationships are morally wrong dropped from 53 to 47 percent.[1] Suppose that two of your friends are discussing the meaning of these statistics. One says, "The statistics mean that gay relationships and having children out of wedlock used to be immoral but now they are moral. On the other hand, abortion used to be moral but now it is immoral." The other responds, "That's ridiculous. If an action was wrong a decade ago, it is still wrong today; and if it wasn't wrong then, it isn't wrong now." Settle your friends' dispute, applying what you learned in this chapter.

2. According to public opinion polls, a majority favor the death penalty for murderers but oppose the military's use of physical torture under all circumstances. Do you share the majority opinion in these cases? If you do not, are you nevertheless willing to agree that these views are morally correct because the majority holds them? Explain.

3. Animal rights activists continue to lobby and demonstrate to outlaw the use of animals in laboratory experiments, particularly those in which the animals suffer extreme pain. Since a majority of Americans have, at least implicitly, supported the use of animals in laboratory experiments, it might be argued that animal rights protests are unethical. Can you find anything in this chapter to support such an argument? Do you support it? Explain.

4. Many people, perhaps a majority, approve of telling lies to employers, co-workers, customers, or clients. Is it ethical to tell lies of this sort? Begin by considering the following situations: (a) a doctor tells a patient he has consulted with a colleague about her condition, though no such consultation occurred; (b) a business executive tells a client that she was tied up in traffic when she really lingered over lunch with friends; (c) a composition teacher tells a student he is making progress in his writing when, in fact, the student is showing no progress. Next, think of several situations you are familiar with in which lies were told in the workplace. Then explain in what circumstances, if any, lying is justifiable.

5. Environmentalists in Oregon, by their own admission, have driven spikes into trees to prevent the lumber industry from harvesting them. If the trees are harvested, the spikes break the huge, expensive saws in the lumber mills and sometimes injure the workers. Is the use of spikes by environmentalists unethical? (*Note:* If your answer to this question differs from your answer to inquiry 3, justify that disagreement.)

6. The great majority of people seem to find nothing objectionable about the use of commercials in children's television programming. Yet a distinguished panel commissioned by the National Science Foundation found reason to disagree. After reviewing twenty-one relevant scholarly studies, they concluded,

> It is clear from the available evidence that television advertising *does* influence children. Research has demonstrated that children attend to and learn from commercials, and that advertising is at least moderately successful in creating positive attitudes toward and the desire for products advertised. The variable that emerged most clearly across numerous studies as a strong determinant of children's perception of television advertising is the child's age. Existing research clearly establishes that children become more skilled in evaluating television advertising as they grow older and that to treat all children from 2 to 12 as a homogeneous group masks important, perhaps crucial, differences.[2]

Do you think the majority view is correct in this case? Do you think the use of commercials in children's television programming raises any ethical questions? Explain.

7. For centuries it was the common belief among Europeans that it is morally acceptable for society to deny Jews the rights of gentiles. That belief resulted in the segregation of Jews in ghettos, the strict regulation of their marriages, the imposition of special codes of dress on Jewish women, the forced attendance at Christian religious ceremonies, and the exclusion from certain occupations, including law, medicine, and education. Was that majority view ethically defensible?

8. After the Japanese attack on Pearl Harbor, President Roosevelt ordered the internment of thousands of American citizens of Japanese ancestry. (They were guilty of no crime but were considered *potentially* disloyal because of their ancestry.) A large number of Americans, possibly a majority, supported the president's action on moral grounds. Then, almost half a century later, Congress awarded every Japanese American who had been interned $20,000 in reparations. Because few people made any public protest, a majority of the American people presumably approved of the congressional action. Was the internment morally justified? Was the paying of reparations?

9. In 1971, a military court found Lt. William Calley guilty of the premeditated murder of twenty-two unarmed civilians in the Vietnam village of My Lai and sentenced him to dismissal from the army, forfeiture of pay and privileges, and life imprisonment. But a national poll revealed that 79 percent of the American public disapproved of the verdict and punishment, presumably on moral grounds.[3] Were the verdict and punishment ethically justifiable?

10. Two years after the U.S. Supreme Court's famous school desegregation order, a national poll revealed that 80 percent of the citizens of southern states opposed school desegregation. The same poll disclosed that 76 percent disapproved of the Interstate Commerce Commission's order banning train, bus, and waiting room segregation.[4] Are such desegregation orders ethically valid?

11. At various times, polls have indicated that a majority of Americans favor outlawing the Communist party. Is it ethically valid in a democracy to outlaw any political party that citizens might in good conscience choose to support?

12. A 16-year-old girl visits a birth control clinic and asks to be put on the pill. Because she is a minor, the clinic doctor who writes the prescription for her notifies her parents of the action. Possibly a majority of Americans would approve of the doctor's action. Is the action ethical?

13. In some parts of the country, a majority of the citizens presumably believe that it is morally acceptable to send people to jail for smoking marijuana. Is that view correct?

14. Advancements in high technology may eliminate many jobs, particularly for the unskilled worker. The majority of labor union members believe that machines should not replace human workers. Is it ethically justifiable for a society to pursue a course of technological advancement that could leave thousands of workers without jobs?

CHAPTER THREE

THE ROLE OF FEELINGS

*If the majority view does not determine the
rightness of an action, should each person
decide on the basis of her or his own feelings,
desires, preferences?*

In certain past times, people took pride in being like their parents and grandparents. Today, however, individuality is so highly prized that being like others is considered shameful. Even people who slavishly adopt the views and values of the majority or of their particular culture manage to maintain the notion that everything about them is as unique as their fingerprints. Not surprisingly, this preoccupation with individuality extends to morality. As we have seen, it is fashionable to believe that morality is subjective and personal—in other words, that no act is always and everywhere right or wrong. This means that whatever a person believes to be right *is right for that person,* and what a person believes to be wrong *is wrong for that person.*

The conclusion that follows from this reasoning is that no one person's view is preferable to another's. Each is good in its own way. One person's sacred ritual may be the next person's cardinal sin. Thus if a man and a woman want to marry, that's fine (the same for a man and a man, a woman and a woman). If a couple choose to live together without marrying, that's fine, too. Indeed, if twenty-two people want to live together in multiple liaison, that is also fine. No one other than the individuals themselves has any right to pass judgment. Freedom is the byword; rules and restrictions are the only heresies.

HOW FEELINGS CAME TO BE EMPHASIZED

Two individuals are especially important in the development of moral relativism and are largely responsible for its emphasis on feelings rather than reasoned judgment. About two centuries ago French philosopher

Jean-Jacques Rousseau wrote, "What I feel is right is right, what I feel is wrong is wrong." The child, in Rousseau's view, is inherently good; the only corrupting influence is society with its artificial constraints. Whether or not today's champions of feelings are aware of the fact, their call to cast aside inhibitions, reject external authority, and follow one's urges is but an echo of Rousseau. That is certainly the case with the ethics education approach known as *values clarification*. This system asserts that there is no universal, objective moral standard and that the only norm is what each person decides to value. The job of the educator, values clarification claims, is to encourage students to decide for themselves and then to affirm and support whatever they choose. The teacher is to be completely nonjudgmental, withholding all criticism of students' choices—the clear implication being that in the area of values *no one can ever be mistaken*.[1]

Also related to Rousseau, but more influential in modern thought than values clarification, is humanistic psychology, especially the thought of Carl Rogers. In phrasing remarkably similar to Rousseau's, Rogers assigned feelings a central role in guiding behavior: "One of the basic things which I was a long time in realizing, and which I am still learning, is that when an activity *feels* as though it is valuable or worth doing, it *is* worth doing. Put another way, I have learned that my total organismic sensing of a situation is more trustworthy than my intellect."[2] Rogers' goal in therapy was to persuade the client not only to "listen to feelings which he has always denied and repressed," including feelings that have seemed "terrible" or "abnormal" or "shameful," but also to *affirm* those feelings. Rogers was convinced that the therapist should be totally accepting of whatever the client expressed and should show "an outgoing positive feeling without reservations, without evaluations."[3]

One becomes a person, Rogers claimed, by self-affirmation rather than self-evaluation or self-criticism. The "only question that matters" for a healthy person, he maintained, is "Am I living in a way which is deeply satisfying to me, and which truly expresses me?" Pleasing others or meeting external, objective standards of behavior—such as the moral code of one's society or religion—has no role in Rogers' process.[4]

Rogers' impact on American thought, and on Western thought in general, has been profound. Together with his associate, William Coulson, Rogers developed and successfully implemented a plan to promote his value-free, nonjudgmental, nondirective approach in the teaching of both psychological counseling and ethics. (Coulson later renounced the approach, claiming that it ruined lives and harmed society.) Subsequently, two generations of psychologists, guidance counselors, student personnel staff in colleges, social workers, and even members of the clergy were trained in Rogers' method and proceeded in good faith to counsel *millions* of people to follow their feelings. Rogers' emphasis on feelings has been most enthusiastically embraced by the entertainment industry, which has made it a central theme of movies and television programs.

In the space of a few decades, feelings have become the dominant ethical standard. As Allan Bloom concluded, "Our desire . . . is now the last word, while in the past it was the questionable and dangerous part of us." As he explains, "choice" used to mean freedom to do what one ought to do, what one determined was right to do, but "now, when we speak of the right to choice, we mean that there are no necessary consequences, that disapproval is only prejudice and guilt only a neurosis."[5]

A number of psychologists have addressed this error. For example, William J. Doherty, a therapist and professor of psychology, argues that "It is time for psychotherapists to stop trying to talk people out of their moral sense. . . . I don't believe that all moral beliefs are created equal. The moral consensus of the world's major religions around the Golden Rule—do unto others as you would have others do unto you—is a far better guide to moral living than the reflexive morality of self-interest in mainstream American society."[6]

ARE FEELINGS RELIABLE?

As we noted in Chapter 2, there is no magic in majorities, so the fact that millions of people have adopted Rogers' implicit faith in feelings, desires, and preferences does not prove that such faith is warranted. Can feelings be trusted to guide human behavior? No reasonable person would deny that *some* feelings, desires, and preferences are admirable and therefore make excellent guides. Albert Schweitzer's feeling of "reverence for life" led him to choose the life of a medical missionary in then-primitive Africa over artistic and scholarly pursuits in Europe. Martin Luther King Jr.'s passion for justice led him to heroic leadership in the civil rights movement. Mother Teresa's compassion for the world's poor and suffering inspired a life of self-sacrificing service to others. And countless caring people the world over, who never become well known, are moved by love of neighbor to make the world a little better. Oseola McCarty is a good example. Forced to go to work in 1919 at age 11, she washed and ironed clothes for a living all her life, always putting as much money as she could afford in the bank. Then at age 87 she donated almost the entire amount—$150,000—to set up a college scholarship fund for deserving young people in her hometown.[7]

Honesty, however, demands acknowledgment of the darker aspect of feelings. When Hitler exterminated more than 6 million Jews and when Stalin massacred 30 million Russian peasants, they were following their feelings, as was their common spiritual ancestor, Genghis Khan, when he led his hordes of Mongols across Asia and into Europe, plundering, raping, and devastating. Serial killer Ted Bundy murdered young women and Jeffrey Dahmer practiced cannibalism for no other reason than to satisfy their desires. And for that same reason a group of Nassau County, New York, men used gifts to lure boys—some as young as 7, most of them fatherless—into homosexual seduction and then threatened them with beatings and even death if they told the authorities.[8]

If Rousseau and Rogers are correct in claiming that everything is a matter of personal preference and whatever feels good is good, then the concept of moral excellence is meaningless and Hitler, Stalin, Bundy, and Dahmer deserve to be considered the *moral equals* of Schweitzer, King, and Mother Teresa. Furthermore, if Rousseau and Rogers are correct, there is no ethical basis for condemning genocide, murder, cannibalism, and child molestation. And without an ethical basis, the laws forbidding these deeds are no longer valid and the people that have been imprisoned for committing them should be released. Logic is uncompromising in such matters and does not allow the luxury of ignoring the implications of ideas. Rather, it demands that we evaluate ideas by their implications. In this case, that means judging Rousseau's and Rogers' idea to be unreasonable.

A BETTER GUIDE IS NEEDED

When we are thinking clearly and being honest with ourselves, we realize that there is a potential in each of us for noble actions of high purpose and honor; but there is also a potential for great mischief and wickedness. Each of us is capable of a wide range of deeds, some that would make us proud if the whole world knew, and others that, if discovered by a single other person, would cause us shame.

A man passing a department store late at night may have a sudden urge to smash the window and steal the cashmere sports jacket he covets. A student may feel like spreading a lie about her roommate to avenge a real or imagined wrong. A bank employee may have the desire to embezzle a million dollars and depart for the South Seas. Any one of us, however placid our nature, may on occasion experience an overwhelming urge to punch someone in the nose. Yet each of these actions is at least of questionable rightness, *despite* the feelings and desires that prompt them.

Similarly, a person walking alone on the shore of a lake may prefer to ignore the call for help that comes from the water. A surgeon relaxing at home may prefer not to answer the call to perform emergency surgery. The father who promised to take his children on a picnic may prefer to play golf with his friends. A lawyer may prefer not to spend the necessary time preparing for the defense of her client. In such situations, the answer "whatever the person prefers to do is right to do" is hollow. Good sense suggests that the right action may be at odds with the individual's preference.

I recently had a personal experience that underscored this point. I was walking with my wife on an exercise trail near our home. The sandy soil that bordered the pavement had eroded in places, and a work crew had dug out the sand to a depth of about six inches in preparation for filling the area with richer soil in which grass could take root. The area extended for about a quarter-mile and the workmen had placed orange cones every twenty feet or so to alert walkers, skaters, and cyclists to the danger. On the return part of our walk, we passed the area again and noticed a teenage boy in front of us, methodically knocking over each cone as he passed it. When we overtook the boy, I spoke to him. The conversation went like this:

> I said, "I'm curious. Do you know why those cones were put there?"
>
> "To warn people," he mumbled.
>
> "Do you realize that by knocking them over you increase the chance that someone might fall and get hurt?"
>
> "Yeah."
>
> "Then why are you doing it?"
>
> "Because I feel like it."

Ironically, morality by feelings *completely ignores other people's feelings.* Those who are acted against surely have feelings, too; in the preceding cases, their feelings presumably run counter to the feelings of those committing the actions. If the murder victims had been consulted, they surely would have expressed a preference not to be so treated. Similarly, few people enjoy being robbed, lied about, assaulted, or neglected in their time of need. To say that we should be free to do as we wish without regard for others is to say that others should be free to do as they wish without regard for us.* If such a rule were followed, the result would be social chaos.

Because our feelings, desires, and preferences can be either beneficial or harmful, noble or ignoble, praiseworthy or damnable, and because they can be either in harmony or in conflict with other people's feelings, desires, and preferences, they obviously are not reliable criteria for moral judgment or trustworthy guidelines for action. Feelings, desires, and

---

*The argument that people may do whatever they desire to do "as long as no one else is hurt" may seem related, but it is really quite different. It has a social dimension (consideration for others) in addition to a personal dimension (what one wants to do). Unfortunately, it begs the question of whether we have a right to injure *ourselves.*

preferences need to be evaluated and judged. They need to be measured against some *impartial* standard that will reveal their quality. To make them the basis of our moral decisions is to ignore those needs and to accept them uncritically as the measure of their own worth.

▦ SAMPLE RESPONSE TO INQUIRIES

Here is a sample response to help you understand the kind of analysis and the form of response appropriate for the inquiries that follow. (You need not agree with the particular viewpoint expressed.) Note that the response expresses not just the writer's moral judgment but also the reasoning that underlies it.

Inquiry: Marian is a 55-year-old widow whose children no longer live at home. Lonely and bored, Marian has sought escape in alcohol. Each night after work, she drinks four or five mixed drinks, sometimes followed by a couple of glasses of wine with dinner. (Not infrequently, she falls asleep on the couch and misses dinner.) When a well-meaning neighbor commented on her drinking, Marian replied, "I feel that if I get up and go to work every day and don't harm anyone, there's nothing wrong with my having a drink at night." Is her feeling reasonable?

Sample Response: *To begin with, five mixed drinks followed by a couple of glasses of wine is considerably more than "a drink." In addition, when she says she's not hurting anyone, she's forgetting at least one person—herself. Using alcohol to cope with life is emotionally harmful, and consuming that much alcohol is physically harmful. It is also difficult to imagine that she performs her work well. Far from guiding her well, Marian's feelings are victimizing her. The moral thing for Marian to do, in my judgment, is to quit fooling herself and get help for her drinking problem.*

▦ INQUIRIES

If you need assistance in composing your responses, read "Writing About Moral Issues" in the Appendix.

1. Read the following passage carefully and then follow the subsequent directions: "Most of the unrest around the world is due to the United States' habit of playing policeman to the world and forcing its view of democracy on countries that desire only to be left alone. This habit is morally offensive and this is why so many people are willing to risk their lives opposing us." Begin by recording your feelings about this passage. Are they strongly positive? Strongly negative? Now put those feelings aside for a moment and examine the underlying idea—that it is morally wrong to force democracy in other countries. List as many pro and con arguments as you can. (If you can only think of arguments on one side of the issue, read a dissenting view and list the arguments presented.) When you have finished examining the underlying idea, revisit your original feelings and decide whether you should modify

them. Be prepared to discuss the differences you noted between responding emotionally and responding rationally.

2. Ada Dupreé died at age 104, and her family intended to bury her in the North Florida town where she had lived all her life and was the oldest citizen—and where she had been a caring friend to whites and blacks alike. That had been her final wish. But then came threats from angry white people to shoot at her hearse and at her mourners if the burial were held in the town's white cemetery. So she was buried in a black cemetery in a neighboring town. The feelings that made those white people oppose Ada Dupreé's burial in the local cemetery evidently were powerful and deeply held. Were they also morally right? (It should be noted that not all white people in the town had these feelings. One white woman offered to give her own burial plot for Dupreé, and others attended the funeral.)[9]

3. Clark lives in a state that has a 7 percent sales tax on automobiles. Even when a person buys a used car from the owner, he or she must file a form with the motor vehicle department, stating the purchase price and paying the appropriate amount of tax. Clark has found the car he wants. The price of $10,000 is within his means, but he doesn't feel that he should have to pay the additional $700 in tax. So he tells the seller, "I'll pay you $10,000 for the car if you give me a sales receipt for $3,000. That way I'll only have to pay $210." The seller shares Clark's feeling about paying the tax, so he agrees. Is their action morally wrong? Explain.

4. Morey is a sadist. In other words, he enjoys causing other people pain. The feelings he experiences when he hurts others are exciting and deeply satisfying. Do these feelings justify the actions that produce them? Why or why not?

5. A Little League baseball coach anticipates a poor season because he lacks a competent pitcher. Just before the season begins, a new family moves into his neighborhood. The coach discovers that one of the boys in the family is an excellent pitcher but that he is over the age limit for Little League participation. Because the family is not known in the area, the coach is sure he can use the boy without being discovered. He wants a winning season very much, for himself and for his team. Is he morally justified in using the boy?

6. Ralph, a college student, borrows his roommate's car to drive to his aunt's funeral. On the way back he falls asleep at the wheel, veers off the road, and rolls down an embankment. Though he emerges unhurt, the car is a total wreck. Because the car is five years old, the roommate has no collision insurance. Ralph is sorry about the accident but feels no responsibility for paying his roommate what the car was worth. Does he have any moral responsibility to do so?

7. The owner of a roadside restaurant prefers not to serve black or Hispanic customers. She paid for the property, she feels, and has spent many years developing the business; therefore, she should have the right to decide whom she serves. Is her whites-only preference ethically defensible?

8. A small city has a zoning ordinance. The spirit of that ordinance clearly prohibits the operating of a business in areas designated residential.

However, the wording is such that a loophole exists. One woman wishes to open a pet shop in the basement of her split-level home. The law is in her favor. Is morality?

9. The executives of three large appliance companies get together to discuss their competitive situation. Among them they account for 91 percent of the U.S. production of their particular products. They decide that by stabilizing their prices, they can benefit their stockholders, invest more money in product research, and thereby deliver a better product to the consumer. They agree to consult one another before setting prices and to price comparable models at the same price. Is this action ethically acceptable?

10. A man buys a house and later realizes he has paid too much money for it. In fact, he has been badly cheated. There is a bad leak in the cellar and through one wall, the furnace is not functioning properly, and the well is dry at certain times during the year. The cost of putting these things right will be prohibitive. He wants to "unload" the house as soon as possible, and he prefers to increase his chances of recovering his investment by concealing the truth about the house's condition. Is it right for him to do so?

11. For more than half a century, a funeral home in Charlotte, North Carolina, displayed an embalmed human body in a glass showcase. The body was that of a carnival worker who was killed in a fight in 1911. The man's father, also a carnival worker, paid part of the funeral costs and asked the funeral home director to keep the body until he returned. Nothing more was heard from him. Thus the body, clad only in a loincloth, remained on display for sixty-one years. Public clamor finally resulted in its removal from public view. However, the funeral home director (the son of the original director) allegedly felt nothing was wrong in exhibiting the body, which he compared to a mummy in a museum.[10] Is his feeling ethically sound?

12. A newspaper columnist signs a contract with a newspaper chain. Several months later she is offered a position with another newspaper chain at a higher salary. Because she would prefer making more money, she notifies the first chain that she is breaking her contract. The courts will decide the legality of her action. But what of the morality? Did the columnist behave ethically?

13. A California businessman started a check-cashing service, operating out of a large commercial van. He charges customers $1\frac{1}{2}$ percent of the face value of the check for the service, and he has plenty of customers, mainly people on unemployment, welfare, social security, and disability, who lack the bank accounts and credit ratings necessary to cash their checks in a bank. His profit is estimated at almost $50,000 per year. He feels there is nothing unethical about his business.[11] Do you agree?

14. In Mineola, New York, a police officer allegedly posed as a clinical psychologist during his off-duty hours and made phone calls to numerous women inquiring about their sex lives.[12] Presumably, he felt that his desire to adopt the pose and make the calls was sufficient to justify his doing so. Do you agree with him?

15. A 16-year-old girl and her father were arrested in Panama City, Florida, for allegedly trying to sell the girl's unborn baby for a ten-year-old car and

$500.[13] Although selling babies is against the law, the two presumably felt that they had the moral right to do so. Is their feeling morally defensible?

16. Two workers were displaced when a company installed a robot to deliver tools and materials to workers in the plant. The robot followed a specially painted track on the plant floor. Several other workers, fearing that their jobs would also be lost, decided to "teach the company a lesson." They repainted the track so that the robot walked off the loading dock and was badly damaged. The workers felt they were justified in their action. Is this an ethically defensible position?

17. An office worker had a record of frequent absence. He used all his vacation and sick leave days and frequently requested additional leave without pay. His supervisor and co-workers expressed great frustration because his absenteeism caused bottlenecks in paperwork, created low morale in the office, and required others to do his work in addition to their own. On the other hand, he felt he was entitled to take his earned time and additional time off without pay. Was he right?

CHAPTER FOUR

THE ROLE OF CONSCIENCE

*If feelings are no better a guide than the
majority view, is the basis of morality
each person's own conscience?
How trustworthy is conscience?*

The term *conscience* is so common and often so carelessly used that for many people it has little meaning. Precisely what is a conscience? Does everybody have one, or are some people born without one? Are all consciences "created equal"? Are our consciences influenced by the attitudes and values of our culture? Can we do anything to develop our consciences, or are they fixed and unchangeable? These important issues must be considered before we can decide whether conscience is a reliable moral guide.

One definition of conscience is an "inner voice," but what kind of voice exactly? The voice of desire or discernment? The voice of emotion or reason? Our own voice? (If so, how does it differ from ordinary reflection?) The voice of society or custom? (If so, how do we explain the many times when conscience urges us to *defy* custom?) The voice of God? (If so, do we explain cases in which conscience fails to inform us that an act is wrong as failures of God?)

Another definition of conscience is a special "moral sense" or "intuition" that is innate in human beings. This comes close to being a workable definition, but it also poses difficulties. The term *sense* usually is associated with a physical organ—the sense of sight with the eyes, the sense of hearing with the ears, and so on. Conscience cannot be that kind of sense. Similarly, equating conscience with intuition ignores the fact that conscience can be *developed* whereas intuition is *inborn*.

Conscience, it seems, cannot be defined in terms of what it is. It can only be defined in terms of what it does or how it occurs. Nor is it unique in this regard. A number of other terms are defined in the same way. In the physical realm, for example, electricity is defined as "a force that . . ." or "a phenomenon that occurs when. . . ." In the metaphysical realm, intellect is defined as "the ability to . . ." or "the capacity for . . . ," and mind is defined as "the collective conscious and unconscious processes . . ." or "the faculty by which we. . . ." Using the same kind of definition, we may define *conscience* as the special awareness that what we have done or are tempted to do is wrong.

CONSCIENCE AND SHAME

We know our conscience has judged us harshly when we feel a sense of shame. The first definition of *shame* in the *Oxford English Dictionary* is "the painful emotion arising from the consciousness of something dishonouring, ridiculous, or indecorous in one's own conduct or circumstances." Because shame is a phenomenon almost everyone has experienced, it is not surprising that it has been traditionally regarded as natural and essentially wholesome. Oddly, however, popular psychology regards it as a sign of emotional instability. One writer describes it as a scourge of the psyche, an emotion totally without redeeming value that is responsible for a broad range of psychological disorders, including depression, addiction, sexual dysfunction, and emotional problems linked to gender, age, and race. Shame, the writer argues, is never appropriate; instead, the proper, healthy emotion is always "self-acceptance."[1]

If this view sounds profound, the reason is simply that we have heard it so often in books, in magazine articles, and on talk shows that we never think to question it. Yet the moment we test it against everyday reality, its absurdity becomes evident. Think back to a time in your childhood when you felt ashamed of something you said or did, such as being disrespectful to a parent or a teacher, hitting your brother or sister, or stealing something from a playmate. If your shame prompted you to apologize, or at least to do the person a kindness to make up for the wrong, your self-respect was restored. Feeling bad about yourself was a necessary step toward feeling good about yourself again.

Think, too, of the "bad actors" you encounter each day or read about in the news: the employers who misuse their employees, the drivers who endanger the lives of others on the highway, the men and women who berate and belittle their spouses and children, and the irresponsible people who cheat and lie their way through life. When you see people behave this way and then show no sign of remorse, are you impressed with their emotional health? Is the fact that many rapists, child molesters, serial killers, and terrorists are not ashamed of their heinous deeds a positive development? Of course not.

The time for celebration is not when people lose their sense of shame but when, after having lost it, they manage to regain it. The following passage from a John Grisham novel describes such a moment:

> At some undefined point in his life, pushed by his work and his addictions, [Nate] had lost his decency and shame. He had learned to lie, cheat, deceive, hide, badger, and attack innocent witnesses without the slightest twinge of guilt.
> But in the quiet of his car and the darkness of the night, Nate was ashamed. He had pity for the Phelan children. He felt sorry for Snead, a sad little man just trying to survive. He wished he hadn't attacked the new experts with such vigor.
> His shame was back, and Nate was pleased. He was proud of himself for feeling so ashamed. He was human after all.[2]

INDIVIDUAL DIFFERENCES

Simple observation will demonstrate that the intensity of conscience differs from person to person. Even as small children most of us have perceived, however vaguely, that our playmates and relatives appear to differ widely in this phenomenon. Preschoolers will often grab toys away from others. Some of them will never show (and, if externals are a mirror to internal states of mind, never *feel*) the slightest remorse. Yet others will be so aware of the offensiveness of such behavior that they will immediately be saddened and repentant; their remorse will be evident. Hours later they will still be trying to make amends.

The classmates of a grade-school stutterer will vary greatly in their attitude toward him. Many will treat him as a nonperson, an object to tease and taunt and mimic. Some will simply know no better and will be unaware that their actions are wrong. Others will at some moment sense that they have caused him pain and will feel ashamed of their behavior.

Such differences in conscience are observable in adults as well. Some people are very sensitive to the effects of their actions, acutely aware when they have done wrong. Others are relatively insensitive, unconscious of their offenses, free from feelings of remorse. They live their lives uninterested in self-examination or self-criticism, seldom even considering whether something *should* be done. Some see right and wrong as applying to only a limited number of matters—sexual behavior, for example, and deportment within the family. The affairs of citizenship and business or professional conduct are, to them, outside the sphere of morality. Still others were at one time morally sensitive but have succeeded in neutralizing the promptings of conscience with elaborate rationalizations. When Claude's wife expresses disapproval of his cramming the hotel's soap and towels and rugs and bedspreads into his suitcase, he says, "Look, the hotels in this country expect you to take a few souvenirs. They build the cost into their room rates. If I take a bit more than they've allowed for, they write it off on their tax returns."

Finally, there are the extremists: the scrupulous and the lax. Scrupulous people are morally sensitive beyond reasonableness, often to the point of compulsion. They see moral faults where there are none. For them, every action, however trivial—whether to peel the potatoes or cook them whole, whether to polish the car today or tomorrow—is an excruciating moral dilemma. Their counterparts at the other pole are virtually without conscience, using other people as things, unmindful of their status as persons, pursuing only what satisfies the almighty *me.*

THE SHAPERS OF CONSCIENCE

Many people have the vague notion that their consciences are solely a product of their own intellectual efforts, not subject to outside influence. They imagine themselves as having devoted a period of time—precisely *when* they are not sure, perhaps during their teenage years—to carefully evaluating various ideas of right and wrong and then forming their own moral perspective. That this notion should exist is understandable. People are naturally more aware of their conscious mental life than of any outside influences, particularly subtle ones. In addition, the thought that one's life is and has always been completely under one's control is very reassuring. In any case, *the notion is wrong.*

Conscience is shaped by two forces that are essentially outside our control—natural endowment and social conditioning—and one that is, in some measure, within our control—moral choice. The specific attributes of our conscience, including its sensitivity to moral issues and the degree of its influence on our behavior, are due to one or more of these forces. Let's examine each of them in turn.

NATURAL ENDOWMENT

A person's basic metabolism and temperament are essentially inborn. Some people are calm, others excitable; some are talkative, others taciturn; some are highly perceptive, others much less so. Such characteristics present certain obstacles and/or opportunities in the development of conscience. For example, the vivacious, energetic person, quick of movement and speech, who constantly performs in metabolic overdrive may tend to be somewhat less disposed to careful analysis of past actions than is the slower, more reflective person. The impulsive person, impatient to do and have done, may find it difficult to consider the consequences of his or her actions; for such a person, conscience may operate only after the fact. It is not, of course, a matter of one metabolic rate, temperament, or disposition being preferable to another. Each presents some fertile areas for the development and employment of conscience, as well as some barren ones.

SOCIAL CONDITIONING

Conditioning is the most neglected shaper of conscience. Yet, ironically, it is in many ways the most important. Conditioning may be defined as the myriad effects of our environment: that is, of the people, places, institutions, ideas, and values we are exposed to as we grow and develop. We are conditioned first by our early social and religious training from parents. This influence may be partly conscious and partly unconscious on their part and indirect as well as direct. It is so pervasive that all our later perspectives—political, economic, sociological, psychological, theological—in some way bear its imprint.

If children are brought up in an ethnocentric environment—that is, one in which the group (race, nationality, culture, or special value system) believes it is superior to others—research shows that they will tend to be less tolerant than other people. More specifically, they will tend to make rigid right–wrong, good–bad classifications. If they cannot identify with a group, they oppose it. In addition, they will tend to need an out-group, some outsiders whom they can blame for real and imagined wrongs. This, in turn, makes it difficult or impossible for them to identify with humanity as a whole or to achieve undistorted understanding of others.[3]

In addition, ethnocentric people, even in childhood, have difficulty dealing with complex situations, and therefore demand simple solutions to problems, even problems that do not admit of simple solutions.[4]

The influence of such training on conscience is obvious. Although few of us are subjected to a *purely* ethnocentric environment as children, elements of ethnocentrism are common in most environments. The effects on us, though less dramatic and pronounced, are nevertheless real and a significant shaping force on our conscience.

Early in life we are also conditioned by our encounters with brothers, sisters, relatives, and friends. We see a sister's observance or disregard of family rules or her habit of lying to parents. An uncle brings a present he has stolen from work. Our playmates cheat in games. More important, we see not only these actions but the reactions of the people themselves and of others who observe them. We are witness to all the moral contradictions, all the petty hypocrisies of those around us. We ourselves act—now in observance of some parental rule, then against another—and we are rewarded or punished. We also imitate others' strategies for justifying questionable behavior.

Next we are conditioned by our experiences in grade school, by our widening circle of acquaintances, and perhaps by our beginning contact with institutional religion. We perceive similarities and differences in the attitudes of our teachers and classmates. We observe their behavior, form impressions, sense (quite subliminally and vaguely, to be sure) the level of development of their consciences. We observe and learn from our priest, minister, or rabbi. Perhaps in all these situations, it is not the formal so much as the informal contact, the simple acquaintance with their personalities, habits, and patterns of behavior, that affects us in powerful, though subconscious, ways. Though memory may cloud, experience remains indelible.

Finally we are conditioned by our contact with people, places, and ideas through books, radio, the Internet, newspapers, magazines, tapes and CDs, and especially television programming. What we see and hear makes an impact on our attitudes and values, sometimes blatantly, sometimes subtly. Situation comedies instruct us as to what may appropriately be laughed at and/or ridiculed. Soap operas and dramatic programs train our emotions to respond favorably or unfavorably to different behaviors. Talk shows inform us of what celebrities think about a variety of subjects, including right and wrong. And commercials incessantly tell us what possessions and living styles will make us happy and are therefore desirable. As the entertainment and communications media have grown more numerous and more sophisticated, the number of individuals and groups involved in social conditioning has multiplied, and their messages are often at odds with those of home, church, and school.

MORAL CHOICE

Long before we were able to make authentic moral choices, heredity and social conditioning had already shaped our conscience, and they continued to do so even when, as small children, we made rudimentary choices. Young children's choices, after all, are not fully *conscious acts* but mere *assertions of will* that express their personality traits or imitation of others' behavior. A toddler's obeying or defying her parents' directions is an example of such an assertion. Only in later childhood do we develop the ability to weigh alternatives and make *reasoned* moral choices. The problem is that by then we will have already developed attitudes and patterns of response to situations and people, at least some of which are likely to be both morally undesirable and difficult to change.

That people tend to behave in ways that are consistent with their thinking is fairly well known. What is not so well known is that the reverse also occurs—they think in ways that justify their behavior. The eminent English scholar Dr. Samuel Johnson explained the two tendencies as follows:

> Not only [do] our speculations influence our practice, but our practice reciprocally influences our speculations. We not only do what we approve, but there is danger lest in time we come to approve what we do . . . for no

other reason than that we do it. A man is always desirous of being at peace with himself; and when he cannot reconcile his passions to [his] conscience, he will attempt to reconcile his conscience to his passions.[5]

Note the word *passions*, a synonym for the term that is causing so much moral confusion today—*feelings*. Dr. Johnson knew what was pointed out in the previous chapter, that feelings are not a reliable guide in moral matters. Furthermore, as he implies here, when feelings are allowed to overrule conscience, conscience loses its moral bearings. It becomes desire's puppet, telling us what we *want* to hear instead of what we *need* to hear. One doesn't have to be morally disreputable to be victimized by this process. It can ensnare respectable, well-intentioned people who not only want to make wise moral choices but *honestly believe they are doing so,* as the following examples illustrate:

> A police detective was investigating a rape case in which the victim had recorded part of the perpetrator's license number. The detective eventually found a suspect who matched the description of a rapist in almost every way. There was only one problem—his license plate number did not match. Rather than lose the case on what seemed a technicality, the detective changed the victim's statement, inserting the suspect's plate number. The detective did not consider this action immoral; he believed he was just bolstering his case, even though his action effectively eliminated exoneration based on "reasonable doubt."[6]
>
> A number of newspapers around the country have a policy of including the cause of death in every obituary, even if the family of the deceased asks that it be omitted. (For example, the obituary might state that the cause of death was suicide by suffocation, slashed wrists, or a gunshot wound to the head.) The editorial staffs that make this policy apparently do so with a clear conscience, despite the fact that many grieving families suffer embarrassment and shame as a result.
>
> When actor Hugh Grant was arrested for consorting with a prostitute in Los Angeles, Grant's friend, Academy Award–winning actress Emma Thompson, described her reaction in an interview: "I thought, thank God, you know, you've broken out." She reportedly went on to say that what Grant had done was not something to be ashamed of but "wonderful, absolutely wonderful."[7] Evidently, from her moral perspective, Grant's unfaithfulness to his fiancée and possible exposure to sexually transmitted disease, including HIV/AIDS, not only posed no moral issue but were in some unspecified way *admirable*!

A BALANCED VIEW OF CONSCIENCE

The unpleasant realities we have noted about conscience demonstrate that it is not an infallible moral guide. However, to leap from that evidence to the conclusion that conscience is without value would be a mistake. For all its imperfections, conscience is the most important single guide to right and wrong an individual can have. It is, as the saying goes, the "proximate norm of morality." For this reason, when circumstances demand an immediate moral choice, we should follow our conscience. (The only alternative would be to violate it, to choose to do what at that moment seems immoral.) However, whenever circumstances allow us time to reflect on the choice conscience recommends, we should use that time to analyze the issue critically and to consider the possibility that a different choice might be better.

In short, we should follow our conscience, but not blindly. True freedom, true individuality, and real moral growth lie in examining conscience, evaluating its promptings, purging it of negative influences and error, and reinforcing it with searching ethical inquiry and penetrating ethical judgment. The chapters that follow contain helpful criteria for further developing your conscience.

Accordingly, for our purposes in examining moral issues in this and subsequent chapters, the answer "It's a matter for the individual's conscience to decide" will be inappropriate. Let's consider a few cases to see exactly why. A high school girl hears a rumor that a classmate is a shoplifter. Is she morally justified in repeating the story to her best friend if she makes the friend promise not to "tell a soul"? A 13-year-old boy walks into his neighborhood grocery store and asks the grocer for a pack of cigarettes "for my mother." The grocer knows the mother doesn't smoke and that the boy is too young to buy cigarettes legally. Should she sell them to him? A weapons manufacturer has an opportunity to make a big and very profitable sale to the ruler of a small foreign country. He knows the ruler is a tyrant who oppresses his people and governs by terror. Is it right for him to sell the weapons? A college student's friends are sexually promiscuous. She has always regarded promiscuity as immoral, but lately she has wondered whether she has been too scrupulous. What should she do?

Whatever we decide is right in these cases, our decision should be based on more than saying "Leave the matter to the individual's conscience." If we say that in the first three cases, we are saying, in effect, "Any action is acceptable," for we can have no way of knowing exactly what those people's consciences will prompt them to do. If we say it in the case of the college student, we are evading the issue, for her dilemma is deciding whether the promptings of her conscience are reasonable.

▦ SAMPLE RESPONSE TO INQUIRIES

Here is a sample response to help you understand the kind of analysis and the form of response appropriate for the inquiries that follow. (You need not agree with the particular viewpoint expressed.) Note that the response expresses not just the writer's moral judgment but also the reasoning that underlies it.

Inquiry: A graduate school professor has several student assistants, talented young men and women pursuing doctorates. He regularly uses their research findings and interpretations, and even their phrasing, in his own scholarly writing, without crediting them either in the text of his articles and books or in the footnotes. "It's part of their job to do research for me," he reasons; "the money they receive from their fellowships for doing the research is credit enough for them." His conscience does not trouble him. But should it?

Sample Response: *His conscience should trouble him because what he is doing is unethical and the argument he offers to support his actions is flawed. Book publishers don't put someone else's name on an author's book on the grounds that the royalties he'll earn will be "credit enough." A person's ideas and the words used to express them are possessions. It doesn't matter whether the person in question is a famous scholar or a student. Taking ideas without permission is no different from stealing the computer that recorded them. There's also the element of deception to be considered. The professor is tricking members of his profession into giving him recognition and honor that he doesn't deserve.*

⊞ INQUIRIES

If you need assistance in composing your responses, read "Writing About Moral Issues" in the Appendix.

1. After *U.S. News and World Report* published an article that discussed cheating in school and pointed out why it is wrong, a student wrote a letter to the magazine arguing that cheating is not morally wrong but merely an efficient way to avoid "busywork" and produce a quality piece of work. Instead of a reprimand, he suggested that cheaters deserve praise for being enterprising and effective.[8] Do you agree with this student? If so, explain why. If not, explain why not in terms of what you have learned in this book.

2. A number of medical centers around the United States now offer "finders' fees" to physicians for referring patients to researchers who are conducting trials of new drug therapies, the side effects of which are not yet known. One researcher, for example, was offering physicians a $350 payment for each referred patient who enrolled in the research project. Many physicians accept the fees and make the referrals, apparently without suffering pangs of conscience. Are their actions ethical?[9]

3. From 1940 to 1970, more than 4,000 radiation experiments were performed on tens of thousands of Americans, many of them poor and uneducated, without their informed consent. Examples of alleged incidents: children in a Massachusetts orphanage were fed radioisotopes; 829 pregnant Tennessee women were fed radioactive iron; patients in Rochester, New York, were injected with plutonium; cancer patients in Cincinnati received heavy doses of gamma rays. Not all of these experiments can be attributed to researchers' ignorance of the harmful effects of radiation; the main purpose of the experiments was to identify those effects rather than to cure the patients. Even so, the researchers do not seem to have thought they were committing a moral offense. Were they?[10]

4. Marvin manufactures locks and keys for automobiles, and his biggest customers are General Motors, Chrysler, and Ford. But he also has a mail-order business, in which he offers (among other products) master keys for automobile locks. He realizes that his mail-order customers include more than a few car thieves, but that does not trouble his conscience. He believes that he is not responsible for the illegal ways his products might be used. Is he correct?

5. When Bruno and Bertha rented their apartment, they signed a lease that included a provision that animals were not allowed. Now they have decided they want to have a cat. They plan to sneak it into the apartment at night so the landlord won't know they have it. Their consciences are not troubled. Comment.

6. Lucille owns a telephone answering service. In order to check on the courtesy and helpfulness of her telephone operators, she often monitors incoming business calls. Though others might consider this to be spying, she believes it is part of her responsibility to her customers. Is it?

7. Sylvester is the descendant of a nineteenth-century robber baron. (A robber baron is an unscrupulous individual who gains wealth by unethical means, such as by paying off legislators, exploiting employees, or savaging the environment.) Though embarrassed by the way his family's wealth was acquired, Sylvester nevertheless believes he is entitled to keep it because he inherited it. Is he correct?

8. For each of the following cases, decide whether the person's conscience was correct. That is, decide whether the action it directed the person to take (or silently approved) is ethically justifiable. Explain your reasoning.

   a. Broderick stops at a pay phone to make a call. As he is talking, he absentmindedly fingers the coin return and finds a dime someone has carelessly forgotten. When he is finished talking, he pockets the coin and walks away. Halfway down the block, he feels guilty for taking it. He returns to the booth and deposits it in the coin return.

   b. A doctor is driving down the highway late at night. She sees a car in the opposite lane swerve sharply off the road and plunge down an embankment. No other cars are around. Her first impulse as a physician is to stop and assist the victims. However, she remembers that the state has no "Good Samaritan law" to protect her from a malpractice lawsuit. Her conscience tells her she is justified in driving on.

   c. A candidate for the local school board has heard the rumor that her opponent gives "wild parties." As she proceeds with her campaign, she visits the homes of many voters. She makes it a point to tell everyone what she has heard about her opponent, always adding, "Of course, it's only a rumor that no one has yet proven to be true." She believes sincerely that it would be dishonest of her not to inform them about the rumor so that they can evaluate it before voting.

   d. In order to beat out the competition for a summer gardener's job at a nearby estate, Alan agreed to work for a wage somewhat lower than the standard of the area. The owner and her family are at the estate only on weekends and Alan works alone. Although his workday is fixed—9 to 5, Monday through Friday—he arrives late and leaves early on most days and occasionally takes an afternoon off. He does not feel guilty because his employer is paying him less than others would have worked for.

e. An enterprising black real estate broker hires a white man and woman to buy a house in a white neighborhood and then transfer title to her. She then visits the white residents of the neighborhood and explains that she owns one house already and plans to buy others and sell them to black families. She tells each white resident that some other white neighbor has secretly agreed to sell. Everyone becomes frightened that property values will plummet, and many are tricked into selling to the broker at much lower prices than their homes are worth. The broker then sells the homes to black families for what they are really worth. Not only does she feel morally blameless, but she regards herself as a heroine of sorts, a fighter against discrimination in housing.

f. Fred is the oldest of seven children of a widow. He is an honor student in a technical program at a nearby junior college. He pays his way by stealing automobile tires, radios, and stereo tape decks and selling them. When he first took up this part-time "occupation," he felt a little guilty. But he no longer does, for he decided that no one is really injured: The owners will be somewhat inconvenienced but not deprived because their insurance will cover replacement costs.

9. The following people all have clear consciences. Decide whether they are entitled to them and explain your decision.

a. George believes strongly that drug use and dealing are a personal matter, outside the sphere of morality. He sells marijuana, cocaine, heroin, anything. Whatever there is a market for, he will deal in.

b. Gus specializes in LSD, which he laces liberally with strychnine to increase his profits.

c. Mary Jane sells marijuana.

d. Connie believes strongly that the use of any drug is a crutch and that hard drugs ruin lives. She volunteers to be an undercover agent at her college, without pay.

10. The consciences of the people in the following cases are confused. As a result, the people cannot decide whether the actions they are contemplating are morally right. Decide for them and present the rationale for your position.

a. A married couple discover that their 22-year-old daughter, a college senior, is a lesbian. They are shocked and dismayed, for they regard this as moral degeneracy. They are thinking of refusing to attend her graduation and refusing to welcome her in their home until she renounces this sexual preference.

b. A student is taking a composition course in college. Her assignment is to write on the morality of war. Back in her room, she moans aloud that she doesn't know where to begin with such a complex subject. One of her roommates declares where she stands on the issue. The other challenges her view. In time, several students wander into the room and get involved in the ensuing discussion. One goes out and gets a term paper she did on a similar subject. She reads it aloud and is interrupted from time to time as someone disputes a statement or expands upon it. After an hour or so, the session breaks up, leaving the student who didn't know where to begin with a different problem: deciding to what extent, if any, she is justified in using in her paper the facts and opinions she heard from the others.

c. Harry has been an officer in the police department of his small city for a year. He has seen many violations of department policy: squad car teams pulling over on lonely streets and sleeping during evening shifts, officers receiving hush money from gamblers and dope pushers, officers conducting sexual commerce with women in the station house while on duty, sergeants and lieutenants spending whole shifts at home and altering duty records to cover their absences. Harry is seriously considering turning these men in, but he is confused about where his loyalty should lie.

d. An airline pilot goes for his regular medical checkup. The doctor discovers that he has developed a heart murmur. The pilot has only a month to go before he is eligible for retirement. The doctor knows this and wonders whether, under these unusual circumstances, she is justified in withholding the information about the pilot's condition.

11. Animal lovers in a suburb of Los Angeles picketed a parochial school to protest the action of a priest-educator. The priest had drowned ten cats because they were too noisy and messy. He explained that his action had been "humane" and added, "I buried them. They're fertilizing our rose bushes."[11] Apparently, the priest's conscience didn't bother him. Should it have?

12. A cosmetologist in a local beauty salon enjoys a high sales record and popularity with his clients. He believes that being attractive is extremely important and that his job is to help his clients feel that they are or could be attractive. Although he realizes that some of his compliments are false and that some of the products he sells do not live up to advertising claims, he feels he is performing a public service by making people feel good about themselves.

13. Rhoda enjoys socializing with fellow employees at work, but their discussion usually consists of gossiping about other people, including several of her friends. At first Rhoda feels uncomfortable talking in this way about people she is close to, but then she decides it does no real harm and so she feels no remorse for joining in.

CHAPTER FIVE

COMPARING CULTURES

*If an action that is praised in one culture
may be condemned in another, would it be
correct to say that all moral values are relative
to the culture they are found in? Isn't it
a mark of ignorance to pass judgments
on other cultures or to claim that
one culture is better than another?*

Before continuing our search for a dependable standard of ethical judgment, it will be useful to consider the issue of whether moral judgments are ever appropriate outside one's own culture. Early anthropological studies of Eskimo, Samoan, and other "exotic" (from the Western perspective) cultures generated considerable debate over this issue. As the twentieth century progressed, cross-cultural communication improved and knowledge of other cultures expanded, and the focus of anthropologists' curiosity shifted from the exotic foreign cultures to the many subcultures within their own country. In the United States, the list of subcultures would include African American, Irish American, Italian American, and Asian American. Narrower divisions according to religion, socioeconomic level, geography, gender, and sexual orientation are all possible. Thus a researcher might examine the attitudes and values of white female yuppies (young urban professionals) living in the southeastern United States.

Contemporary scholarly discussion of cultures and subcultures is significantly affected by the social movement known as *multiculturalism*. Among the central tenets of this movement are that every race or ethnic group has its own values and characteristic behaviors, that no group's values are any better or worse than any other's, and that criticism of another culture's ideas and actions is wrong. Our concern in this chapter is not with multiculturalism itself but only with its influence on ethics. We'll begin our analysis by considering differences in ethical standards among cultures.

DIFFERENCES AMONG CULTURES

Cultures differ in their ideas about right and wrong, and the differences are not always slight. In some instances, one culture's sin is another's virtue. For example, the conception of marriage that Americans are most familiar with—one wife and one husband joined for life—is not universal. In some cultures, serial monogamy—marrying several times—is not merely tolerated (as it is beginning to be in the United States) but is regarded as neutral or even good. In Siberia, "a Koryak woman . . . would find it hard to understand how a woman could be so selfish and so undesirous of female companionship in the home as to wish to restrict her husband to one mate."[1]

Sex before marriage has been generally viewed as immoral in the West. Yet in some island cultures, it is encouraged. Homosexuals are hounded and tormented as immoral deviants in some cultures; in others they are accepted without reservation.

Such differences are not limited to sexual morality. It is considered a person's moral obligation in some cultures to assist a blood relative in any enterprise, even stealing from others. Certain tribes of headhunters may raid neighboring villages and return with the villagers' heads for no other reason than that their supply of names has been used up, and before a new name may be claimed one must possess the head it belonged to.[2]

It is commonly thought that at least one action—the taking of life—would be unanimously condemned by people of all cultures. Here is what anthropologist Ruth Benedict has to say about that idea in her classic study, *Patterns of Culture:*

> On the contrary, in a matter of homicide, it may be held that one is blameless if diplomatic relations have been severed between neighboring countries, or that one kills by custom his first two children, or that a husband has right of life and death over his wife, or that it is the duty of the child to kill his parents before they are old. It may be that those are killed who steal a fowl, or who cut their upper teeth first, or who are born on a Wednesday. Among some peoples a person suffers torments at having caused an accidental death; among others it is a matter of no consequence. Suicide also may be a light matter, the recourse of anyone who has suffered some slight rebuff, an act that occurs constantly in a tribe. It may be the highest and noblest act a wise man can perform. The very tale of it, on the other hand, may be a matter for incredulous mirth, and the act itself impossible to conceive as a human possibility. Or it may be a crime punishable by law, or regarded as a sin against the gods.[3]

In *Patterns of Culture,* Benedict details the customs, values, and beliefs of three cultures. One of them is the culture of several groups of Indians of the Northwest Coast of America, mainly the Kwakiutl of Vancouver Island, whose traditional way of life survived until the end of the nineteenth century. Among those tribes, it was an accepted practice to murder a man to acquire the rights to his name, his special dances, his personal crests, and his symbols. Similarly, when a loved one died, the mourners would search for someone of equal rank in a neighboring tribe, announce their intention of killing that person, and then proceed to do so. In this way, they vanquished fate and the pain of sorrow not by reacting passively, but by striking back.[4]

Another interesting culture described by Benedict is that of Dobu Island off the coast of New Guinea. At one time a cannibal culture, Dobu had "no chiefs . . . no political organization . . . no legality" when Benedict studied it. A Dobuan's entire life was spent in vicious competition. The rule of virtually every social enterprise was *cheat your neighbor.* The virtuous man, the respected man, was the one who had succeeded in injuring his rival in some way. Unlike the Northwest Coast Indian, the Dobuan who wished to rob or kill someone did not announce his plan but pretended affection and performed his treachery in secret or by surprise. The sorcery that the Dobuans practiced on one another was, in their view, made more potent by closeness to the victim.

So institutionalized had this practice become that the Dobuans had a special term for it: *wabuwabu,* the achievement of "reap[ing] personal advantage in a situation in which others are victimized." Typical examples of *wabuwabu* were promising to trade the same valuable possession to several traders and breaking an engagement for marriage after obtaining the usual property settlement from the father of the betrothed. Given the unrelenting emphasis on the ill treatment of others, it is not surprising that the Dobuans scorned laughter and refrained from pleasurable activities or expressions of happiness.[5]

During the mid-1960s, another anthropologist, Colin Turnbull, conducted an in-depth field study of an equally fascinating culture, that of the Ik tribe of Central Africa. The Ik acknowledge no moral or social obligation to anyone or anything. Their standard of value is the self; their rule of life, to do whatever they wish. At age 3, children are put out of their parents' huts and thereafter sleep in the open, rain or shine. To survive, they gather in bands and form not friendships but temporary alliances, which are betrayed whenever convenience dictates. Not surprisingly, children learn to cry tears of malice, anger, or hate, but never of sorrow. Because family life and community are foreign to their world, the Ik live out their lives without ever experiencing love, affection, or a sense of belonging, painfully aware that if illness or age weakens them, they will be left to die.

The Ik's sexual expression typically is adulterous and is driven less by passion than by the desire to profit at someone else's expense. A neighbor's suffering evokes not pity or kindness but malicious glee.

On one occasion observed by Turnbull, when an emaciated little girl lay dying of hunger, her playmates put a bit of food in her hand and then, as she raised it to her mouth, beat her savagely. Similarly, mothers laugh when their infants fall and hurt themselves; if a leopard carries off a child, the parents' reaction is delight.

From the beginning of Turnbull's stay, he searched the tribe's daily behavior for some small evidence of love, some gesture of self-sacrifice for a loved one or a principle. He found none, although he did find "ample evidence" in their language and oral traditions that they had at one time known the meaning of values such as goodness and happiness. Turnbull concluded that the Ik had at some time abandoned their humanity for an existence of passionless mutual exploitation.[6]

INTERPRETING THE DIFFERENCES

What do anthropologists make of such differences between the traditional moral standards of our culture and the standards of the Kwakiutl, Dobuans, and Ik? What conclusions do anthropologists draw about the appropriateness of judging other cultures? The principle that has governed such matters is a complex and, in some ways, controversial principle known as *cultural relativity*. It derives from observation of cultural differences and two important realizations: (a) that a culture's values, rituals, and customs reflect its geography, history, and socioeconomic circumstances and (b) that hasty or facile comparison of other cultures with one's own culture tends to thwart scholarly analysis and produce shallow or erroneous conclusions.

In themselves, these realizations are truisms; no reasonable person would deny that a people's experience influences its beliefs and behaviors or that careful, objective thinking is preferable to careless, biased thinking. Difficulty has arisen only because some anthropologists (and many other individuals) have leaped from these realizations to the conclusion that *whatever a culture considers morally acceptable is by that very fact morally acceptable.* Two facts about this conclusion are noteworthy. First, it is closely related to the majoritarian view discussed in Chapter 2 and has the same flaws. Second, this conclusion represents a crossing from one academic domain to another—from anthropology to ethics. Because academic boundaries are not well marked, such wandering is not uncommon. Unfortunately, it tends to compromise the quality of both scholarly and popular discussion. That is exactly what has happened in the case of cultural relativism.

Some anthropologists have challenged extreme interpretations of cultural relativity. Clyde Kluckhohn, for example, argues that "the principle of cultural relativity does not mean that because the members of some savage tribe are allowed to behave in a certain way that this fact gives intellectual warrant for such behavior in all groups. Cultural relativity means, on the contrary, that the appropriateness of any positive or negative custom must be evaluated with regard to how this habit fits with other group habits."[7] However, this argument merely adds a condition of consistency to the formula, saying, in effect, that whatever a group decides is moral will be moral *as long as it is consistent with other behaviors of the group*. It leaves unanswered the very relevant question, Is it possible for a custom or habit within a culture to be long-standing and completely consistent with other behaviors of the group *yet at the same time be immoral*? Before we address that question, let us balance our discussion of the differing values among cultures with consideration of similarities.

THE SIMILARITY OF VALUES

Not long ago my wife received a letter from a relative. The letter described a spiritual retreat he was about to begin. He wrote as follows: "The whole retreat comes right back to the virtue of generosity and giving. The first step is to give gifts that are of value to others. The next step is to give one's self to goodness, which entails having good manners, good deportment, and kind speech, so that others will be uplifted in spirit. To accomplish this takes a lot of looking inside one's self and asking frequently 'What am I doing now and why? Is this act coming from a kind and caring mind or is it coming from anger and frustration or some other negative impulse?' "

As you read, did you get the impression that the young man is a born-again Christian? Many people would, but they would be wrong. He happens to be a young American who moved to Thailand five years ago to become a Buddhist monk. The values he described are Buddhist values. Even so, they would be meaningful to people around the globe, regardless of their racial, ethnic, or cultural differences. Catholics, Methodists, Mormons, Amish, Muslims, Taoists, and more than a few agnostics and atheists would affirm them.

The point is not that there are no differences among cultures—we have already affirmed that there are. It is that the currently fashionable focus on diversity—that is, on the things that divide people—often obscures the many values people have in common.

You may think Christianity is unique in affirming the importance of keeping a pure and honest mind, yet one of the greatest literary works of early Buddhism, the *Dhammapada,* begins with these words: "Those who harbor resentful thoughts toward others, believing they were insulted, hurt, defeated, or cheated, will suffer from hatred, because hate never conquers hatred. Yet hate is conquered by love, which is an eternal law.

Those who live for pleasures with uncontrolled senses will be over-thrown by temptation. Those who cleanse themselves from impurity, grounded in virtues, possessing self-control and truth are worthy of the yellow robe. Those who imagine truth in untruth and see untruth in truth follow vain desires."

You may be similarly surprised to learn that the values of humility, modesty, control of passions and desires, truthfulness, integrity, patience, steadfastness, and fulfilling one's promises are not peculiar to the Judeo-Christian tradition but are honored in other cultures. For example, they are mentioned again and again in Islam's sacred book, the Koran. As Dr. Shadid Athar notes, even the Ten Commandments have almost exact counterparts in Islam. Here are just a few examples:

The Bible	**The Koran**
Thou shalt not use God's name in vain.	Make not God's name an excuse to your oaths.
Thou shalt honor thy mother and father.	Be kind to your parents if one or both of them attain old age in thy life, say not a word of contempt nor repel them but address them in terms of honor.
Thou shalt not kill.	If anyone has killed one person it is as if he had killed the whole of mankind.

Where differences exist, it is easy to misinterpret their nature and extent. For example, we might assume a value is absent when, in fact, *it is merely subordinated to another, higher value.* To the casual observer, for example, the Hindus' refusal to use cattle to feed starving people shows a wanton disregard for human life. Yet the real explanation for the refusal is that their religion prevents them from killing cattle for any purpose. Another way to misinterpret other cultures is to assume that a value is absent when *it is merely considered inapplicable to the situation in question.* Consider two cases mentioned earlier in the chapter: the man who helped his relative steal and the headhunters who replenished their supply of names. Although it certainly seemed that they were act-ing without a sense of justice or fairness, both were in fact acting on the idea that outsiders, people alien to their family or tribe, are "beyond the pale of moral consideration."[8] Justice and fairness are seen as inapplica-ble to them. They are not persons; hence, they have no rights. (If such reasoning seems bizarre, remember that many American slaveowners had similar attitudes toward their slaves and that the domestic and for-eign policies of "civilized" countries do not always, even to this day, coincide.)

The conclusion that even these brief examples suggest is that though behavior may vary greatly from culture to culture, the underlying values are, as a rule, remarkably similar. We find justice and courage, respect for one's relatives and tribal members, subordination of individual whim to custom or the judgments of tribal sages. If it is a mistake to deny the differences in human values, as manifested in the behaviors of the Ik and the Dobuans, then surely it is an even greater mistake to deny the similarities.

In 1967 at the Aspen Institute of Humanistic Studies, a famous Oriental scholar, Wing-sit Chan, and a famous Occidental scholar, Mortimer Adler, conducted a joint seminar. After reviewing the teachings of Confucius and Aristotle, and noting similarities and differences, seminar participants agreed that the main differences were style and method. Further, "it seemed equally clear to all present that the fundamental notions and insights were either the same or closely parallel."[9] Adler also rejects "the illusion that there is a Western mind and an Eastern mind, a European mind and an African mind, or a civilized mind and a primitive mind." In his view, "there is only a human mind and it is one and the same in all human beings."[10] In other words, all people have the same basic physio-logical, psychological, and intellectual equipment. They receive data from the same five senses; react with the same range of emotions; form attitudes, desires, dispositions, and intentions in the same ways; form ideas in the same manner; and even make the same kinds of mistakes—for example, overgeneralizing, oversimplifying, and jumping to conclusions.

IS JUDGMENT APPROPRIATE?

We have noted that people who accept an extreme interpretation of cul-tural relativism say that moral judgment of other cultures is never ap-propriate. We have also noted that multiculturalism extends that view-point to *subcultures*. In other words, multiculturalism clearly implies that within the larger American culture, Jews should not comment on the behavior of Protestants, and neither of these groups should criticize the actions of Roman Catholics. Similarly, African Americans should remain silent about the behavior of Asian or European Americans, and vice versa. And Lithuanian Americans, Japanese Americans, and Peruvian Americans ought to remain mutually mute on moral issues outside their own ethnic groups. By this logic, your author, an Irish-Italian Caucasian American, has no business writing this book for a general audience. But, then again, by the same logic, no one else has either!

This point of view may sound reasonable when presented in the abstract, but the moment we apply it to concrete cases, its shallowness becomes evident. What is wrong with African Americans denouncing white racism; Jews denouncing Nation of Islam leader Louis Farrakhan's anti-Semitic statements; Christians denouncing the assassination of Israel's Prime Minister Rabin; and people all over the world denouncing apartheid in South Africa, Saddam Hussein's invasion of Kuwait, and the atrocities committed in Bosnia? The answer, most reasonable people would agree, is *nothing at all.* Such judgments are not only appropriate but also morally responsible.

In some cases, we cannot avoid making moral judgments even if we try. In a 1973 decision (*Roe* v. *Wade*), the U.S. Supreme Court declared that the human fetus is not entitled to the protection of the law and abortion is therefore legal. Yet in 1975, the Constitutional Court of Germany reached the exact opposite legal opinion—that "the life of each individual human being is self-evidently a central value of the legal order . . . [and] the constitutional duty to protect this life also includes its preliminary stages before birth." The German high court reaffirmed this view in 1993, holding that the state has "a duty to place itself protectively before unborn human life, shielding this life from unlawful attacks" and calling for penal laws against anyone who would pressure pregnant women into having abortions.[11] *Holding either of these views necessarily entails rejecting the other.* We may, of course, try to reconcile the two views in the manner of cultural relativists or multiculturalists, but we will encounter mind-boggling difficulties. If a pregnant American woman visits Germany, for example, does her fetus magically gain moral and legal rights when the plane lands in Frankfurt? And what of the woman's German counterpart? Does her fetus leave Hamburg a person and arrive in New York a nonperson?

Earlier in this chapter we asked, but postponed answering, this question: "Is it possible for a custom or habit within a culture to be long-standing and completely consistent with other behaviors of the group *yet at the same time be immoral*?" History answers in the affirmative. Every age has moral issues that challenge all thinking, caring people, regardless of their race, creed, or ethnic heritage. During World War II, for example, the Nazis invaded their neighbors, hauled off many millions of people to concentration camps, performed hideous experiments without anesthesia, and conducted mass executions. For the Allies to have ignored these heinous deeds on the grounds that whatever was approved in Nazi Germany was morally acceptable for Nazi Germany would have violated the memory of the Nazis' victims. When the war was finally won, the Allies, to their credit, held the famous Nuremberg trials, at which the responsible individuals were called to account for their "crimes against humanity." The United Nations based its well-known Declaration of Human Rights on essentially the same idea—that some actions deserve condemnation no matter where, when, or in what cultural circumstances they are performed and that no decent person or nation will shrink from condemning them.

The key to appreciating the appropriateness and, in some cases, the necessity of making moral judgments about other cultures and subcultures is to acknowledge three facts. The first is that cultures are dynamic rather than static (though the rate at which change occurs may vary greatly). Ancestral behaviors are not always mindlessly repeated but are often evaluated, embellished, refined, and/or reformed. Over time, the resulting changes can be significant. (Remember Colin Turnbull's observation that the Ik tribe at one time had a more civilized moral code but for some reason abandoned it.) Also, if a culture has contact with the outside world, some borrowing of ideas, beliefs, and values from other cultures is inevitable. Modern communications technology has provided unprecedented opportunities for intercultural borrowing. Communications satellites enable people in remote areas to receive television programs from any country. Personal computers, fax modems, and access to the Internet invite global exchange of ideas.

The second fact to be acknowledged is that the revolution in communications technology has profoundly altered the process by which cultural values are reaffirmed or modified and imparted to subsequent generations. Historically, those values were acquired in the home, the church, and the school, agencies that, though far from perfect, nevertheless took the welfare of children and society very seriously. In technologically advanced countries, the entertainment and communications media have become more influential than these agencies. American youngsters, for example, spend roughly twice as much time watching television as they do in the classroom and countless more hours listening to CDs and playing video games; they also see more than 750,000 commercials and print advertisements by age 18. Moreover, the media are driven more by the desire for profit than by commitment to truth, dedication to moral excellence, or concern for the emotional and intellectual welfare of the public. Accordingly, as ratings competition has increased, the media have not hesitated to embrace sensationalism and to glamorize ideas, attitudes, and values that directly oppose the teachings of home, church, and school. Mass culture (also known as popular culture) is being exported to virtually every corner of the world; and wherever it goes, it tends to undermine the traditional culture.

The third and most important fact, so obvious that theorists often overlook it, is that all of the people referred to in the previous two paragraphs are fallible creatures. This includes the ancestors who formulated cultural customs and moral codes; the progeny who preserved or changed those customs and codes; the parents, clergy, and teachers who perpetuate them; and the purveyors of mass culture who challenge them.

At times, these people will have made the effort to become well informed and will have raised important questions about issues, reasoned carefully and well, and produced genuine insights. At other times, their emotions, preconceptions, and assumptions will have biased their thinking and resulted in shallow or erroneous conclusions.

The only way we have of determining which customs, codes, beliefs, values, and behaviors are wise and which are foolish is to examine them carefully and judge them honestly and fairly. The notion that other people's cultures (or our own culture) have in some mystical way escaped the effects of human fallibility does a disservice to the subject of ethics and to the men and women in every culture who have striven for moral excellence.

THREE IMPORTANT CAUTIONS

To say that moral judgment of other cultures is appropriate or necessary is not to say that it should be undertaken casually. To ensure that your judgments are fair and reasonable, keep these cautions in mind:

1. *Understanding is no substitute for moral judgment.* Because speaking from ignorance is irresponsible, we should refrain from judging any act until we understand the context in which it occurred. However, we should also avoid the mistake of ending our inquiry when we reach that understanding. An example will illustrate how this mistake occurs. Suppose we encounter a reference to the ancient Spartan practice of whipping young boys viciously. Resisting the temptation to judge without fuller understanding, we inquire further and learn that the whipping was part of a ritual marking the boy's initiation into manhood and that it symbolized the physical toughness required of a citizen in a warrior state. Our curiosity about context thus satisfied, we may have the vague feeling that we have settled the moral question *when all we have really done is sharpened its focus.* We now need to find out whether the ritual initiation of young boys into manhood by viciously whipping them was a moral practice.

   The details of what was done, the cultural situation in which it occurred, and the motivation of the person doing it are all very useful kinds of knowledge, but they are not the same as knowledge of the moral quality of the action itself. That kind of knowledge is the most important kind in ethics. This leads us to the second caution.

2. *The essential moral quality of an action does not change from time to time or place to place.* Admittedly, in many cases the moral quality can seem to change. Many actions we would unhesitatingly denounce in our own time and place have a way of sounding morally acceptable for other times and places. If CNN reported that ritual human sacrifices had been performed last week in Kansas City to ensure a good harvest, we would be outraged and alarmed. But when we are told

that many ancient cultures slaughtered people to ensure a good harvest, to dedicate a new temple, or to provide servants for a deceased monarch in the afterlife, our reaction may be "Oh, that's interesting." In such cases, we are tricked into attaching more significance to incidental details of time and place than to essential matters, as if the subtraction of a few centuries or even millennia, a geographical shift, and the adding of strange costumes and undecipherable incantations could transform an immoral act into a moral one. Ritual human sacrifice was as wrong a thousand years ago as it is today, and we can confidently say that it will be wrong a thousand years from now. The same is true of rape and plunder and genocide.

Let's examine some less dramatic cases, as well. Today, if doctors went through hospital wards touching patient after patient without ever washing their hands, they would be committing an ethical offense (and could also face legal action). Yet up until the mid-nineteenth century, doctors didn't bother to wash their hands. Similarly, if modern soft-drink manufacturers put cocaine in their products or cigarette manufacturers wrote "beneficial to your health" on their labels, they would be behaving unethically. Yet in the early twentieth century, cocaine was an ingredient in at least one soft drink and cigarettes were widely advertised as healthful.

What changed with the passing of time? Not the actions themselves, and certainly not their effects. People became ill and sometimes died from the doctors' spread of bacteria then, and they would now. Cocaine-laced soft drinks caused addiction then, and they would now. Cigarette smoking resulted in lung cancer and other diseases then, and it continues to do so. The only thing that changed was human knowledge. That leaves us with a dilemma. We can't classify the acts in the distant past as ethical or morally neutral, even though people thought them so. On the other hand, it doesn't seem reasonable to say the acts were unethical, because the people who performed them had no way of knowing the harm that would result. Perhaps the dilemma cannot be completely resolved. The third caution provides a way to address this dilemma.

3. *Culpability for immoral acts may vary widely.* Culpability is moral responsibility or blame. Most people are familiar with the concept as it applies in law. They know that taking another person's life warrants the death penalty or life imprisonment if the act was premeditated, a term of perhaps twenty years if it was committed in a moment of passion, and no punishment at all if it was done in self-defense. Although the act is identical in all three cases, the responsibility of the perpetrators varies according to the circumstances.

The concept of culpability applies in ethics as well as in law, and it is particularly relevant to the case of the doctors who unwittingly spread bacteria and the cases of the people who put cocaine in soft drinks and proclaimed that smoking is beneficial. However much harm their acts did, the individuals were not culpable.

By separating the act from the person who performs it, we are able to make more accurate and reasonable ethical judgments. For example, we may denounce the cannibalism, infanticide, and human sacrifice and yet acknowledge that primitive tribes lacked the insight necessary for moral responsibility.*

▥ INQUIRIES

1. The Makah tribe claim to have hunted gray whales for more than 2,000 years. They stopped in the 1920s due to a decline in the number of gray whales. Now they want to return to the hunt to provide food for their tribe and to restore the young men's sense of discipline and pride in their traditions. Proponents of the hunt claim that a majority of the tribe support the hunt, which is expected to take fewer than the five whales they are permitted by law to kill. Tribal leaders claim they will take no pregnant or nursing females. Some Makah elders disagree, however, pointing out that the tribe survived for most of the twentieth century without eating whale meat and claiming that there are better ways to instill pride and discipline. The environmental community argues that the whale hunt is immoral because it violates the whales' right to exist on the planet. Is it appropriate for nonmembers of the Makah tribe—for example, students in your class—to evaluate the morality of the Makah whale hunt? Explain.

2. In each of the following cases, the behavior illustrated seems to suggest that the people's values differ significantly from our own. Consider the possibility that, beneath appearances, the values are similar. Develop a plausible explanation for the difference in behavior.

a. In one culture, the elderly and those with severe handicaps are put to death. It would appear that this culture does not recognize human dignity as a value.

b. In another culture, this habit is observed: A person will ask a relative to do a task that requires days of labor and, when it is completed, never even thank the relative. On the other hand, if a stranger renders anyone the slightest service, the stranger is lavishly rewarded. It would appear that a sense of fairness is lacking in this culture.

c. Members of a tribe living in a remote jungle area commonly shun the sick. The moment members of the tribe become seriously ill, they cease to exist in the tribe's view. They must leave the village and care for themselves. If they recover, however, they are restored to tribal membership. Apparently, the tribe lacks compassion for the afflicted.

d. A group of young boys are gathered together. Several men approach them, brandishing sticks and whips. They beat the boys viciously. The other male members of the tribe sit by and watch, laughing and

*Culpability is discussed more fully in Chapter 11.

obviously enjoying the event. It would seem that the men of this culture are sadistic, deriving pleasure from seeing others in pain.

e. Whenever hunters in a certain culture are asked how their day's hunting went, they say "very well" and go on to declare that their relatives and friends and ancestors will be pleased with them. They say this whether they return heavily laden or empty-handed. It appears that truth-telling has no value in this culture.

f. One woman finds another eating a piece of wild fruit. She calls to her neighbors and they stone the offender to death. Because the punishment does not fit the crime, it would appear that this culture lacks a sense of proportion and fails to recognize the value of human life.

g. In an island culture, the men are seen returning from a fishing expedition. One man runs his canoe happily up on the beach. The villagers cheer him. Then a second canoe arrives. The second fisherman leaps out, runs to the first man, seizes his basket of fish, and throws it into the sea. He goes unpunished. The tribe seems to tolerate stealing.

h. In some technologically advanced cultures, young people are "tracked" early in life to certain vocations and training programs. As adults, they have few career options and are expected to follow a path chosen for them. Apparently, the cultures do not value self-determination and individual well-being.

3. When Hua, a Chinese woman, gave birth to a daughter rather than a son, her husband refused to look at the child. Later he punished his wife for the "offense" by withholding money and hitting her without provocation. When the child contracted pneumonia, he suggested she be left to die. Eventually, he divorced his wife—the decree cited his disapproval of having a girl baby and specified that the wife would keep the child and he would get their apartment. This story is not that uncommon in China, where masculinity is defined as producing a son to maintain the family line. This cultural value is so ancient and so strong that it is even reflected in the language—the character for the word *good* is a combination of the sign for "woman" and the sign for "son."[12] Evaluate this cultural value.

4. Soviet dictator Joseph Stalin ordered the killing of 30 million peasants and filled the gulags (forced labor camps) with another 15 million, many of them guilty of nothing more than publicly disagreeing with his policies. Some people would say it is inappropriate for us to judge the morality of Stalin's actions because they took place in a different culture and at a different time. How would you answer them?

5. In some cultures, mutilation is considered an appropriate punishment for certain crimes. For example, if a man is caught stealing, his hand is cut off. Since such a punishment is unheard of in our culture, we tend to consider it morally insupportable. Do you agree or disagree with this moral assessment?

6. Imelda Marcos, wife of former Philippine dictator Ferdinand Marcos, reportedly spent millions on antiques in a single day. When her husband was deposed, her closet was found to contain 3,000 pairs of shoes and hundreds of priceless gowns. All this occurred at a time when most of the people of that country lived in poverty. Her culture is not our culture, so is it proper for us to judge the morality of her actions? If so, what is your judgment? If not, why not?

7. The Eskimo husband's sense of hospitality requires him to offer his wife to an overnight guest. In our culture this is considered wrong. Is one view more justifiable than the other? Explain your reasoning carefully.

8. In some ancient cultures, a young maiden was sacrificed each year to ensure a good harvest. In others, when the king died, many servants were killed and buried with him so that his needs in the afterlife could be suitably attended. Such practices are understandable, given the beliefs of the people. Are they morally right? Why or why not?

9. In ancient Rome, Sparta, and China, unwanted children were abandoned to die. Comment on the morality of this practice.

10. In some cultures, a person who kills someone by accident must support the victim's family thereafter. In our culture we expect life insurance and social security to cover the family's needs. If the one responsible for the accident is found to be legally blameless, he or she is customarily considered morally blameless as well. Compare and evaluate these moral views.

11. Review the Dobuan moral code and underlying view of life presented in this chapter. To what extent is the code ethically justifiable?

12. When a Christian missionary is sent to preach the Gospel to members of a newly discovered tribe, she has the following experiences:

a. After arriving in their primitive jungle settlement and establishing a friendly relationship with them, she learns that they encourage extramarital promiscuity. She believes that this is morally wrong. She therefore explains to them that such promiscuity is immoral, an offense against God. Is the missionary's action ethical?

b. The same Christian missionary next learns that once each year, as an inducement to the god of the hunt to smile upon their efforts, members of the tribe cut off someone's right hand. (Whose right hand is determined quite democratically, by lottery.) The missionary is appalled by this custom and explains to the tribe that it is based on pure superstition. Is the missionary's action justifiable?

c. The missionary now makes an even more startling discovery. Because tribe members believe women are inferior to men and a tribe with a large number of women is an outrage to the god of good sense, they strictly control the female population. Whenever the number of girl babies exceeds the percentage approved by the wise men of the tribe, they permit no more girl babies born that year to live. More specifically, they take newborn babies out into the wilderness to die. The missionary tries to persuade them that such behavior is wrong. Is this action justifiable? Does your answer to this question agree with your answers to the first two questions? If not, explain why.

II

A STRATEGY

CHAPTER SIX

A FOUNDATION FOR JUDGMENT

*If both individuals and cultures can be
mistaken in their moral reasoning, we need
a basis for evaluating their judgment. If the
majority view, feelings, and conscience do not
provide that basis, what does?*

The first fact to note about our search for a surer foundation for moral judgment than the majority view, feelings, or conscience is that some philosophers say no such foundation exists! This skeptical assessment can be traced to the eighteenth-century English philosopher David Hume, who argued that there is no logical way to get from knowing what *is* (factual knowledge) to knowing what *ought to be* (objective moral standards). In other words, Hume held that no amount of observation of the way people actually behave can ever lead to a conclusion about the way they should behave. Hume was not denying morality, but only denying that *reason* can tell us what is moral. He believed that we all have a "moral sentiment" that guides us by responding to sensations of pleasure or pain. According to the *Oxford English Dictionary*, the word *sentiment* had several meanings in Hume's time, so we can't be absolutely certain what meaning he had in mind. However, given that he denied the applicability of reason in moral judgment, he most likely regarded moral sentiment as a feeling or intuition, a meaning that survives today.

Hume's conclusion about *is* and *ought* has profoundly influenced English and American thought and deserves to be closely examined. As we proceed, remember that the best tribute we can pay the thinkers of the past is to examine their ideas with the same passion for truth they displayed and that rejecting an idea is not a sign of disrespect for the person who advanced it.

ASSESSING *OUGHT* STATEMENTS

If morality were subjective and knowing what *is* could never lead to knowing what *ought to be,* we might reasonably expect that (a) only foolish or irresponsible people would say what other people should or should not do and (b) the statements they utter would be demonstrably shallow and irrelevant to other people's lives. If that is what a fair and impartial search reveals, then Hume's view will be vindicated. On the other hand, if intelligent, responsible people make such statements and the statements prove to be reasonable and relevant, then we are justified in concluding that Hume was mistaken. Let us see.

OUGHTS IN ANCIENT CULTURES

Here is a selection of moral prescriptions from a variety of ancient cultures.

> Slander not. (Babylonian)
>
> One should never strike a woman; not even with a flower. (Hindu)
>
> He who is asked for alms should always give. (Hindu)
>
> Never do to others what you would not like them to do to you. (Chinese)
>
> The Master said, Respect the young. (Chinese)
>
> Love thy wife studiously. Gladden her heart all thy life long. (Ancient Egyptian)
>
> Be blameless to thy kindred. Take no vengeance even though they do thee wrong. (Old Norse)
>
> Choose loss rather than shameful gains. (Greek)
>
> Death is to be chosen before slavery and base deeds. (Roman)
>
> Nature and Reason command that nothing uncomely . . . [and] nothing lascivious be done or thought. (Roman)
>
> Let him not desire to die, let him not desire to live, let him wait for his time . . . let him patiently bear hard words, entirely abstaining from bodily pleasures. (Ancient Indian)
>
> I sought no trickery, nor swore false oaths. (Anglo-Saxon)
>
> In the Dalebura tribe a woman, a cripple from birth, was carried about by the tribespeople in turn until her death at the age of sixty-six. . . . They never desert the sick. (Australian Aborigines)
>
> You will see them take care of . . . widows, orphans, and old men, never reproaching them. (Native American)[1]

Because we do not know the specific individuals who authored these sayings, we cannot judge them personally, but we do know that their words were generally regarded as wise sayings in their cultures. Also, even though we are ages removed from those times, they still speak meaningfully to the contemporary human condition.

GOVERNMENTAL *OUGHTS*

The Declaration of Independence is not usually thought of as a collection of moral judgments, but it is that. It begins with the moral judgments that "all Men are created equal, that they are endowed by their Creator with certain unalienable Rights, that among these are Life, Liberty, and the Pursuit of Happiness"; further, it states that the people empower the government to "secure these Rights" and, when the government fails to do so, the people have not only a right but also a duty to overthrow it. The Declaration proceeds to present a lengthy list of "Injuries and Usurpations"—that is, moral offenses—allegedly committed by King George against the colonists. The U.S. Constitution was created out of that same moral frame of reference. The Bill of Rights, in fact, is properly viewed as a safeguard that the moral obligations affirmed in the Declaration of Independence would not be violated. Its preamble makes clear that the amendments were proposed "in order to prevent misconstruction or abuse of its [the Constitution's] powers. . . ."

Were the Founding Fathers foolish or irresponsible individuals? Hardly. Historians agree that they were among the most intelligent, accomplished men who ever gathered for a common purpose. The documents they produced, far from being shallow or inappropriate, are universally regarded as profound and timeless in their application.

The United Nations' Declaration of Human Rights contains similar references to rights. It begins, for example, by declaring that "human rights should be protected by the rule of law" and goes on to say that all human beings "should act towards one another in a spirit of brotherhood." And the Nuremberg Code, enacted after the Second World War in response to Nazi atrocities, specifies the rights and safeguards that should be guaranteed in medical experiments.

ORGANIZATIONAL *OUGHTS*

The search for organizational statements of right and wrong behavior is not difficult to conduct. Virtually every sizable corporation has a carefully framed code of ethics. The same is true of virtually every professional organization, including the American Academy of Forensic Sciences, the American Institute of Chemists, the American Pharmaceutical Society, the American Psychological Association, the American Society of Zoologists, and the American Medical Association. (A notable exception is the American Philosophical Association, which has no published code of ethics. This situation is ironic because ethics has historically been a subdiscipline of philosophy.)

The American Medical Association's code of ethics states that "physicians are ethically and legally required to protect the personal privacy

and other legal rights of patients" and that they "have an ethical obligation to report impaired, incompetent, and unethical colleagues." The
American Historical Association's code includes numerous *should* statements. Here is a sampling:

> All historians should be guided by the same principles of conduct. . . .
> Historians should carefully document their findings, . . . should acknowl-
> edge the receipt of any financial support, sponsorship, or unique
> privileges (including privileged access to research material) related to
> their research, . . . should also acknowledge assistance received from
> colleagues, students, and others, . . . should be careful not to present
> [interpretations and judgments] in a way that forecloses discussion of
> alternative interpretations by charging that they are not qualified to speak
> on an issue or are biased, . . . should be prepared to explain the methods
> and assumptions in their research and the relations between evidence and
> interpretation and should be ready also to discuss alternative interpreta-
> tions of the subjects being addressed.[2]

Organizational codes of ethics typically are created by well-qualified,
respected individuals, endorsed by the highest ranking officers, and
regarded by everyone as the standard of behavior in organizational
affairs. Violations of the code generally result in formal reprimand or, in
serious cases, dismissal. In the case of professional organizations, violations can result in the loss of one's license to practice the profession. Far
from being shallow or irrelevant, codes of ethics provide essential guidance in the conduct of a business or profession.

OUR OWN EVERYDAY *OUGHTS*

Each day's news brings a wide assortment of reports that prompt us to
make moral judgments. A mother locks her children in the car and lets it
roll into a lake, then tells police they were kidnapped. College students
rape a coed. Computer hackers shut down a number of Internet businesses. A candidate for high office misrepresents her opponent's voting
record. A highly paid professional athlete is exposed as the deadbeat father
of five illegitimate children by different women. A group of scam artists
cheat hundreds of retired people out of their life savings. Suicide bombers
kill themselves and scores of innocent strangers in crowded marketplaces.

When we encounter such stories, we don't say, "I myself wouldn't do
such a thing, but I can't say whether others ought not do it." No, we say
exactly what millions of other morally sensitive individuals say—"That is
a moral outrage and the perpetrators ought to be held accountable." We
judge the deed to be wrong no matter who does it. In other words, we
express not a personal moral *sentiment* but an objective moral *assessment*.

In summary, we have the choice of saying that David Hume was
right and all the *oughts* we have considered—the sayings of the ancients,

the Founding Fathers' historic documents, innumerable organizational codes of ethics, and our own daily moral judgments—are shallow and irresponsible. Or we can conclude that David Hume was mistaken. Surely the weight of the evidence supports the latter judgment. Every day millions of people succeed in getting from factual knowledge of the world (what *is*) to objective moral assessments (what *ought to be*), so it must be possible to do so. The only question is how.

THE PRINCIPLE OF RIGHT DESIRE

One of the foremost interpreters of the Western philosophic tradition, Mortimer Adler, explains how to get from *is* to *ought*. He begins by acknowledging that the problem Hume identified about *is* statements and *ought* statements is a real problem—in other words, the fact that people *do* act in a certain way does not prove that they *should* act in that way. Let's say we want to establish that we ought to be kind to animals, so we gather some facts, and after each we pause and ask, "Have we proved we ought to be kind to animals yet?" Here are the facts. You ask the question after each.

> Harry is kind to his cat. Mary is kind to her lamb. Bruno is mean to his dog. Harry's cat never scratches him. Mary's lamb is gentle. Bruno's dog snarls and snaps at people. Many pets are abandoned every year. The animal shelter is forced to destroy those animals that are not adopted. Trainers who mistreat elephants sometimes get stomped.

Were you able to say after any sentence, "Hold it. Now it's been proved that we ought to be kind to animals"? No. The paragraph could be extended for a dozen more pages, fact piled upon fact, and still we wouldn't have that proof because, though the *is* sentences can be tested against reality and proved true or false, there is nothing to test the *ought* sentence against. Hume used different examples, of course, but reached the same conclusion. As a result, he decided that it is impossible to get from *is* to *ought*.

However, Adler demonstrates that it is possible. He found the key in a little-noticed passage in the ancient Greek philosopher Aristotle's *Nicomachean Ethics*. There Aristotle noted that although prescriptive (ought) statements cannot be tested for their correspondence with reality, they can be tested for *conformity with right desire*. The principle of right desire, which Adler terms "the first principle of moral philosophy," is as follows:

> "We ought to desire what is really good for us and nothing else."

Adler notes that this principle is self-evident, meaning that the words "ought" and "really good for us" are related in such a way that the sentence *cannot be contradicted.* (To say that we ought *not* desire what is really good for us or that we ought to desire what is really *bad* for us would be illogical.)

With this self-evident principle as our major premise, we can confidently make moral judgments. Adler offers this example:[3]

> We ought to desire what is really good for us.
>
> Knowledge is really good for us.
>
> We ought to desire knowledge.

The premise "Knowledge is really good for us," of course, like any other premise inserted in that position, cannot be assumed to be true; its truth must be demonstrated. But if this can be accomplished, the conclusion is inescapable. Skeptics may object that the kind of demonstration that can be made for statements of what is good for us does not provide absolute, scientific certainty and is therefore unacceptable. But this argument requires ethics to meet a more stringent standard than other disciplines. Every day in virtually every academic field, including the sciences, a lesser standard than certainty is accepted. For example, Darwin's theory of evolution is taught as fact despite science's failure to find the "missing link," and the scientific community endorses the idea that cigarette smoking causes lung cancer without absolutely conclusive evidence. Similarly, assertions are made about the origin of the universe despite the fact that the reality in question has never been, and indeed may never be, known with certainty. Whenever certainty is unachievable in these and other academic fields, the less demanding standard of *probability* is considered adequate. Fairness demands that the subject of ethics be treated no differently.

THE PRINCIPLE OF CONTRADICTION

One of the most dramatic ethical issues of the millennium exploded during the final decade of the twentieth century. That issue is the creation of human embryos for research. Advances in medical technology have made possible *in vitro* fertilization, which unites sperm and egg outside the female body in a test tube. The initial intention of this technology was to accomplish pregnancy for couples who, for medical reasons, could not conceive a child in the natural way. The fertilized egg would be implanted in the woman's uterus and the pregnancy would proceed. In a proposed controversial use, an egg would be fertilized in a test tube, allowed to develop into an embryo, used for scientific experimentation, *and then discarded after fourteen days,* the point at which the embryo's nervous system begins to function. The procedure was unanimously recommended by a National Institutes of Health advisory committee, the Human Embryo Research Panel. The committee stated that such research would improve infertility treatment and provide new methods for birth control, new cancer therapies, and increased understanding of birth defects. (Aware of the controversial nature of the proposal, then president Bill Clinton imposed a ban on federal funding of the research.[4])

A *Washington Post* editorial denounced the panel's recommendation, commenting that "The creation of human embryos specifically for research that will destroy them is unconscionable." And the Ramsey Colloquium, a group of Jewish and Christian theologians, philosophers, and scholars that meets periodically to consider questions of ethics, religion, and public life, issued a formal statement of opposition. The Ramsey statement concluded that the panel's recommendation "is morally repugnant, entails grave injustice to innocent human beings, and constitutes an assault upon the foundational ideals of human dignity and rights essential to a free and decent society." It also expressed concern that panel members were themselves engaged in the very research for which they recommended funding, a situation that raised questions of conflict of interest.[5]

Controversial issues like this one often generate considerable intellectual tension. People form strong convictions on one side of the issue or the other and attempt to persuade others of the rightness of their viewpoint. Even relativists can be found arguing passionately for one side of an issue despite their professed belief that all views are equal. Underlying all such debates is a principle that both sides acknowledge, either consciously or unconsciously. In other words, whether or not they give verbal affirmation of the principle, whether or not they have even conceptualized it, they attest to it by the very act of debating. This principle is known as the principle of contradiction and is expressed as follows: *An idea cannot be both true and false at the same time in the same way.*

The qualifying terms "at the same time" and "in the same way" are crucial. If George died this morning, the sentence "George is alive" was true yesterday and is false today, yet it was *not true and false at the same time.* If one of your professors presents intellectually challenging ideas in a dull monotone, the sentence "That course is stimulating" is both true and false at the same time, yet *not in the same way.* Where we are dealing with a genuine contradiction, on the other hand, we can no more imagine both sides being true than we can imagine a stick with one end or a square circle.

Contradiction is not always blatant; sometimes it is subtle and thus may escape detection for years. For example, in the very same book in which he denounced the use of *never, always,* and similar terms denoting absolutes, Joseph Fletcher, the founder of "situation ethics," wrote "love is the only norm" and "no unwanted babies should ever be born."[6] Those are absolute statements. As one critic of situation ethics has pointed out, "Fletcher's claim that all is relative . . . is self-destructive. It says in effect, we should never use the word never. Never! Or we should always avoid using the word always. Always!" (Fletcher could have avoided this embarrassing problem by moderating his assertion, saying "Be careful in using words like *always* and *never.* Often they overstate the case.") This critic goes on to argue that the relativists' quandary is that they must either be absolutely sure that there are no absolutes, in which case they have contradicted themselves, or they are not absolutely sure, in which case they admit there may be absolutes.[7]

CHALLENGES TO JUDGMENT

The principle of right desire, in bridging the gap between *is* and *ought,* provides a foundation for judgment. The principle of contradiction gives assurance that critical thinking is relevant to ethical controversies, that when two ethical judgments are diametrically opposed, one must be mistaken. Thus these two principles offer us confidence and encouragement in ethical analysis and judgment, no small contributions. They do not, however, answer the questions, What is really good for us? What criteria and approaches are most effective in examining moral issues? and What pitfalls should we be aware of and strive to avoid? All these challenges will be the focus of subsequent chapters, but the third deserves preliminary consideration here.

In Greek legend, sailors had to negotiate their ships between twin perils: Scylla, a female sea monster, and Charybdis, a deadly whirlpool. If they drifted too far to either the right or the left, they were doomed. Anyone who undertakes ethical analysis and judgment is similarly challenged to steer a course between the "monsters" of relativism and absolutism.

RELATIVISM

As we have noted, relativism is the view that no objective moral standard is possible; hence, issues of right and wrong are personal and subjective and may be decided by each person for himself or herself without danger of being wrong. As the dominant moral perspective of our age, it undoubtedly claims more victims than its evil twin, but absolutism is no less objectionable for that fact.

ABSOLUTISM

A great deal of confusion exists about absolutism. Many people define it as the belief in moral absolutes. That is incorrect—it is possible to believe in moral absolutes and at the same time reject absolutism. A moral absolute is a norm or principle that is true at all times and in all places and admits of no exceptions. Almost everyone regards some norms or principles as absolutes. For example: "Every human being has an inalienable right to life, liberty, and the pursuit of happiness"; "The basic rule of morality is to do good and to avoid evil"; "One should never act dishonorably"; "Slavery is a moral offense"; and "Rape is never morally acceptable."

After the Nazi trials for crimes committed against humanity during World War II, the international community created the Nuremberg Code, which forbade experiments on human beings without their explicit consent; it also forbade experiments that exposed patients to unnecessary suffering, disabling injury, or risk of death even *with* their consent. The 1975 Helsinki Declaration of the World Medical Association stated: "Concern for the interests of the subject [the person used in research] must always prevail over the interest of science and society." Both the Nuremberg prohibition and the Helsinki Declaration's principle are moral absolutes, and both are almost universally accepted.

Many moral norms, however, do admit of exceptions and therefore cannot be considered absolute. At first thought, the principle "Taking what does not belong to us without the owner's permission is wrong" may seem like a moral absolute, especially if we realize it is found in almost every culture and religion—for example, "Thou shalt not steal" (in the Bible) and "As for the thief, male or female, cut off his or her hands" (in the Koran). But what about removing a pistol from the home of a friend who has threatened to use it to kill someone, or secretly taking a friend's car keys when you know the friend is too intoxicated to drive? No reasonable person would consider these actions unethical.

When we say that a norm or principle is not absolute, are we claiming that it has no value? And in cases where it is a religious norm, are we diminishing its sacred nature or importance for believers? The answer to both questions is emphatically no. To say that a norm does not apply in a small number of unusual situations in no way lessens its applicability to the vast number of usual situations.

If, as we have seen, believing in moral absolutes does not necessarily make one a moral absolut*ist*, what does? The belief that the circumstances of a case make no difference, that moral judgment consists solely in applying rigid inflexible rules to cases.

The reason we should avoid the extremes of absolutism and relativism is that both trivialize the subject of ethics. If, as the relativist believes, no objective moral standard is possible and everything is a matter of personal preference, then the terms *right* and *wrong* have little practical application and ethics is without real value. On the other hand, if, as the absolutist believes, circumstances make no difference, then there is little point in studying the details of cases and making comparative studies of similar cases. Your challenge is to steer a course between relativism and absolutism. You are not likely to have a problem with both extremes; instead, you will undoubtedly be inclined toward one or the other. Determine now which one that is and try to assess its influence on your judgment. Whenever you are analyzing a moral issue, be alert to that influence and take whatever measures are necessary to overcome it.

▨ INQUIRIES

1. Extend the list of historical examples of *oughts* by adding others that you learned at home, in school, or in church.

2. Consult the ethics code of an organization you belong to and are familiar with. If you don't belong to any organizations, visit the library or the Internet and consult the code of a professional organization. List the main moral prescriptions included in that code.

3. Consult print and broadcast sources for one or more current news stories that have evoked moral judgment from the general public. Summarize each story, describe the dominant public view of the moral issue involved, and then decide whether you agree with that view.

4. Examine each of the following ethical questions in light of what you have learned in this chapter and previous chapters. In each instance, answer the question and state the reasoning that led to that answer. (*Note:* Save your response to this inquiry; you will be asked to refer to it in a later chapter.)

a. Copyright law makes it illegal to copy computer software programs. Yet sometimes students want or need a program that is too expensive for them to buy. In such cases, is it morally acceptable for students to copy a friend's software?

b. Often a person will work for someone; learn all the procedures, formulas, and strategies of the business; and then quit and take a job with a competitor or start a new, competing, business. Is it morally acceptable for her to use what she learned on the previous job? To approach her previous employer's customers and try to persuade them to do business with her? To use her previous employer's "secrets" (recipes in the food industry, for example, or formulas in the cosmetics industry)?

c. Is it morally acceptable for store owners to include subliminal messages ("Don't steal") in the music piped into the store? What about subliminal appeals ("Buy now") to spend money in the store?

d. Is drag racing on the highway ethical?

e. Is it morally right for old people to be put in institutions when their children have room for them in their homes?

f. Is it permissible to kill animals of an endangered species?

g. Is it ethical for the United States to train the police and military forces of dictatorships that use those forces to suppress their citizens?

h. Is it ethical for the United States to continue diplomatic relations with countries that deny women the basic rights of citizenship?

i. Is it morally acceptable for children to be used in pornographic films? Does it make a difference if their parents approve?

j. There are more than four hundred pet cemeteries in the United States. People often spend hundreds of dollars to bury their dogs, cats, birds, goldfish, and hamsters. Is this practice morally acceptable?

k. Many countries employ secret agents, spies whose duty is to learn the military or diplomatic secrets of other countries. Is it morally permissible to be a secret agent? Is it morally permissible to be a double agent (one who works for both sides while pretending to work exclusively for each)?

CHAPTER SEVEN

THE BASIC CRITERIA

*What is really good for us? What criteria and
approaches are most effective in examining
moral issues? What pitfalls other than
relativism and absolutism should we
be aware of and strive to avoid?*

In previous chapters we noted that religion and law cannot substitute
for ethics, although they are related to and compatible with ethics; that
the majority view is as apt to be mistaken as correct; that feelings are
often capricious and therefore unreliable; and that conscience, though
in some cases trustworthy, is susceptible to negative influences and
error. We also found that, contrary to popular opinion, moral judgments
of other cultures are appropriate when they are based on understanding
and thoughtful analysis. Next we observed that despite skepticism's
claim that moral prescriptions (*ought* statements) are illogical, such prescriptions have been made throughout history and are still made today
by respectable individuals and organizations. Most important, we identified a sound basis for making moral prescriptions—the principle of right
desire. This principle, together with the principle of contradiction,
enables us to approach ethical analysis with confidence. In this chapter
we will build on this understanding.

The standard we will need for judging the morality of actions is one
that is acceptable to men and women of various moral perspectives and
that reflects the principles most ethical systems have in common. Such a
standard helps us set aside defensiveness, frees us from the entangle-
ments of prefabricated interpretations, and elevates our dialogue to a
more analytic and objective level.

A FUNDAMENTAL GOOD: RESPECT FOR PERSONS

One example of something that is "really good for us," as we noted in the
previous chapter, is knowledge. Another significant good is *respect for*

persons, which, as Errol E. Harris explains, includes the following three requirements:

> First, that each and every person should be regarded as worthy of sympathetic consideration, and should be so treated; secondly, that no person should be regarded by another as a mere possession, or used as a mere instrument, or treated as a mere obstacle, to another's satisfaction; and thirdly, that persons are not and ought never to be treated in any undertaking as mere expendables.[1]

Respect for persons is an important value in most ethical systems. (The Dobuans and the Ik are noteworthy exceptions.) This is not to say that respect for persons is always interpreted in the same way or that it is always given precedence over other values. In some cultures *person* is defined not broadly, as "all members of the species *Homo sapiens,*" but narrowly, as "a member of our tribe" or "one who enjoys the rights of citizenship." In some tribal languages, the word used to denote a person is the tribal name; to be outside the tribe is thus, by definition, to be a nonperson. In the Roman Empire many of the freedoms now associated with personhood were denied to noncitizens, notably slaves. (Roman citizenship could, however, be bestowed on anyone, even a slave.) Yet even in such cultures, where personhood is more narrowly conceived, respect for persons is nevertheless honored.

One reason respect for persons historically has been—and continues to be—universally accepted is that it is affirmed theologically as well as philosophically and thus is acceptable to believers and nonbelievers alike. The many variations of the Golden Rule, "Do unto others as you would have them do unto you," illustrate this universality. Following is a sampling of those variations:

> What you do not want others to do to you, do not do to others. (Confucius)
>
> Love your neighbor as yourself. (Moses, Jesus)
>
> No man is a true believer unless he desireth for his brother that which he desires for himself. (Muhammad)
>
> Do naught unto others which would cause you pain if done to you. (Mahabharata)
>
> No one of you is a believer until he desires for his brother that which he desires for himself. (Sunnah)
>
> Whatever is disagreeable to yourself do not do unto others. (Zoroastrianism)
>
> Hurt not others in ways that you yourself would find hurtful. (Buddhism)
>
> What you would avoid suffering yourself, seek not to impose on others. (Epictetus)

And if thine eyes be turned towards justice, choose thou for thy neighbour that which thou choosest for thyself. (Baha'i faith)

What you dislike for yourself do not like for me. (Spanish proverb)

In the philosophical sense, respect for persons may be considered an extension of the principle of right desire. Just as we should desire only what is really good for ourselves, so should we desire the same thing for other people because they are essentially no different from us. In the theological sense, respect for persons reinforces the idea that all human beings are created in the image and likeness of God and therefore are, their many differences notwithstanding, children of God.

THREE BASIC CRITERIA

As the requirements stated by Errol Harris suggest, respect for persons is not merely a theoretical construct but a practical standard for the treatment of others in everyday situations. Over the centuries three basic criteria have been associated with that standard and have informed ethical discourse. These criteria—*obligations, moral ideals,* and *consequences*—will be our principal concern in this chapter and in subsequent chapters. Generally speaking, a moral action is one that demonstrates respect for persons by honoring the relevant obligations and ideals and by producing favorable consequences.

OBLIGATIONS

Every significant human action occurs, directly or indirectly, in a context of relationships with others. And relationships usually imply *obligations,* that is, restrictions on our behavior, demands to do something or to avoid doing it. The most obvious kind of obligation is a formal agreement. Whenever a person enters into a contract—for example, to sell something or to perform a service—we consider that person ethically (as well as legally) bound to live up to his or her agreement.

There are other kinds of obligations. Obligations of friendship, for example, demand the keeping of confidences. Obligations of citizenship in a democracy demand concern for the conduct of government and responsible participation in the electoral process. There are also business obligations. The employer or supervisor, for example, is morally bound to use fair hiring practices, judge workers impartially, and pay them a reasonable wage that is consistent with the demands of their position and the quality of their work. The employee, in turn, is morally bound to do a job as efficiently and competently as he or she is able to. And both employer and employee have moral obligations to their customers.

In addition, there are professional obligations. Lawyers are obligated to protect the interests of their clients, doctors to promote or restore the health of their patients, teachers to advance the knowledge and wisdom of their students, and elected officials to serve the interests of their constituents.

It should be noted that there can be no obligation to do something morally wrong. In other words, if one person promises another to tell a lie, steal something, or give inappropriate assistance during an exam, the promise is not binding.

MORAL IDEALS

In the general sense, *ideals* are aspects of excellence, goals that bring greater harmony within one's self and between self and others. In the moral sense, they are also specific concepts that assist us in achieving respect for persons in our moral judgments. One group of moral ideals that can be traced back to the time of ancient Greece and continue to be relevant to contemporary living is the *cardinal virtues*—prudence, temperance, justice, and fortitude. The word *cardinal* derives from a Latin word for *hinge,* and it would not be an exaggeration to say that moral living, in large part, hinges on these ideals. Religious thinkers have added another group of ideals, the *theological virtues* faith, hope, and charity. Other moral ideals are loving-kindness, honesty, compassion, forgiveness, repentance, reparation, gratitude, and beneficence. We will discuss these ideals and the cardinal virtues further in Chapter 9.

Different cultures interpret the same ideal differently, of course. As we have seen, the way a culture interprets its ideals and relates one to another will affect its judgment of particular actions. The Eskimo accepts the ideal of respect for the aged, but some of the Eskimo's ways of honoring it—for instance, walling them up in an igloo to die when they are too old to contribute to the community and are a drain on its resources—are very different from ours. Furthermore, the same ideal of justice that we honor may impel someone in another culture to do something we would never think of doing: for instance, to cut out the tongue of one who has uttered a taboo word. These variations in the ways of viewing and pursuing ideals can pose exquisite dilemmas for those engaged in cross-cultural studies and those whose occupations involve them directly with other cultures (diplomats, for example, and medical and religious missionaries). They present less difficulty for us in the examination of our own culture.

The distinction between ideals and obligations is not always clear, and, paradoxically, the more we learn about ethics and strive to behave morally, the more blurred the distinction becomes. The reason is simple:

Highly ethical people tend to regard ideals as obligations. For them, fairness, compassion, forgiveness, and the other moral ideals are more than lofty notions of excellence—they are also personal standards of conduct that they hold themselves responsible for meeting in everyday situations.

CONSEQUENCES

Consequences are the beneficial or harmful effects that result from an action and affect the people involved, including, of course, the person performing the action. Some consequences are physical; others are emotional. Some occur immediately; others occur only with the passing of time. Some are intended by the person performing the act; others are unintended. Finally, some consequences may be obvious, and others may be subtle and even hidden by appearances. The ethicist is concerned with all significant consequences of actions occurring in a moral context. Because consequences can be complex and difficult to pinpoint, ethical analysis often requires not merely an examination of indisputable facts but also speculation about possibilities and probabilities.

ANALYZING ETHICAL ISSUES

As your analyses of the inquiries in previous chapters have undoubtedly revealed, the job of examining issues and making judgments can be a difficult one, even when the cases are relatively simple. The fact that you now have a set of criteria to use can be of considerable help if you apply the criteria thoughtfully and systematically. The following approach will help you accomplish this.

STEP 1: STUDY THE DETAILS OF THE CASE

Study the details of the case carefully. Look closely at any circumstances that set it apart from otherwise similar cases. Keep in mind that "circumstances alter cases." Suppose, for example, that a computer operator used her employer's computer for her own personal project. Is such an action morally acceptable? It is impossible to give a meaningful answer without knowing more of the details of the case. You must identify the important questions that a meaningful answer would depend on. *Did she use the computer on her own time or on company time? Was she expressly forbidden to use it? Was her personal project in any way competitive with or harmful to her employer's business?* These are the key questions.

If, as often happens, you have insufficient details about a case to answer one or more of your important questions, speculate about *possible* answers. For example, if the issue were the firing of a teacher because of his homosexuality and you didn't know the specific cause of his being fired, you would consider the possibilities that (a) he was propagandizing for homosexuality in his class, (b) he was enticing his own students, and (c) he was merely living with another homosexual. For the first two causes the firing may be morally defensible, but for the third it would undoubtedly be indefensible.

STEP 2: IDENTIFY THE RELEVANT CRITERIA

Identify specific criteria that are relevant to the case. In other words, ask these questions: Are there any *obligations*? What *ideals* are involved? What are the *consequences* of the case? Whom will they affect? In what way? After identifying the criteria, decide where the emphasis should lie. Sometimes the issue will be mainly a matter of obligation; at other times, an ideal will be most important; at still other times, the consequences will be. Not infrequently, the force of all three will be very nearly equal.

STEP 3: DETERMINE POSSIBLE COURSES OF ACTION

Determine all possible choices of action that are—or, in the case of a past action, were—available. Usually, there will be several alternative choices. By determining what they are, you increase your chances of making a reasonable moral judgment.

STEP 4: DECIDE WHICH ACTION IS MOST ETHICAL

In light of your findings in steps 1 through 3, decide which action is most ethical.

This four-step approach will help you cut through the confusion that surrounds many complex moral issues, overcome indecision, and reach a judgment. It will also help you express that judgment to others. Let's look at three cases and see how the approach works in practice.

THE CASE OF PROFESSOR WOEBEGONE

Midwestern University is a national football power. The alumni association, which exerts considerable influence on the university's affairs, does not tolerate losing teams, and no faculty member or administrator who stands in the way of victory is tolerated. This year Professor Woebegone has had the misfortune of having Roger Rapid, star halfback, in his mathematics class. Roger is, to put it delicately, mathematically challenged. After spending many extra hours with Roger in hopes of dragging him through the course successfully, the professor has been forced to admit failure. On the final exam, Roger has scored 27. Judged by the grading scale in the course, he has failed miserably. Because he is a borderline student in other courses, an F could put Roger on academic probation and make him ineligible for the last crucial game of the season. Without Roger, the team will surely lose the conference title, and Professor Woebegone, who is untenured, will just as surely lose his job. The deadline for submitting grades is fast approaching, and Professor Woebegone has to make a decision. He is inclined to assign Roger a failing grade.

STEP 1: THE DETAILS OF THE CASE

You would note the details of the case given and identify any important questions that are not answered in the statement of the case. For example, you might ask the following questions:

> Has Professor Woebegone checked with his colleagues who have had Roger in class this semester? Is there any chance that Roger earned passing grades in their classes? (If that were the case, Professor Woebegone's grade of F might not cost Roger his eligibility.)

> What are Professor Woebegone's chances of getting a position at another college or university (perhaps one that is not a national athletic power)?

STEP 2: RELEVANT CRITERIA

You would identify the obligations, moral ideals, and consequences involved in the case. Professor Woebegone has several *obligations*. His primary one is the obligation to be diligent in his efforts to help students meet the course objectives; this has already been met. The professor also has the obligation, both to the university and to his profession, to set a reasonable grading standard and apply it impartially and honestly. (Contrary to what many alumni might believe, the professor has *no* moral obligation to guarantee athletes' continuing eligibility.)

At least three *moral ideals* are involved: the virtues of justice and courage and the general ideal of fairness. Justice in this case would be giving to each student the grade he or she has earned. Courage would mean doing what the professor determines is the right thing to do regardless of the personal consequences. Fairness would mean giving no special consideration to one student that is not offered to all students.

One probable *consequence* of failing Roger Rapid would be his ineligibility for the crucial game; that, in turn, would make the loss of the game likely. (Of course, if Roger's grades in other courses offset his F in mathematics—a rather unlikely scenario—both these consequences might be avoided.) Another predictable consequence would be the firing of

Professor Woebegone, although he could conceivably manage to escape that penalty. However, even if both unfortunate consequences occurred, at least one positive one would occur—Professor Woebegone would have set an example of integrity for his colleagues.

STEP 3: POSSIBLE COURSES OF ACTION

You would consider the possible actions open to Professor Woebegone. At first thought, there are only two: to violate his obligations and the relevant moral ideals and give Roger Rapid a higher grade than he deserves, or to fail Roger and risk losing his position. However, there is a third possibility—to fail Roger and let the administration know that if they succumb to alumni pressure and fire him, he will file a lawsuit for wrongful dismissal, in which case the university would receive a good deal of most unwelcome publicity.

STEP 4: THE MOST ETHICAL ACTION

In light of your analysis, you would no doubt conclude that although the consequences are mixed, both the obligations and the moral ideals in this case suggest that the most ethical action for Professor Woebegone would be to fail Roger. The professor might also try to preserve his teaching position, but ultimately he should be willing to be dismissed rather than compromise his integrity.

THE CASE OF THE SHIRKING MANEUVER

Florida residents enjoy two advantages not available in many other states: They pay no state income tax, and they are granted a $25,000 homestead exemption on their real estate taxes. To be a legal resident, however, a person must live in the state at least six months out of every year. Realizing that enforcement of this requirement is lax, retired California residents Lester and Myra Shirking buy a small condominium in a Florida coastal town and fill out the necessary forms declaring themselves to be Florida residents, even though they have no intention of spending more than a few weeks in the state each year. They are granted a homestead exemption, begin filing their federal tax returns from Florida, and stop filing California state tax returns. Because they are in a high tax bracket, this maneuver saves them tens of thousands of dollars per year.

STEP 1: THE DETAILS OF THE CASE

After a close reading, you would probably decide that the statement of this case leaves no significant questions unanswered.

STEP 2: RELEVANT CRITERIA

The Shirkings clearly violated the law, because they knowingly claimed residence without meeting the requirements. Our focus, however, is on moral rather than legal considerations. The most important moral *obligation* in this case is one of citizenship—specifically, to assist in contributing to the cost of maintaining highways, providing police and fire department services, and supporting public schools and hospitals (in short, all the expenses covered by taxes).

Among the *moral ideals* that are relevant to this case, the most prominent are fairness and honesty. Fairness requires that the Shirkings refrain from placing their share of the tax burden on their neighbors. (On this point, the obligation of citizenship and the ideal of fairness are mutually reinforcing.) The latter ideal, honesty, requires that the Shirkings make no representation that is at odds with the truth.

The most obvious *consequence* of the Shirkings' declaring residence in Florida is that they significantly reduce their tax burden by gaining a real estate tax reduction and by eliminating their state income tax obligation. However, the consequences to the states of California and Florida are not so salutary. California loses the tax income that the Shirkings, as residents, are required to pay; Florida loses the real estate tax that people who don't qualify for a homestead exemption are required to pay. And the citizens of both California and Florida are required to make up the difference between what the Shirkings should have paid and what they did pay.

STEP 3: POSSIBLE COURSES OF ACTION

Perhaps the Shirkings believed the tax burden in California was so difficult to bear that the action they chose was the only one open to them. ("I had no choice but to do what I did" is a common lament when defending moral transgressions.) But they did have an alternative—a rather obvious one, in fact. Instead of pretending to move to Florida, they could have actually moved there or to some other no-tax or low-tax state. Many people do so, even when they have to give up their jobs. In the Shirkings' case, the choice would have been less difficult because they were retired.

STEP 4: THE MOST ETHICAL ACTION

This case is easier to decide than the other two cases because all three criteria point to the same conclusion: The Shirkings' maneuver was unethical.

THE FINANCIAL CRISIS CASE

The causes of the financial crisis that began in 2007 and has not yet fully abated are numerous and complex. But one factor is generally acknowledged to have been significant, if not central: government's effort to pressure financial institutions to relax their standards for lending. (This effort was made by both Democrats and Republicans, specifically in the Carter, Clinton, and George W. Bush administrations.) As a result, loans were made to three groups of people at high risk of defaulting—people who had bad credit histories, people whose incomes were low or unstable, and people with stable incomes who requested large loans that strained their budgets. In addition, many loans were written for significantly more than the assessed value of the homes.

To protect themselves, large lending institutions adopted the practice of "bundling," which consisted of combining high risk loans with less risky loans and selling the bundle to other institutions. Because it was difficult to distinguish the quality of the loans in the bundles, the financial stability of the receiving institutions was weakened, often without their knowledge.

During this period, the easy availability of loans led the real estate market to flourish and property values to soar. Tempted by quick profits, many people engaged in buying homes for the sole purpose of selling them again, a practice known as "flipping." When the housing market peaked and began to return to normal, financial institutions were left holding mortgages worth much less than their face value. To make matters worse, many homeowners defaulted on their mortgages, some because they could not afford to pay, others because they saw no reason to keep paying for a home worth much less than its purchase price and in which they had little or no equity. When many financial institutions were on the verge of bankruptcy, the federal government spent massive amounts of money in "bailouts" and "stimulus packages."

STEP 1: THE DETAILS OF THE CASE

Because of the complexity of the case, you would narrow your focus and deal with one aspect at a time. Given space limitations, we will address only the government's effort to pressure financial institutions to relax lending standards. (Separate analyses could be made of the morality of "bundling" mortgages and other factors.) Among the questions you would ask are: What was government officials' motivation in bringing pressure on the banks? (Answer: They wished to make housing available to all Americans, regardless of their economic status. This is clearly a noble motive. Some, less altruistically, may have wished to increase support by low-income voters in their reelection campaigns.) Was this kind of pressure significantly different from previous governmental efforts on behalf of low-income Americans? (Answer: Yes. Past efforts had been to provide governmental financial support for low-income housing and to create anti-discrimination laws but not to interfere in banking standards and regulations.)

STEP 2: RELEVANT CRITERIA

The federal government has a number of moral *obligations* that are relevant to this case: to protect citizens from dishonest practices, to ensure the integrity of financial institutions, and to maintain the health of the economy for the good of the citizens. (However, the government has no moral, or for that matter legal, obligation to use financial institutions as instruments of social change, or to take them over and/or manage them.)

The principal moral *ideals* that apply to government officials in this case are fairness and prudence. Fairness entails refraining from actions that hinder banking institutions from doing their jobs, as well as refraining from actions that put the financial welfare of citizens at risk. Prudence consists of behaving judiciously in the consideration, framing, and enactment of laws and regulations that govern the banking institutions.

The immediate *consequences* of the government pressure on the banks to relax their lending standards were the issuing of hundreds of thousands or perhaps millions of risky loans and the placing in financial jeopardy of all the people who were encouraged to apply for those loans. Eventual consequences included the banking industry crisis, the corresponding decline of the stock market and the loss of hundreds of billions of dollars in people's retirement accounts, and the incurring of monstrous "bailout" debt that rich and poor Americans will bear for generations.

STEP 3: POSSIBLE COURSES OF ACTION

The government did not *have* to make the banking industry the instrument of its social agenda. Instead, they could have let the industry continue the lending practices proven over centuries to ensure economic stability—notably, the practice of objectively determining which loan applicants were qualified and which were not. Incidentally, this approach in no way prevented the government from finding other ways to assist people who were rejected for home loans. They could have heightened monitoring of banks to ensure that no one was rejected for a loan simply because of race or ethnicity, expanded educational opportunities for low income citizens, and given additional support to low cost housing programs such as Habitat for Humanity.

STEP 4: DECIDE WHICH ACTION IS MOST ETHICAL

Your analysis would probably lead you to conclude that the government's pressure on the banks to relax their lending standards both violated their obligations and the ideals of fairness and prudence and resulted in tragic consequences, and was therefore unethical. (Note that this case involves other moral questions that could be addressed separately, notably the morality of "bundling" loans.)

In all three of the preceding cases, and in all the cases you encounter, the moral action is the action that most fully honors the obligations, ideals, and consequences involved, the action that best fits the situation. It is the action that ought to be chosen, not just by the person in the case in question, but *by anyone in the same circumstances.* As subsequent chapters will reveal, the solutions to moral problems are seldom perfect solutions; they usually are only the best choices from among the imperfect solutions that are available.

A CAUTION ABOUT GENERALIZING

The temptation to move beyond the criteria we have been discussing and to develop a set of firm generalizations or rules of ethics is a common temptation. Although it arises from a very legitimate desire to simplify and streamline the process of analysis, it usually causes many more problems than it solves and is best avoided.*

Let's say we are analyzing a situation in which someone has taken something belonging to someone else. If we begin by applying an unqualified general rule, such as "It is wrong to take what does not belong to us," *we will have already judged the situation in question.* After making such a judgment, any analysis we do is likely to be little more than a listing of the reasons to support our predetermined conclusion. Like the juror who makes up his mind that the defendant is guilty the moment he sees her, we may appear to be weighing the evidence and may even believe that we are. Yet, in fact, we will have already made up our minds.

But, someone might object, what is wrong in starting with a rule like "It's wrong to take something that does not belong to us"? Doesn't such a generalization fit most cases? Certainly, and that is just the problem. The generalization about the wrongness of taking what doesn't belong to us would cover numerous situations from bank robbery to embezzlement to stealing hubcaps and even to pocketing the extra change the supermarket cashier gave us by mistake. But it doesn't cover the exceptions, such as finding some change in a public telephone booth or taking in a stray dog and (after advertising in the local paper and not finding the owner) keeping it. In judging any particular case, we must be concerned with precisely that: *whether there is anything about the case that makes it an exception to the rule.*

---

*It is possible to construct ethical rules that are so carefully shaped and qualified as to withstand even the most subtle objections. But that kind of construction is an activity that only the most advanced students of ethics should undertake. The safest and most profitable focus is on individual cases, not on generalizations.

It is tempting to protest that there must be some generalization that applies in all cases. "Do unto others as you would have them do unto you" comes to mind. What, after all, is more basic to morality than this Golden Rule found in virtually all advanced moral systems? And yet, as Paul A. Freund has pointed out, even this rule has its exception, for a masochist's application of it would prompt him to torture others.

An interesting illustration of the danger of relying on sweeping ethical generalizations and the importance of inquiring into the circumstances of a case occurred some years ago. In Willowbrook State Hospital, an institution for the retarded, medical doctors intentionally injected entering children with an infectious hepatitis virus. On first consideration, such behavior seems outrageous. It calls to mind the barbarisms of Nazi concentration camps. In fact, not a few critics regarded the action as precisely such a moral atrocity.

The details of the situation, however, undermine that judgment. It was known that a mild form of hepatitis was rife in the institution. Historical data showed that most of the newly admitted children would be infected by natural means. By deliberately infecting newly admitted patients, the doctors could assure them a milder case of the disease, and they could be given special housing and care while ill. Moreover, the plan had been reviewed and approved by several agencies, and parental consent was obtained before a child was infected.[2]

The tendency to respond to issues with unqualified generalizations, though natural enough, should not be indulged. The people we are writing for or speaking with deserve better from us. Every important ethical issue demands our careful attention, not only to its similarity to other issues, but also to its dissimilarity, to its uniqueness. To give less, to merely mouth an overall, ready-made response, is not to use moral rules but to be used by them; not to be guided by our experience but to be controlled by it. It takes wisdom to know when the case at hand fits the rule and when it is the exception to it. Such wisdom does not come easily. And if we substitute generalization for analysis, it does not come at all.

AVOIDING OTHER ERRORS

In addition to overgeneralization, five other errors are common in the analysis of moral issues: "Mine-is-better" thinking, double standard, unwarranted assumptions, oversimplification, and hasty conclusions.

"MINE-IS-BETTER" THINKING

This error is rooted in the perspective almost all of us had in early childhood. We thought and even said to others, "My mommy is prettier than yours," "My dad is stronger," "My teddy bear is cuddlier," "My tricycle is faster." As we grew older, we stopped making such statements and may even have stopped thinking such thoughts, at least about Mom and Dad, teddy and trike. But some vestiges of the old habit remain evident in the way we regard our opinions. And that can be an obstacle to ethical analysis and judgment by closing our minds to perspectives different from our own.

Whenever you find yourself objecting to another viewpoint on an ethical issue, ask yourself, "On what basis am I objecting?" If the answer is "Nothing more than 'mine-is-better' thinking," suppress your objection and give the other viewpoint a fair hearing.

DOUBLE STANDARD

The error of the *double standard* consists of using one set of criteria for judging cases that concern us or someone we identify with and another set for judging other cases. It involves viewing evidence selectively or twisting it to serve our own interests. It is especially common in cases where we have a strong commitment to a certain action, often because we have chosen it ourselves in similar cases and wish to avoid self-condemnation.

For example, we may judge most cases of taking what does not belong to one according to the criteria of obligations, ideals, and consequences. However, when we encounter a case that comes close to home—let's say, taking clothes from a roommate or taking money from a parent without permission—we tend to set aside the criteria and construct irrational arguments or rationalizations to justify the action. Such lapses are understandable but not justifiable. Similar cases should be judged similarly. The fact that a case involves us in some way or causes us to feel shame or regret should make no difference.

To find the error of the double standard in your moral reasoning, be alert for situations in which you have a personal emotional stake. When you encounter such situations, ask yourself whether you have applied the criteria consistently, as you would in any other case. Look for signs that you have slipped into special pleading.

UNWARRANTED ASSUMPTIONS

The error of *unwarranted assumptions* consists of taking too much for granted. The fact that it usually occurs unconsciously makes it a particularly troublesome error. We usually make unwarranted assumptions whenever we read a case carelessly and fail to distinguish between what it says and what it does not say—in other words, when we read into the case details that are not known or stated. Does this mean you should never speculate about what is not known or stated? Not at all. It means only that you should do so responsibly, as the following example illustrates.

Inquiry 2 in Chapter 4 concerned the morality of physicians receiving "finders' fees" for referring patients to researchers who are conducting trials of new drug therapies, the side effects of which are not known. The case did not state whether the physicians informed the patients about their fees and the possible dangers of the experimental therapies. To take for granted that they did or didn't inform their patients would be an unwarranted assumption. Instead of making that assumption, you should ask, "Would it make a difference if the doctors fully informed their patients?" Then, after considering your answer, you should make your decision and express it in the "If . . . then" format, as shown next. (Your position on the issue, of course, might be different than is expressed here.)

> If the doctors told their patients nothing about the fee they receive for referrals or about the risks involved, then they would be guilty of a serious ethical offense. If they informed their patients about both the fee and the risks, then the offense would be less serious. Even in the latter case, however, the practice of referring patients for a fee would be unethical because it compromises the physician's obligation to make the individual patient's health paramount.

OVERSIMPLIFICATION

It is natural enough to want to simplify matters. It is often necessary to do so to make sense of cases and to communicate our judgment to others. Simplification is not objectionable; it is *over*simplification that is an error. Oversimplification exists whenever our treatment of a case goes beyond reducing it to manageable proportions and *distorts* it. In moral reasoning, oversimplification is usually caused by omitting consideration of some important criterion—an obligation, for example, or a significant consequence. In the case of Professor Woebegone, if our analysis overlooked his obligation to apply his grading standard impartially and not give special consideration to any student, including a star football player, we would be guilty of oversimplifying the issue.

Unfortunately, oversimplification is fairly common in the discussion of ethical issues. Consider, for example, the discussion of the practice popularly known as whistle-blowing. Some people make it seem that the decision to report wrongdoing at one's place of work is a simple matter of picking up the phone and dialing the authorities. In reality, the situation is usually much more complicated. The potential whistle-blower must consider whether the wrongdoing is real or only apparent, serious or trivial, and also what the consequences of reporting the offense are likely to be to self and family. Loss of one's position is a likely effect; being blackballed in the job market, sued, and even physically harmed are possibilities. At the very least, these factors affect the level of obligation.

The continuing debate over the morality of affirmative action programs also provides numerous illustrations of oversimplification. Many who oppose such programs ignore the reality of past and present discrimination against women and minorities. On the other hand, many who support the programs ignore the unfairness involved in present racial or gender preferences.

To avoid oversimplification, be thorough in your identification of the relevant criteria. Do not be satisfied with acknowledging the most obvious ones; consider all of them. In addition, be prepared for complexity and address it carefully when you find it.

HASTY CONCLUSIONS

Drawing *hasty conclusions* refers to embracing a judgment before examining the case fully. Sometimes it results from lack of time to do a thorough analysis. More often, however, it results from accepting first impressions uncritically or from approaching the case with a preconceived notion of what the solution will be. Such impressions and preconceived notions are natural enough. Whenever we encounter a case, our mind begins making associations with thousands of experiences. As quickly as a fast computer, it identifies those experiences that are analogous and presents to us the conclusions we have reached for those cases or have decided to apply to all such cases. The problem is that those conclusions may not really fit the case in question.

To avoid making a hasty conclusion, make *no* conclusion until you have completed your analysis of the issue. Whenever a possibility occurs to you, write it down for later consideration. But resist the temptation to embrace any conclusion immediately, even if, at first thought, it seems unassailable.

Being familiar with the errors discussed here and using the strategies suggested for avoiding them will help you keep your moral reasoning sound. There is, however, one additional approach you can take: Think of yourself as two people, an *idea producer* and an *idea evaluator*. Let the producer generate as many varied ideas as it wishes, but before accepting them or presenting them to others in speaking or in writing, submit them to the scrutiny of the evaluator. This approach will help you form the habit of going beyond mere thinking to *thinking about thinking*. That is the habit of the philosopher.

▦ INQUIRIES

1. (*Note:* This inquiry is related to, but nevertheless distinct from, inquiry 1 in Chapter 6.) For many years hordes of people have been coming across the U.S. border in violation of existing immigration laws. The number of people in this country illegally is now well over 10 million. Many solutions have been proposed, including building a fence across the border, adding thousands of border patrol officers, using the National Guard for border patrol, and enforcing the law by seeking out and deporting illegal immigrants and punishing employers who knowingly hire them. (In 2010, Arizona passed a law permitting police to check the immigration status of anyone who has been detained for a separate violation.) The vast majority of Americans support one or more of these solutions; a good number support all of them. However, some people reject all of these solutions on moral grounds. They believe further that illegal immigrants should receive the same rights and privileges accorded to citizens, including drivers' licenses, social security, and health and education benefits. Evaluate this issue according to the criteria presented in this chapter.

2. Another, broader issue concerning immigration concerns the morality of the borders that separate nations. Some people argue that freedom of movement around the globe is a human right and that all nations have a *moral obligation* to open their borders and let anyone enter, rather than set immigration restrictions. Others not only deny that there is any such right but argue that the *consequences* of opening borders would create social and economic chaos in developed countries without improving the conditions of poorer countries. Research this issue using the terms "open borders issue" and "open borders arguments," then make your judgment in light of what you have learned in this chapter.

3. The idea of "redistributing wealth" is not new, but it has gained prominence during the administration of President Barrack Obama. Those who support such redistribution argue that the widespread economic inequality that exists in America and around the world is unjust and therefore immoral, and that it is the obligation of government to overcome such inequality through the capping of executive salaries and significantly raising taxes for everyone above a certain income level. With increased tax revenues the government could create and/or maintain programs that lift the economic status of the poor. Opponents argue that redistribution of wealth is a form of stealing that punishes achievement and rewards irresponsibility and indolence. They also believe that governments who engage in this practice greatly exceed their authority. Research this issue using the terms "pros and cons of redistribution of wealth," then make your judgment in light of what you have learned in this chapter.

4. On a Sunday morning in the spring of 2010 in New York City, a homeless man attempted to save a woman from an attacker and was stabbed in the process. For over an hour he lay bleeding on the sidewalk in plain view of passersby. Several people stopped to look at him. One man shook him. Another took a photo of him with a cell phone. But no one helped him or called 911. The man died there. Evaluate the morality of the passersby behavior in light of what you learned in this chapter.

5. Mr. Barker is returning to a town he once lived in and a position he once held. He and his wife visit several real estate brokers there in hopes of finding a house. One broker mentions that Horace's house will soon be for sale.

"Oh," Barker says, "I know Horace; is he leaving the area?" The broker explains that he is not, but he is moving to a larger house she showed him because his family has outgrown their present home. As they are driving to inspect Horace's property, Barker casually asks the broker which house Horace is buying. The broker tells him. She innocently adds that he is paying $178,000 for it. After leaving the broker, Barker goes directly to the owner of the house Horace is planning to buy, inspects it, is impressed with what he sees, and says to the owner, "Look, I know Horace has offered you $178,000. I'll pay $179,000, and what's more, you won't have to pay any broker's commission." The owner agrees and Barker buys the house. Was Barker's behavior unethical? Apply the criteria presented in this chapter and decide.

6. Review your responses to the ethical issues in Chapter 6, inquiry 4. Decide which responses should be modified or expanded in light of what you have learned in this chapter. Identify those responses and explain your changes.

7. Futurists are already talking about the use of modern technology for "virtual sex." The approaches that are being contemplated are more sophisticated than the use of virtual reality headsets. People will be able to have *realistic but nonphysical* sexual contact with virtual men and women created from real-life models, such as celebrities or acquaintances, or purely from their imagination.[3] Will virtual sex be ethical? In deciding, be sure to consider the obligations, moral ideals, and consequences that are involved in real sexual relationships and determine which, if any, would apply to virtual sex.

8. *Consumer Reports* magazine examined the growing practice of advertising in and around schools. The school buses that transport many children to school are decorated with advertisements, as are hallways and restrooms. School corridors and cafeterias pipe in popular music punctuated by commercials. Workbooks, instructional videos, and other classroom materials contain messages from sponsors. For example, the National Live Stock and Meat Board claims that meat consumption makes people taller, and Procter & Gamble suggests that clear-cut logging (the equivalent of strip mining) is beneficial to the environment. More significantly, Channel One, a daily news broadcast, is mandatory in many school systems. Roughly two students out of every five enrolled in U.S. schools watch Channel One, which consists of ten minutes of news and two minutes of commercials for Snickers, Rold Gold pretzels, Carefree bubble gum, Pepsi, and Reebok shoes, among other products. Advertisers pay the schools substantial fees, which can be used to purchase school supplies and equipment.[4] Apply the ethical criteria presented in this chapter and decide whether such advertising practices are morally defensible.

9. Apply what you have learned in this chapter to the following questions. Explain your answers.

   a. While driving a car, it is morally acceptable to talk or text on a cell phone? Is it morally permissible to drive a car after having one drink? Two? Three? After how many drinks would it be wrong to drive a car? After how many drinks would it be wrong for an airline pilot to fly a commercial airplane?

b. Is it ethical to take habit-forming drugs? Is it ethical to use a substance for which the research evidence is not yet conclusive and which might be harmful?

c. Is it wrong for people to starve themselves as a means of political protest?

d. Is it ethical for the United States to sell weapons to other countries?

e. Do people who take the lives of others have any moral responsibility to their victims' families? (For example, are they obligated to provide financial assistance to the families?) Would a case of accidental death be different from a case of murder?

Evaluate the action in each of the following cases, applying what you learned in this chapter and explaining your reasoning carefully.

10. Claude challenges the principle of respect for persons with the following argument: "Past ages were simpler. Our grandparents knew personally the people they had contact with every day. Yet today the world has grown impersonal. We deal with telephone operators, airline personnel, cab drivers, people at the other end of computer lines. We don't know them and they don't know us. So the idea of respect for persons no longer holds." Construct a reply to Claude's argument.

11. The science of genetic testing is fast reaching the point where it can be determined whether people carry genes for crippling, often fatal, diseases. Before long, employers may be able to know in advance whether job candidates are likely to need time off for illness; they can reject such candidates in advance. Further, health insurance companies may deny policies to such individuals. They may even refuse to reimburse parents for the delivery of a child known to be disabled before birth.

12. A seventh-grade teacher divides his class into teams to research some history topics and report to the class. Each team consists of four students. One team presents a report that is excellent in substance. However, two members of the team behave childishly while making their contributions, so the overall presentation is flawed. The teacher lowers the team's mark a full letter grade. Because the grade recorded for each team member is identical to the team grade, each member is penalized.

13. A businessman is waiting for an elevator in his office building. A stranger motions him aside and whispers, "Wanna buy a fur coat for your wife? Two hundred dollars. No questions asked. What say?" He opens a large paper bag to reveal the coat. The businessman looks at it, touches it, and realizes that the coat is unquestionably mink and worth at least ten times what the man is asking for it. He takes out his wallet, hands over the $200, and takes the bag.

14. A common method for dispatching animals in slaughterhouses is to hit them on the head with a sledgehammer as many times as necessary to drive them into semiconsciousness, then to pierce one of their rear legs with a hook, hoist them into the air, and slit their throats, leaving them to bleed to death.

15. A woman learns that her son-in-law fathered an illegitimate child several years before he met her daughter. (He and his wife have been happily married for ten years. They are childless.) She is sure her daughter is not aware of this and has reason to doubt that she would ever find out about it by herself. The woman feels obliged to tell her, however, and does so.

16. The executives of a large company are planning their advertising campaign for the coming year. They would prefer to use a simple and honest approach, but they know that their competitors use devious psychological approaches and even outright lies in their advertising. The executives fear that if they do not use the same approaches as their competitors, their company's profits will suffer and they may lose their jobs. They decide to play it safe and use those approaches.

17. A man and a woman, both college students, have been living together off campus for three years. They have never considered marrying, and it has always been implicit in their relationship that each should be free to leave the other any time he or she wishes. Unexpectedly, the woman becomes pregnant. Because she is opposed to abortion, she resigns herself to having the child. When she is seven months pregnant, the man decides to leave her. One day when she is out shopping for groceries, he gathers his belongings, scribbles a hasty note ("Our relationship was beautiful while it lasted, but it's over"), and leaves.

18. A businessman wishes to invest some money in wooded land. He knows that he can sell the trees for lumber, plant more trees, and sell them when they mature. He will be serving the cause of ecology at the same time he makes a modest income. After finding a parcel of land that is appropriate for his purposes, he asks the owner the selling price. The price is so ridiculously low that the man realizes the owner is unaware of the value of the trees as lumber. He ponders whether it is immoral to buy the land at such a price. He decides it is not and buys it.

19. A young woman has a serious kidney disease. She undergoes expensive care while awaiting the availability of a donor's kidney. One day she receives word that a donor has been found. She looks forward happily to the transplant operation. Then she finds out that the donor is an institutionalized person with mental retardation who is unable to understand the nature of the operation and the remote possible danger to him should his other kidney ever become damaged. The surgeon will be removing the organ without his permission. The young woman accepts the kidney anyway.

20. Knowing that after negotiations with management are completed they will get less than they ask for in wages and fringe benefits, some labor unions begin negotiations by demanding more than is reasonable.

21. Allegedly, the U.S. Army has researched mechanical ways to control human behavior. For example, they conducted experiments with devices that used "flickering light of varying intensity" to render the brain incapable of controlling the body and with devices that emit inaudible sound to confuse the mind and cause pain. (An Army spokesman stated that such devices might be useful in controlling crowds.)[5]

22. A newspaper carrier begins his job with enthusiasm. His supervisor explains that once or twice a week, advertising inserts will be delivered with the papers and must be placed inside them. The job of insertion is a time-consuming chore, the supervisor explains, and paper carriers are easily tempted to discard the inserts. However, the supervisor warns, discarding them is grounds for dismissal, because the advertisers pay for them and have a right to expect them to reach the customers. Not only is each newspaper carrier expected to handle his or her own inserts properly, but the carrier is also expected to report any other paper carrier who does not do so. Two weeks later, the boy notices that all the other delivery people in his town regularly throw the inserts in a trash barrel. He reports them to his supervisor.

23. A businesswoman realizes that with the local college enrollment burgeoning, an investment in a trailer court will be profitable. It happens, too, that a perfect site is available. The one complication is that the owner of the land, who lives across the highway, would not sell it if he knew it would be put to such use. The businesswoman therefore pays a young married couple to buy it for her. They approach the owner, explain that they want the land to build a home on, and even show him fake building plans. After he sells the land to them, they turn it over to the businesswoman.

24. Residents of a poor neighborhood are plagued with a drug problem. Five pushers operate openly on their streets and brazenly try to entice neighborhood children to take free samples. A committee of residents has approached the police and begged them to arrest the pushers, but they have done nothing. There is reason to believe some of the police are sharing in the proceeds of the drug trade. The residents decide that their only hope for a safe and decent neighborhood for their children is to take the law into their own hands. Accordingly, one calm summer night they unceremoniously execute the five pushers.

25. A nurse in a nursing home dispenses medication to elderly patients. The home is understaffed and, though the existing staff is efficient, there is such a demand on their time that they have difficulty doing a quality job. The nursing supervisor frequently orders the nurse to give the patients unprescribed tranquilizers to keep them quiet and docile. This allows the staff to attend to critical needs.

26. A large grocery chain orders its personnel department to screen out all grocery clerk applicants who have a prison record, a history of alcohol/drug abuse or mental illness, or a problem with obesity.

CHAPTER EIGHT

CONSIDERING OBLIGATIONS

*What do we do in situations where there
is more than a single obligation? How can
we reconcile conflicting obligations?*

In Chapter 7 we defined obligations as restrictions on our behavior, demands to do something or to avoid doing it. We also noted the relationships that most commonly give rise to obligations. The most obvious one is a contractual relationship, which spells out in more or less formal terms what is required of each party and often specifies penalties for noncompliance. Other relationships include those with friends, to our country, to the companies or institutions we are associated with, and to our professions. Let's consider the latter relationships more closely and examine the obligations they entail.

> *Obligations of friendship:* Friendship entails mutual respect and a special interest in the other person's well-being. It requires one to rejoice at the other's success and good fortune and to share the pain of the other's disappointment and failure. It also requires one to be trustworthy about confidences, to provide emotional support when it is needed, and to restrain the urge to be critical in small matters.

> *Obligations of citizenship:* Citizenship obligates a person to promote the well-being of the country and fellow citizens by respecting and observing the law and respecting the legitimate initiatives of the country's leaders, even if one disagrees with their political perspective. In a democracy, it also requires participation in the electoral process. When the country is unjustly attacked, it is also a citizen's responsibility, conscience permitting, to support the country's response and even, if one is young and healthy enough, to play an active role in the country's defense.

> *Employment obligations:* This category of obligation covers employees' relationships with employers and, by extension, students' relationships with teachers. An employee has the duty to accept assigned

tasks cheerfully and perform them punctually and well, to work cooperatively with others so that the workplace atmosphere remains productive and pleasant, to follow established rules and regulations, and to be diligent in serving the customers' or clients' needs and interests. (Employers have corresponding relationships to employees, and teachers to students.)

Professional obligations: Most professional organizations have detailed codes of conduct that specify the obligations members are expected to honor. Here is a brief sampling from a variety of professions:

A physician shall always bear in mind the obligation of preserving human life. (World Medical Association)

In research, an anthropologist's paramount responsibility is to those he studies. (American Anthropological Association)

We have a special obligation to ensure the free flow of information and ideas to present and future generations. (American Library Association)

It is the individual responsibility of each sociologist to aspire to the highest possible standards of conduct in research, teaching, practice, and service. (American Sociological Association)

Advertising agencies must recognize an obligation, not only to their clients, but to the public, the media they employ, and to each other. (American Association of Advertising Agencies)

When Obligations Conflict

Sometimes a single obligation will be present in a moral situation. But often two or more will be present, and many times they will conflict. In such cases, the challenge is to choose wisely among them.

The executives of a corporation, for example, must make a difficult decision. Their profit picture has been dismal. If they do not find some way to cut back their expenses, they may be driven into bankruptcy. Because their biggest expense is salaries, it is clear they must make economies there. After analyzing the various operations of the corporation, they determine that they can effect significant economies by curtailing certain services to customers and combining the work of three departments.

This reorganization will make it possible to reduce the work staff by twelve people and result in savings of tens of thousands of dollars. However, each of the people involved has been employed by the company for more than fifteen years, and all are between ages 45 and 55. They are too young for retirement and too old to find other positions very easily.

The dilemma the executives face is the conflict between their obligation to longtime and faithful employees and their obligation to stockholders. Both obligations demand fulfillment. Both obviously cannot be fulfilled. There may be some middle ground possible—some special waiving of the retirement rules that will permit at least some employees to retire early. But even in cases where the executives have the power to grant such a waiver, it is unlikely that they could do it for all twelve people. Choice is unavoidable. They must give preference to one obligation or the other.

Another common moral dilemma caused by conflicting obligations is that faced by the person who is asked to give a job reference for a colleague or subordinate whom he or she believes may not be able to perform the job in question. The chairman of an academic department, for instance, may be called by his counterpart in another school. "I'm calling about an applicant of ours who worked for you until last year," the caller says. "His name is Dr. Elmo Ryan, and he's applying for a position in sociology." The chairman winces. He remembers Ryan all too well. For three years the poor man struggled to teach his courses well. The chairman visited his classes and tried to help him improve. Several of his colleagues in the department did likewise. Finally, everyone was driven to the same conclusion that the students who were unfortunate enough to be in his classes had long since reached: Ryan simply was not meant to be a teacher.

Now the chairman must answer a direct question about him to a prospective employer. If he tells her the truth about Ryan—that he is a hardworking, personable, cooperative *incompetent*—Ryan will surely lose the job. The chairman feels a certain obligation to Ryan. And yet he feels obligated to the woman on the phone and to all the students Ryan might be assigned to teach. Whatever the chairman decides to do, the decision will not be easy. It will require breaking one obligation.

Does everyone have an obligation to assist in the rehabilitation of former thieves and rapists by giving them a chance to return to society without discrimination? Most of us would agree that there is such an obligation, at least one of beneficence. But if a banker wants to honor that obligation and hire the reformed thief, he or she must also consider the obligation owed his or her customers and the Federal Deposit Insurance Corporation to maintain the security of the bank. If the owners of a girls' camp wish to honor that obligation and hire the reformed rapist, they must consider their obligation to ensure the safety of their clientele.

WEIGHING THE OBLIGATIONS

In cases where two or more obligations are in conflict, the best we can do is to *consider the relative importance of each and give preference to the more important one.* Of course, which obligation is more important is often a decision about which honest, intelligent people may disagree. To judge well we need a sense of proportion. That is, we need to perceive what balance among the obligations will serve each one to the extent appropriate and thereby make the best of a difficult situation. Whenever both obligations can be partly served, they should be. Whenever only one can be served, the more important one should be.

If a person owes $200 to someone who needs the money and then, just when he is able to pay, he reads in the paper that contributions are being sought for flood relief in a neighboring state, he may be torn between settling his debt and donating to the flood victims. Which should he do? A rationale could be developed to support either. But a better case could be made for settling his debt, not only because it existed prior to the other, but also because the creditor is in need. The obligation of justice in this case would be more important than the obligation of beneficence. (It is not necessarily so in every case where two obligations conflict. If the creditor did not need the money immediately and the act of charity was to a family that had no income and neither qualified for public assistance nor was likely to find any other private benefactor, beneficence might be more important.)

A merchandiser for a clothing concern is in her busiest season of the year. Moreover, the demands of her job this year are even greater than usual because two very different and daring fashion trends are competing with a well-entrenched mode. The right judgment on the merchandiser's part in assessing the buying public's taste will make a great deal of money for her company; the wrong judgment could ruin the company. Meanwhile her husband, whom she loves, is in a state of depression. He feels he has disappointed her by losing his job, he suspects her (wrongly) of infidelity, and he is given to periods of depression during which he contemplates suicide. The psychiatrist he has been visiting says he is not dangerously ill but could easily become so. He advises the merchandiser to take her husband on a month's vacation.

What should the wife do? She owes her employer her expert judgment during the next month. Yet she owes her husband help and attention. Which obligation is greater? Most ethicists would undoubtedly rule in favor of the husband for two reasons: first, because the wife's obligation to him derives from a solemn vow to care for him "in sickness and in health"; second, because his condition may be a matter of life and death.

To the extent possible she should, of course, try to serve both obligations. She might, in other words, postpone the vacation for a week or ten days and during that period work sixteen- or eighteen-hour days. She might even take work with her on the vacation or telephone or e-mail the office every day to provide whatever guidance she can to her employer. Nevertheless, it would be a graver fault to neglect her husband's needs than to neglect her employer's.

Two Moral Dilemmas

Such choices challenge lawyers and doctors virtually every day. Clarence Darrow, the famous attorney, is said to have won a case by stealing the jury's attention during the prosecutor's summation. He smoked a cigar in which he had placed a wire to prevent the ashes from falling. With each puff the ashes would grow longer . . . and the jury would sit a little farther forward on their chairs. When would those ashes fall? They never did. However brilliant the prosecutor's closing words might have been, they were ineffective. The jury was too busy watching that cigar to pay any attention to them.

Darrow's bit of vaudeville represented a choice between his obligation to his client and his obligation to courtroom procedure. Obviously, in his judgment no trick was too cheap to play if it helped his client. Was his action morally blameless? Hardly. It was an open-and-shut case of wrongdoing, though one that we might be tempted to approve if our life were in the balance.

A similar case of a lawyer forced to choose between obligations occurred more recently in New York City. Martin Erdmann, a Legal Aid defender, remarked publicly that judgeships today must either be bought or won through political influence. He was brought before the New York City Bar Association for violating the group's code of ethics. (The association recommended that no action be taken against him.) Erdmann had an obligation to the legal profession to protect it from scandal, and he had an obligation to that profession, and to the citizens it represents, to speak out against abuses within the profession. Undoubtedly he judged the latter obligation to be more important.

How do we judge his action? To judge fairly we would have to know more than the details given here or available in the news accounts of his case. If the situation concerning the selection of judges is as he described it, then it makes a mockery of our system of jurisprudence and of the very concept of justice. Because it cries out for denunciation, his obligation to speak out would indeed take precedence over his obligation to protect his profession. On the other hand, if the situation was not as serious as he described it, or if he wasn't sure and didn't bother to determine the validity of the description, then the obligation to be silent and not scandalize the courts would take precedence. If he had knowledge of some abuses but did not know how widespread they were, the requirement of proportion would demand that he modify his statement to reflect his degree of knowledge rather than speak in general terms and indict, by implication, all judges.

(Look back at the previous paragraph and note the two "if . . . then" sentences. This device, which is helpful in analyzing ethical issues, was explained in Chapter 7 on page 93. Use this device whenever you lack some of the facts necessary to make a categorical judgment.)

THE ALABAMA SYPHILIS CASE

In the summer of 1972, a shocking disclosure was made about a government-sponsored medical experiment that had gone on, unnoticed, for *forty years.* The experiment concerned the effects of syphilis. The Public Health Service had begun the experiment in Alabama. Its purpose was to determine the extent of the damage that syphilis will do if left untreated. (Its effects, most of them known or at least surmised at the time the experiment was begun, are blindness; deafness; degeneration of the heart, bones, and central nervous system; insanity; and death.) Six hundred black men were selected for the experiment. They were promised free transportation to the hospital, free medical treatment for diseases other than syphilis, and free burial. Apparently they did not receive clear explanations of the possible harm the disease could cause them if left untreated.

Of the six hundred, one-third never developed syphilis. One-third received the arsenic-mercury treatment that was standard before the discovery of penicillin. The remaining one-third got no medication. Even after the discovery of penicillin a decade later and its widespread use as a cure for syphilis, they received no treatment. They remained human guinea pigs.

There were several obligations the researchers should have weighed. First, there was their obligation as physicians to care for their patients. Second, there was their obligation to justice, to respect other human beings and treat them in a manner consistent with their humanity. Third, there was their obligation as researchers to serve mankind by seeking cures for deadly diseases. The researchers seem to have ignored the first two obligations completely. Apparently they thought of the men not as patients, but as the "subjects" of the experiment—as phenomena to be studied rather than as persons to be cured. If they recognized the inhumanity of their handling of the two hundred men, they failed to act on their recognition. (There is a bitter irony in this case. During the very period in which the experiment was conducted, Nazi doctors performed similar barbarities on the inmates of concentration camps. After World War II, at the Nuremberg trials, the United States and its allies condemned those doctors for "crimes against humanity.")

The shock felt by every sensitive person at this disclosure reveals the importance of choosing well among conflicting moral obligations. It was not wrong for the doctors in the Alabama case to honor their obligation as researchers. What was wrong was their ignoring the two other obligations, both of which were more important.

On May 16, 1997, at a White House ceremony, then president Clinton told the five survivors of the Alabama syphilis experiment: "The American people are sorry for the loss, for the years of hurt. You did nothing wrong, but you were grievously wronged. I apologize, and I am sorry this apology has been so long in coming."[1]

THOROUGHNESS IS IMPORTANT

It is difficult enough to reach wise decisions in cases with conflicting obligations when we have identified all the obligations. To judge wisely when we have overlooked one or more obligations is impossible; our analysis is bound to be oversimplified. For this reason it is important to consider all possible obligations—including those of reparation, gratitude, justice, and beneficence, as well as those of fidelity—before attempting to judge.

▦ INQUIRIES

1. Historically, the method of determining whether the employees of a company wanted to be represented by a union was a secret ballot election, for which the National Labor Relations Board had oversight to avoid coercion. The "card check" approach, known more formally as the Employee Free Choice Act, would do away with the secret ballot election. Employees would just sign petition cards and if enough cards were obtained, the union would be recognized. Supporters of card check say it is fairer because it is conducted in the open, without any secrecy, and the cards are available for all to see. Opponents say taking away the secret ballot opens elections to intimidation and harassment. Research this issue using the search term "pro and con union card check." Then decide what moral criteria are applicable and decide whether card check is more or less preferable than the present system from a moral perspective.

2. A number of cases of publicizing classified government information have received national attention in recent years. One of the most serious cases occurred in June 2006 when someone leaked information to the press about a secret program to identify the financial backers of international terrorism. The program had been in effect since shortly after 9/11, was conducted with the cooperation of a Belgian banking organization, aided in the monitoring of Al Qaeda activities, and resulted in some significant arrests and prosecutions. When administration officials learned of the leak, they requested that the *New York Times* and other newspapers refrain from divulging the information. Even though it was clear that the program was legal and that the White House had kept congressional leaders informed of its progress, the *Times* decided to reveal the program to the public. Did the leaker behave ethically in revealing the existence of the program to the press? Did the *New York Times* behave ethically in publicizing it?

3. Warren Buffett, the famous financier, has a personal fortune estimated at $1.5 billion. Nevertheless, he is reported to have prepared a will that leaves almost all his wealth to charity and only a few hundred thousand dollars to each of his three children. Buffett's decision was not based on any animosity toward his children but, instead, on his belief that inheriting great wealth is more harmful than helpful to a person. Comment on his decision in light of what you read in this chapter.

4. Your grandfather is in a nursing home and you are responsible for his medical decisions. Formerly a tall, strapping man who spent most of his life engaged in physical labor and was proud of his work ethic and his independent spirit, he has suffered a stroke and lost the use of both legs and one arm and much of the ability to speak. Moreover, the staff must feed him pureed food, and even so his difficulty in swallowing causes him to aspirate small particles of food and drink, which causes frequent episodes of bacterial pneumonia. The nursing home physician poses the medical options listed here. Decide which option is the most ethical and defend your choice with references to the criteria of obligations, moral ideals, and consequences.

> **a.** Have a feeding tube surgically inserted in his throat so that he will not be required to swallow and thus can be fed without danger of aspirating food.

> **b.** Have the staff continue to offer him food and drink and, when he contracts pneumonia, administer antibiotics intravenously.

> **c.** Have the staff continue to offer him food and drink, but withhold antibiotics when he contracts pneumonia.

> **d.** Have the staff discontinue both food and drink and antibiotics.

5. In 1999, when the Brooklyn Museum of Art displayed works by Chris Ofili, it set off a furor that continued for many months. What caused the controversy was a particular painting, *The Holy Virgin Mary*, which presented a likeness of the Virgin Mary spattered with dung and covered with designs depicting female genitalia. Then mayor Rudolph Giuliani threatened to cut off $7 million in funding if the museum did not remove the painting, arguing that taxpayers should not have to support exhibits that make a mockery of their religious beliefs. When a solution was not reached, the matter was taken to court, with the museum's director claiming that the exhibit was covered by the constitutional guarantee of free speech. Begin by conducting an Internet search using the terms "Charles Ofili controversy" and "sensation exhibition." Then consider the relevant obligations, moral ideals, and consequences and decide which view of the issue was more defensible from an ethical standpoint.

6. Nineteen-year-old Joshua Davey, a freshman student at Northwest College in Kirkland, Washington, who is majoring in Pastoral Ministries and Business Management, was awarded $1,125 for the 1999–2000 school year through the Promise Scholarship. This scholarship provides financial assistance to students from low- and middle-income families who exhibit high academic credentials and are enrolled in an accredited public or private postsecondary school within the state of Washington. The college later notified Davey that state officials were denying him the funds because he is pursuing a degree in religious studies and "students who are pursuing a degree in the-ology are not eligible to receive any state-funded student financial aid, including the new Washington Promise Scholarship." Davey's attorney has filed a lawsuit in the matter.[2] Was it ethical for the state of Washington to deny Davey the scholarship? Explain your answer in terms of obligations, moral ideals, and consequences.

7. It has become fashionable for political candidates to hire private investi-gators to find embarrassing information about their opponents so that they can leak it to the press and discredit the opponents. Discuss the morality of hiring private investigators for this purpose and the morality of the investi-gators' accepting such an assignment.

8. James Q. Wilson argues that "a moral life is perfected by practice more than by precept" and that social institutions, notably the family, have the power to encourage that practice and create the climate in which it takes place.[3] Would it be correct to say that the family has a moral obligation to use this power? If so, do other social agencies—for example, school, church, entertainment and communications media, government—have a similar obli-gation? Explain.

Directions for inquiries 8–20: In each case, identify the conflicting obligations and decide whether the action taken is morally right. Be sure to consider the requirement of proportion.

9. In studying the subculture of a particular group, a sociologist must be accepted by the people and gain their trust. One such researcher is studying the people in an urban slum. She learns through their confidence that certain members of the community are involved in a car-theft ring. She does not report them to the police.

10. A Roman Catholic priest disagrees with his church on the issue of abor-tion. A parishioner comes to him for guidance. He does not mention the Church's official position on the subject, but instead gives his own moral judgment.

11. An executive of a large company learns that the company is violating the state antipollution law by dumping chemicals into the lake bordering its plant. The state inspectors are being bribed to ignore the violation. The exec-utive takes no action.

12. A senator believes strongly that the country has oversubscribed the de-fense program to the detriment of other programs. Yet he is from a state that receives a large number of defense contracts, and if he introduces legislation to curtail defense spending, he is likely to be defeated in the next election. He decides not to introduce it.

13. A very competent druggist, well versed in the latest pharmacological studies, receives a prescription from a physician and recognizes that it is for a dangerous, highly addictive, and largely discredited medication. She calls the physician and is told curtly to mind her own business. As the customer waits in the front of the store, the druggist ponders the situation. "Should I refuse to fill it? Should I tell the customer I am certain the doctor has made a mistake?

Should I call the medical board and report the incident?" She decides to fill the prescription.

14. An Old Testament professor in a Protestant seminary does not accept the school's literal interpretation of the Bible. In his classes he introduces his students to a number of philosophies of interpretation, including liberal ones. Learning of this violation of the school's traditional theological perspective, the faculty deliberates about it at length. Finally they reach a decision. The professor is to be fired.

15. A doctor on duty in a hospital emergency room one Halloween night treats a 15-year-old boy whose eye was injured by an exploding firecracker. He notices the boy is drunk. Because the extent of the injury is not certain, he has the boy admitted to the hospital and notifies his parents. When they arrive, the boy is under sedation, so his drunken condition escapes their detection. Nevertheless, the doctor informs them that their son had been drinking.

16. A psychiatrist is treating a very disturbed and potentially violent man. One day the man tells her that he has recurring thoughts of killing a stranger, whom he will choose at random. He details exactly how he will carry out the crime. A few days later the psychiatrist reads in the newspaper that the very same crime her patient described has been committed. She has no doubt that her patient committed it; every detail is identical. The psychiatrist would like to inform the police, but she decides not to.

17. A company president receives an angry letter from a high government official. It seems an executive of the company has written a letter to a large daily newspaper criticizing the official's policy decisions. (She wrote as a private citizen, not as a representative of her company.) The government official is demanding that the executive be fired. If she is not, he warns, the company will lose some lucrative government contracts. The president ponders the matter and decides to fire the executive.

18. When Sally's father was gravely ill, he called her to his bedside and said, "I'd always hoped I'd see you graduate from college and go on to become a physicist, but I know death is near. Promise me one thing—that you'll keep on studying hard and become a physicist." Sally was deeply moved. "I will," she responded; "I swear to you I will." Her father died shortly thereafter. Now it is two years later, and Sally is ready to graduate from college. But she will not become a physicist. She has decided to go to law school.

19. A carpenter with a wife and three children works for a home construction firm that is barely able to make its payroll. The current job is for ten houses in a new development. The carpenter is aware that the lumber for the inside walls is inferior to the grade required in the architect's specifications; eventually, the walls could warp. However, he does the job as he is told and says nothing.

20. Portia is a legal secretary hired with the understanding that all office information will be confidential. Her boss, a criminal lawyer in a large city, defends a man accused of vicious attacks on several elderly women. In the course of her work, Portia learns that the accused has told her boss that he committed the crimes and feels no remorse. A plea of "not guilty" is being entered and there is a good chance the man will serve no time for his crimes. What, if anything, should Portia do?

21. Claude, a college freshman, learns that his roommate and friend is pushing hard drugs on campus. Claude is not opposed to drug use. He smokes marijuana himself, though he has never used any hard drugs. Neither does he believe that drug pushing is wrong. But he does fear for his own safety, because if his friend is discovered and their room searched, his own marijuana might be found. After removing his marijuana from his room, he slips an anonymous note under the dean's door, informing on his roommate.

CHAPTER NINE

CONSIDERING MORAL IDEALS

How can we reconcile conflicts
between moral ideals or between
a moral ideal and an obligation?

In some contemporary contexts, the word *ideal* has acquired the connotation of impracticality. Thus we may say something is ideal when we really mean unrealistic; we may call people idealistic when they produce grand but unworkable ideas. From that perspective, having and valuing ideals understandably seems naive and even foolish. Yet there is nothing impractical or unrealistic about the word *ideal* as it is used in ethical analysis. As noted in Chapter 7, to an ethicist ideals are not only notions of excellence, goals that bring greater harmony in ourselves and with others, but also specific concepts that assist us in achieving respect for persons in our judgments and actions. Also noted was the fact that for highly ethical people, the line between obligations and ideals tends to be blurred—in other words, such people tend to view ideals as obligations that they hold themselves responsible for meeting.

IMPORTANT MORAL IDEALS

Now let us look more closely at the specific moral ideals—the *cardinal virtues*—mentioned earlier. (Note that the less fashionable term *virtue* is a near-synonym for *moral ideal*.) Although this list is not exhaustive, it covers most of the ideals that continue to be prized in our own and many other cultures.

PRUDENCE

This virtue, known also as *practical wisdom*, consists of choosing one's behavior judiciously by consulting experience and deliberating thoughtfully about what response is most appropriate. Prudence is the exact opposite of rashness and impulsiveness. The American Society of Mechanical Engineers is referring to prudence in their stipulation that "engineers shall associate only with reputable persons or organizations."

JUSTICE/FAIRNESS

Justice denotes the evaluation of situations according to their merits, fairly and without prejudice, as well as giving each person his or her due. The ideal of justice opposes "playing favorites" and giving unfair advantage to one person or group. This ideal is also the cornerstone of law. (*Note:* Some ethicists regard justice and fairness as separate ideals, but in everyday English usage there is little difference. Each implies the other.)

TEMPERANCE

The Greek philosopher Socrates considered temperance to be almost synonymous with self-mastery. The temperate person, he argued, is the one who exercises control over his or her desires and thereby escapes domination by them. Aristotle took a similar view, holding self-indulgence to be childish. For these philosophers, and for many of the ethicists that followed them, the hallmarks of temperance are moderation and restraint of one's desires and passions.[1]

COURAGE

This virtue "does not consist only in conquering fear and in withholding the body from flight no matter what the risk of pain. It consists at least as much in steeling the will, reinforcing its resolutions, and turning the mind relentlessly to seek or face the truth."[2] Thus courage has an intellectual and a moral, as well as a physical, dimension.

LOVING KINDNESS

This moral ideal is perhaps the most fundamental and universal of all. It is the essential meaning of *agape*, the ancient Greek word for love of neighbor. It is also mentioned thirty separate times in the Hebrew Bible (known to Christians as the Old Testament). The New Testament does not use that term, but its many references to love of neighbor convey the same idea—for example, "Love your neighbor as yourself." "Loving kindness toward all creation" is a central concept of Buddhism. And the Golden Rule—"Do unto others as you would have them do unto you"—is best understood as an exhortation to loving kindness. As noted in Chapter 7, some form of the Golden Rule is found in virtually every religion, from Baha'i to Zoroastrianism, as well as in secular philosophy.[*]

*For a detailed treatment of this ideal, see Vincent Ryan Ruggiero, *The Practice of Loving Kindness* (Hyde Park, NY: New City Press, 2002).

HONESTY

The word *honesty* derives from the Latin word for "honorable." This ideal entails being truthful to others and refusing to mislead or deceive.

COMPASSION

This ideal is a sentiment that occurs in response to other people's suffering, emotional as well as physical. It is characterized by feelings of pity and sympathy and the desire to alleviate the other person's pain. When intensely felt, compassion becomes empathy—that is, not only understanding the other person's difficulties but also vicariously experiencing them.

FORGIVENESS

This ideal consists in granting others absolution for their offenses against us. It is found in most secular and religious ethical systems. In Christianity it is also considered a requirement for asking God's forgiveness: If we aren't willing to forgive others their offenses, Christianity teaches, we shouldn't expect God to forgive ours.*

REPENTANCE

To repent is to feel remorse for having offended others and, by extension, to express that feeling in the form of an apology.

REPARATION

This ideal is defined as undoing the harm we have done to others—for example, by returning something we have taken without the person's permission or, if we have told a lie about someone, by revisiting the person we told and admitting we lied. When the harm is of such a nature that it cannot be undone, some other way of making amends can be sought.

GRATITUDE

This ideal is defined as a sense of appreciation and thanks for an act of generosity. The act may be as small as the loan of a few dollars or a ride home on a rainy day or as great as years of love and nurture from our parents. We may also be grateful for a sound mind and body and the good fortune to live in a country that, however imperfectly, safeguards its citizens' basic freedoms.

---

*The Lord's Prayer contains the clause "forgive us our trespasses *as we forgive those who trespass against us.*" [Emphasis added.]

BENEFICENCE

This ideal is defined as the performance of good acts for no other reason than that they are good. A popular phrase used to describe this ideal is "random acts of kindness."

British ethicist W. D. Ross classifies some of the moral ideals mentioned above—specifically, justice, reparation, gratitude, and beneficence—as obligations rather than ideals.[3] (He also includes two others in his list, "self-improvement" and "non-maleficence.") We are classifying them as ideals *because they are not associated with specific relationships* but instead are generally applicable. This distinction is helpful in differentiating obligations from ideals.

IDEALS IN CONFLICT

Ideals, like obligations, are not always in harmony with one another. In fact, they often compete with one another. Consider this case. A kindergarten boy from a poor family rides the school bus to and from school. On the half-hour ride, many of the other children on the bus entertain themselves by teasing him about his plain clothes, his unkempt hair, his worn shoes. Day after day the abuse continues, becoming more and more cruel. An 11-year-old girl, sensitive to the feelings of others, notices the boy suffering in silence, unable to understand why the other students want to make him feel bad. The girl is repulsed by his appearance and is not at all eager to alienate her friends. Honesty bids her stay out of the affair. But kindness prompts her to sit with him, speak with him, become a "big sister" he can look forward to seeing each day on the bus so that the rejection of the others will not scar him emotionally.

By choosing to honor the ideal of kindness, the girl necessarily violates the ideal of honesty. Does she do right? If we believe kindness to be the higher ideal in this situation, we will agree that she does.

An interesting case of conflicting ideals occurred in the filming of a documentary account of the life of a young evangelist who later became a movie actor, Marjoe Gortner. The film shows how Marjoe perfected and used his pentecostal pitch on crowds of believers. He didn't believe he was preaching a "miracle of God." In fact, he didn't even believe in God! The producers intended the film to reveal this and thus to serve the ideal of honest reporting. However, in filming the revival meeting scenes they used real revival meetings that were set up by Marjoe. Thus the crowds who appear on the screen were exploited, and their religious beliefs by implication were mocked in the film.[4]

Was the use of real believers in real revival meetings morally justified? To decide, we must consider whether the ideal of honesty in reporting outweighed the ideals of respect for the many sincere believers and tolerance of their beliefs. In other words, we must determine which ideal represented the *greater good* (or the lesser evil).

If there had been no way to create a set and use actors, or perhaps if the point of the film had never been made before, then the ideal of honesty in reporting might have taken precedence. But there was a way, and though it would have cost more in time and money, the cost would not seem to have been prohibitive. Furthermore, the point had previously been made in books and films. Therefore, the offense to the people and the insult to their beliefs outweighed the authenticity achieved. The producers' decision did not represent the greater good.

THE MUNICH INCIDENT

Several decades ago the world shared the dilemma of West German police officials when Arab guerrillas held members of the Israeli Olympic team hostage and attempted to leave the country with them. The police were faced with the decision of how best to free the Israelis with a minimum of harm to everyone concerned. The ideal of respect for the rights and safety of the victims clashed with the ideal of respect for the lives of the guerrillas. If the guerrillas were allowed to leave the country with their hostages, the hostages faced almost certain torture and death. Yet if the police tried to prevent them from leaving, the lives of both groups would be threatened.

The police tried to minimize the danger by tricking the guerrillas, gaining entry to the buildings they had taken over, and subduing them. But after this and other efforts failed and the guerrillas and their captives were at the airport, the police were left with their final plan—to separate the guerrillas, kill their leader, and either overpower the others or persuade them to surrender. (The plan did not work as intended.)

Was the plan to murder the leader justified? Had it been the first response, it surely would have been questionable. Human life, even the life of a criminal, is a precious thing and should not be treated lightly. In this case, however, it was a last resort, put into effect only after other, less violent, actions had failed. Finally, since it was designed to save lives, it was surely justified. The only alternative to it would have been to stand by while many innocent people were taken to their deaths. Was it, then, a desirable action that decent men could be proud of performing? No. But it was the lesser of two evils.

The Issue of Affirmative Action

The debate over the wisdom of affirmative action has taken place mainly in the political arena. Yet the issue is essentially a moral one involving conflicting ideals—or, more precisely, conflicting expressions of a single ideal, fairness. Affirmative action was conceived as a means of overcoming the effects of centuries of discrimination. Several decades ago more and more people became convinced that denying education and employment opportunities to women merely on the basis of their gender and to black (or Hispanic) men merely on the basis of their color (or ethnicity) was unfair and therefore unethical.

Clearly, decency required that something be done to correct the situation. But what was the best and most reasonable approach? One idea was to guarantee equal educational and employment opportunity to all citizens and to create laws providing for the prosecution of individuals who failed to honor that guarantee. Critics responded that such a guarantee was fine for the future but did nothing to correct past injustices. Another idea was to provide special educational catch-up programs to offset academic deprivation. Critics argued that this solution would not achieve results quickly enough; the only fair solution, in their view, would be to give women and minority men *preference* over white men in college admissions and employment. Such preference generally took the form of set-asides and hiring quotas.

Although arguments against preferences were initially dismissed as shallow and, in some cases, racist, in recent years they have been given a more impartial hearing. Some such arguments are that preferences cause racial animosity, that they cheat the very people they are designed to help by putting them in educational or employment situations for which they have not been prepared, or that they deprive society of the most highly trained and qualified people. But the most common, and perhaps most substantive, argument is that preferences have resulted less in fairness toward women and minority men than in unfairness toward white men. Those who advance this argument maintain that the only fair system is one that is completely blind to gender, race, and ethnicity and judges each individual solely on his or her qualifications. However the affirmative action issue ultimately is resolved, it offers an unmistakable lesson: Even when an ideal is universally accepted, it can still be very difficult to achieve.

Ideals Versus Obligations

Frequently, moral ideals compete not with one another but with obligations. Every time a police officer takes a gun from a criminal, he or she is choosing the obligation to prevent crime over the ideal of respecting private property. Every time a doctor prescribes a placebo for a hypochondriac patient, he or she is placing the obligation to care for the patient over the ideal of honesty. Most people would agree with the choices made in such cases. There are situations, however, in which the promptings of ideal and obligation are more nearly balanced.

The body of a man who died from cancer has just been delivered to the funeral home. As the mortician begins to prepare the body for burial, the telephone rings. The caller is the director of a nearby medical school. It seems that the type of cancer the man had is very rare and the opportunity to study it more closely could provide valuable insights in the fight to cure cancer. The director and his staff, as well as the medical staff of the hospital, had suggested that the man will his body to the medical center, but he had refused. After his death they pleaded with the man's relatives to permit an autopsy. They refused. The purpose of his call, the director explains, is to request that the mortician cooperate with them and permit the autopsy to be done without the relatives' knowledge.

The mortician is being asked to set aside his obligation to the relatives to treat the body as they wish and instead to honor the ideal of concern for the suffering of other human beings. If the autopsy were certain to provide needed insights in the study of cancer, we might conclude that he should agree to it. Because it offers only a possibility, and because his obligation to the family is not casual but serious and formal, the mortician should refuse.

Consider still another case. Simone's cousin comes to her house one evening and explains that he is in a desperate situation. He has been in debt to loan sharks for some time and has been able to postpone the due date several times. Now his time is up. He has received the final warning: Pay up tonight or die. He must raise $23,000 in five hours. It is futile even to try to raise the money. He could turn himself in to the police, but that would be only a temporary solution. The moment he was released from their custody, his life would again be in jeopardy. All he can hope for is to hide out for a week or ten days and then attempt to slip out of the country. He begs Simone to hide him in her home for a while.

Simone weighs the matter. She and her cousin have never been close. She hasn't even seen him in ten years. But his life is at stake. Simple charity demands that Simone honor his request. On the other hand, if Simone harbors him in her home, he will surely be endangering her husband and children, whom she has an obligation to protect. The people who will be searching for her cousin are not likely to look kindly on witnesses who can identify them. Furthermore, they are probably not above harming women and children.

If there is any way that Simone can help her cousin without endangering herself and her loved ones, morality demands that she do so. However, for Simone to choose to help her cousin at the expense of endangering herself and her family would be a greater wrong. It is not necessary that Simone be certain that her immediate family would be harmed. The likelihood that they would be is sufficient cause for her to deny her cousin the act of charity.

To summarize, in cases in which there is a conflict between ideals or between an ideal and an obligation, we should choose the action that will achieve the greater good. Where the choice of actions is such that no good can be achieved, we should choose the action that will result in the lesser evil.

🔲 INQUIRIES

In each of the following cases, identify the ideals, or ideals and obligations, that are in conflict. Examine the action taken or proposed and decide whether it achieves the greater good (or lesser harm).

1. The issue of using animals to test consumer products has been with us for many decades. Supporters of the use of animals maintain that the practice enables researchers to ensure the safety of consumer products and medicines for humans. Opponents argue that it causes unnecessary pain and suffering to animals and, in many cases, does not achieve its objective because of the anatomical and physiological differences between animals and humans. More recently, "cruelty-free" testing and product labeling has been introduced, but critics say the standards are porous and provide little protection for animals. (Search terms: "animal testing pros and cons" and "cruelty-free labeling."

2. The issue of health care rationing was an important factor in the debate over the health care bill that President Obama signed into law in 2010. Whether such rationing will occur remains to be seen. If it does, though, it will undoubtedly have the greatest effect on the elderly—that is, some government administrator or health care panel may decide that certain expensive medical procedures will not be approved for people above a certain age. Similar decisions could also be made about the level of care given in assisted living facilities and nursing homes. (Search term: "health care rationing.")

3. The world's largest cigarette company, Philip Morris, donates millions of dollars to museums, theaters, dance companies, and arts groups in New York City, where its corporate headquarters are located. When the city was about to enact tough smoking restrictions, Philip Morris reportedly contacted the various groups and let them know that future grants would be affected by the level of support they received in their fight against the city. Many of the groups joined the lobbying effort and barraged city hall with calls and letters opposing the smoking restrictions. Editorials in the *Chronicle of Philanthropy* and elsewhere criticized Philip Morris for its pressure tactics.[5]

4. As a child, Nathan was taught to avoid speaking ill of his country, especially in public. However, since he graduated from college and became a journalist, Nathan has been an outspoken critic of his country, blaming it for most of the problems that exist in the world—including the behavior of tyrants and dictators in other countries.

5. Trudy is an executive with a large corporation. After reading a confidential memorandum revealing that her corporation is concluding negotiations to buy several smaller companies, she realizes that an immediate investment in those companies before news of the buyout becomes public will result in a handsome profit. So she invests $10,000 of her own money and tells her family and friends to do likewise.

6. Ronald, a senior editor at a publishing house, receives a book manuscript written by a celebrity. He skims it and immediately recognizes that it is filled with details about the personal lives of dozens of prominent people. Unquestionably, it will ruin reputations and cause many people pain. On the other hand, given the public's taste for scandal, it is bound to make the best-seller list and earn his company a lot of money. He decides to offer the celebrity a contract on the book.

7. It is standard practice for advertising people to create ads that play on people's needs and desires. For example, they choose words and images that convey the idea that buying a certain brand of clothing will bring friendship, athletic or professional success, love, and happiness.

8. Cibella Borges had been a police officer in New York City for more than eighteen months when nude photographs of her appeared in a girlie magazine. (The photographs had been taken before she was appointed to the department.) She was subsequently dismissed from the department for "conduct prejudicial to the good order and effectiveness of the police department."[6]

9. A columnist for a college newspaper writes a column praising the American Nazi party and arguing that the security of the United States depends on the elimination of Jews, blacks, and Catholics from positions of importance and influence. Someone on the staff notifies the dean of student affairs that the column is scheduled for publication, and the dean forbids the editor to publish it.

10. A police officer is on duty in the station house when he overhears the victim of a robbery describing the robber to the desk sergeant. The officer realizes that the description fits his older brother perfectly. He pretends not to have heard the discussion.

11. Eight-year-old Tom receives a new and expensive toy from his parents for his birthday. They emphasize that they expect him to take special care of it. While playing with his friends, Tom notices that one boy keeps staring at the new toy. Realizing that the boy is poor and would be thrilled to have such a toy, Tom gives it to him to keep.

12. A young police officer is assigned to plainclothes duty at a local college. She attends classes, lives in a dormitory, and cultivates friendships with many students. Through those friendships she identifies the campus drug pushers, sets them up, and arrests them.

13. A team of doctors has been assigned the difficult duty of deciding which of two patients will receive the next heart transplant when a heart is available. The patients are Anne, 12 years old, the only child of a laborer and his wife, and Mark, 48, an executive and the father of four children. They choose Anne.

14. An 18-year-old student, home from college during the semester break, stumbles onto the fact that his father, whom he thought to be a business machines salesman, is actually a gunman for the mob. Moreover, he recently killed a member of a rival mob faction. The son considers going to the police and turning his father in, but he does not do so.

15. Raoul is a private detective. He specializes in cases in which husbands or wives suspect their spouse of infidelity. In the performance of his service, he hides microphones in offices and homes (including bedrooms), breaks into homes and searches for incriminating evidence, and steams open private correspondence.

16. Two weeks ago Arthur was hospitalized for a series of tests. Yesterday the doctor called his wife in and explained that he has a fatal disease and has at most six months to live. The doctor adds that, in his judgment, Arthur would experience great difficulty coping with the truth. Today, sensing that something is troubling his wife, Arthur guesses and probes, "You're hiding something, aren't you, Martha? Is it about my tests? Am I going to die?" She has never lied to him and cannot bring herself to lie now. She tells him the truth.

17. A social caseworker learns that one of her clients is secretly playing in a band two nights a week and earning $20 a night. Because the client is physically disabled and receiving full welfare benefits for himself and his family, he is required by law to surrender any other income to the welfare department. He is breaking the law by keeping the money. The caseworker, knowing that the welfare benefits are based on an unrealistically low cost-of-living index, does not report the man.

18. Elvira is very much in love with her fiancé, Ethelred. Though they have been engaged for over a year (and sexually intimate for almost as long), Ethelred balks at setting a date for the marriage. Elvira is convinced that his obstacle is not disaffection, but fear, and that once he can be moved to action, he will be relieved and happy. She therefore feigns pregnancy and plans to feign a miscarriage after they are married.

19. A man is elected to the presidency of a small country. Soon after his inauguration, he begins quietly to undermine the other branches of government and to assume more and more power himself. Within a few years his control is absolute. A large army and secret police force assure that his will is obeyed. Taxes rise, private businesses are taken over by the government, and the standard of living of the average citizen plummets to a mere subsistence level. Protests are met with imprisonment and, in some cases, execution. A small band of men and women assassinate the tyrant and a half dozen of his lieutenants.

20. A high school basketball coach has a rule against smoking. Any team member who is caught violating the rule is supposed to be dropped from the team for the remainder of the season. Several days before the big game of the season, the game that will determine the league championship, the coach catches a star player violating the rule. He decides not to suspend him.

21. On October 13, 1972, a plane crashed high in the Andes mountains, killing almost two-thirds of its forty-five passengers and crew and leaving the others exposed to below-zero temperatures and the threat of starvation. More than three months passed before they were found. After their rescue it was revealed that the survivors had resorted to eating the flesh of their dead companions as a means of survival.[7]

22. Sharon and her friend Bill are both lab technicians at a blood bank. Sharon knows that Bill is going through a pretty tough divorce and that Bill's work hasn't been up to par. Sharon accidentally learns that Bill has mixed up several patients' blood samples. If Sharon corrects the errors, the director of the blood bank will find out and Bill will be fired. If she doesn't correct them, several doctors will receive incorrect information about their patients' physical condition. Sharon decides to correct the errors.

23. Tina and Frank apply for the same job. Tina is the more qualified applicant, but Frank is the personnel officer's friend and next-door neighbor. The personnel officer knows that Frank's family needs the income badly. She screens out Tina and sends only Frank to interview with the boss.

24. A restaurant cook is working a busy dinner shift on Friday night. In his hurry, he drops two expensive cooked steaks on the floor. He picks the steaks up, puts them on two platters, and calls for them to be served.

25. A hijacker is holding a jetliner and 192 passengers hostage until his demands are met. He is demanding $500,000 and a guarantee of safe passage to a country that will not return him for prosecution. The airline authorities and the police agree to his demands, and he releases the plane and the hostages. Then the police seize him and take him to jail.

26. A professor of psychology wishes to learn the effects of various conditions on students' learning. He significantly varies the heat, lighting, noise, and humidity of his classroom during examinations. On occasion he also purposely garbles half a lecture or repeats a previous day's lecture verbatim without comment.

27. According to the philosophy known as *objectivism,* created by Ayn Rand, no person has any obligation to his or her fellow human beings, selfishness is more virtuous than altruism, and the best principle to follow is the principle of self-interest. Thomas Cannon is a retired postal worker who came from a poor family and never earned more than $30,000 annually. Yet he managed to give away more than $96,000 over the years, most of it in $1,000 grants to individuals he hears or reads have done something exemplary.[8] What do you think Ayn Rand would say of him? Do you agree with that assessment? Explain with references to what you learned in this and previous chapters.

CHAPTER TEN

CONSIDERING CONSEQUENCES

*How do we deal with cases in which
the consequences are not neatly separable
into good and bad, but are mixed?*

The relationship between actions and consequences is a cause-and-effect relationship, but not the kind we associate with the motion of physical objects, such as a row of dominoes tumbling down in predictable response to the falling of the first one. In human affairs the responses are never completely predictable. If Lucy curses Pauline, Pauline might well respond in kind, but then again she might bless Lucy instead. If Clyde strikes Hector, chances are Hector will strike back, but it is possible that he will turn the other cheek. Similarly, some people who grow up in crime-ridden, drug-infested neighborhoods become criminals or drug users, but others remain honest and drug-free.* And though children who have been neglected or abused by their parents often harbor anger and resentment throughout their lives, in some cases animosity gives way to forgiveness and love.

The main difference between the laws of cause and effect in the physical universe and cause and effect in human affairs is that humans have the capacity to choose how they respond to events. To be sure, natural endowment and social conditioning exert a powerful influence and make some patterns of response more likely than others. (In Chapter 4 we discussed how these forces influence the development of conscience.) But in the vast majority of cases, these forces only *diminish*, rather than eradicate, one's freedom to choose. Free will enables people to resist outside influences, defy psychological and sociological axioms, and behave unpredictably.

---

*For a fascinating and highly readable study that debunks media stereotypes of inner-city neighborhoods, see Mitchell Dunier's award-winning *Slim's Table: Race, Respectability, and Masculinity* (Chicago: University of Chicago Press, 1992).

Let's be clear that free will doesn't suspend the laws of nature. If a woman jumps out a fiftieth-floor window, she is not likely to get up and walk away, no matter how robust her will to survive. If a man sprinkles his mashed potatoes with cyanide, we can safely bet that he won't report for work tomorrow. (Chances are, he won't even make it through dessert!)

DEALING WITH PROBABILITY

The fact that people can and do behave unpredictably makes consideration of consequences more difficult than it might otherwise be. Often as not, we are unable to arrive at certainty but must be content with probability. A case introduced earlier (Chapter 1, inquiry 10) will illustrate. That case recounted the poignant situation of a young girl who was raised by foster parents from infancy and then, at age 9, returned by court order to the former drug addicts who had neglected her. The effects that must be considered in this situation include those on the real parents, the foster parents, and the girl herself. The effects on the real parents, of course, are beneficial. They gain a purpose for living and for remaining off drugs. They can overcome the terrible sense of loss and of failure that must have plagued them ever since their child was taken from them. Unfortunately, the foster parents experience almost the opposite effect: a feeling of helplessness, a profound sense of loss, and perhaps a bitterness about the seeming unfairness of the court decision.

The obvious effect on the little girl is sadness and confusion at being separated from the only parents she has ever known and at being given, like some inanimate object, to two strangers. But a deeper, delayed effect is also possible. Such an experience could leave an emotional scar on her. Will she be made bitter and cynical about human relationships? Will she be driven inward, avoiding the sharing of love and affection with others because of the subconscious fear that they, too, may be taken from her? Will she be filled with resentment toward her real parents and turn against them and all they try to do for her?

Each of these possibilities is very real. Although there is always the chance that none of them may happen, and instead her suffering may enrich her life and her trauma may lead her to become deeply sensitive to the sufferings of others, such a happy ending seems rather unlikely. The effect of lasting emotional damage is more probable and thus is the best measure of the morality of the court's action.

MAKING THE ANALYSIS THOROUGH

For moral judgment to be reliable, all significant consequences must be identified—the indirect as well as the direct, the subtle as well as the obvious, the unintended as well as the intended, the delayed as well as the immediate, the emotional and intellectual as well as the physical. The temptation to judge quickly and/or self-servingly poses a serious obstacle to thorough analysis.

Chapter 4, inquiry 8f, for example, presented the case of Fred, the son of a widow with six other children, who pays his way though college by stealing and selling automobile tires, radios, and stereo tape decks. He has decided that his behavior is justified because it helps him without hurting others; the owners are a bit inconvenienced, he reasons, but the insurance companies replace the stolen property.

Fred's examination of the consequences of his action is shallow. He has recognized only one dimension of one effect. There are other dimensions of that effect—and other effects—to consider. There is the effect on the insurance companies and their stockholders—making them pay for the stolen items. There is the effect on all the people who take out insurance policies with those companies—making them pay higher premiums. There is the effect on every citizen's attitudes—contributing to fear and anger and suspicion. Not least, there are the effects on Fred himself—reinforcing the habit of solving problems the easy way, blurring his sense of right and wrong, stilling his conscience with excuses and rationalizations.

To ensure that you account for all significant consequences, develop the habit of using your imagination: Visualize the action taking place at a particular time and place, and ask probing questions. In this case, some of the appropriate questions would have been, Who reimburses the victims of Fred's crimes? Where does the money come from? What is the public reaction to such crimes?

THREE DIFFICULT QUESTIONS

The basic rule of ethics is to do good and avoid doing evil. But real-life situations are often messy and raise difficult questions, notably the following ones.

> *Is it justifiable to perform an evil act in order to achieve good consequences?*

Many ethicists answer no, arguing that an evil act remains evil and therefore unacceptable even when done with good intentions or with good effects. This reasoning—that "the end does not justify the means"—becomes clearer in the context of actual cases.

During the period from 1940 to 1970, more than four thousand radiation experiments were performed on tens of thousands of Americans, many of them poor and uneducated, without their informed consent. Examples of alleged incidents: children in a Massachusetts orphanage were fed radioisotopes; 829 pregnant Tennessee women were fed radioactive iron; patients in Rochester, New York, were injected with plutonium; cancer patients in Cincinnati received heavy doses of gamma rays. In many of these cases, the researchers understood the harmful effects of radiation but performed the experiments anyway in order to obtain valuable scientific knowledge.[1]

A similar case occurred during the early days of World War II. In order to determine how the enemy's use of chemical warfare would affect U.S. soldiers, U.S. military commanders secretly subjected thousands of troops to mustard gas and other chemicals without their approval. The troops were ordered to enter a gas chamber as many as six times. The poisonous effects of the gas proved to be harmful and, in many cases, long lasting. Decades later, the health of many individuals continued to decline. However, when they applied for medical benefits, they found that their records had disappeared.[2]

In these cases, the end was ethically acceptable and even noble— gaining scientific insights that could spare thousands, perhaps even millions, of people pain and suffering. However, the action taken to achieve the end—subjecting innocent individuals to immediate and potentially long-term pain and suffering without their permission—was morally unacceptable. Therefore, the reasoning goes, the action is unethical. The good end did not justify the evil means.

Is it justifiable to perform an act that is not in itself evil but produces mixed consequences, some of them beneficial and others harmful?

Most ethicists would say yes, provided three conditions are met: that the good consequences are inseparable from the bad, that the good consequences outweigh the bad, and that the bad consequences are not directly intended. These conditions form what is called the "principle of the double effect."

This principle is neither new nor radical. In fact, it is a conservative ethical approach that has traditionally been applied by Roman Catholic ethicists in cases of fallopian pregnancy. In such abnormal pregnancies, the fetus fails to move down the fallopian tube and lodge in the uterus. Instead, it remains in the tube. If it cannot be dislodged and made to continue its course to the uterus, it will develop in the tube and cause the woman to hemorrhage and die. Despite the well-known Catholic opposition to induced abortion, Catholic ethicists approve surgical removal of the fetus in such cases because the three conditions specified above are met.

The principle of the double effect has application in other situations, as well. Consider this one. Sophie has been kidnapped. For three days she has been held captive in a shack in the mountains, hoping that the ransom will be paid and she will be released. But now her captor is planning to kill her. "I'm really sorry, but I can't take the chance that you'll identify me," he says as he unties her legs and orders her to walk out of the cabin. Just then, hearing a noise outside, he turns to look out the window. Sophie, her hands still tied, grabs the bread knife lying on the counter and stabs him in the back. He falls dead at her feet.

In Sophie's case, and other self-defense cases, many ethicists would say the action was permitted because the good effect—escaping—was inseparable from and outweighed the evil one—stabbing—and the evil effect was not directly intended. (Some ethicists take a different view. Although they, too, would approve of Sophie's action, they would classify it as an *exception* to the principle that "the end does not justify the means.")

When only two actions are possible and both produce good consequences, which should be chosen?

In such situations, the morally preferable action is the one that produces *the greater good*. Similarly, as noted in Chapter 9, in cases where two actions are possible and both produce harmful effects, the morally preferable action is the one that produces *the lesser evil*.

Two examples from World War II will further illustrate this principle. In the North African theater of operations many hospitalized soldiers awaited the arrival of the first large shipment of the new wonder drug penicillin. When it arrived, high military medical officials had to decide which of two groups of patients to use it on, those with infected battle wounds or those with sulfa-resistant gonorrhea. Those with gonorrhea got the penicillin. The decision may at first seem absurdly wrong. But consider the reasoning that led to it. Large numbers of patients with gonorrhea were crowding hospitals and posing the threat of infection to others. Within a week these men could be returned to the battle lines where, because there was a shortage of manpower and because victory was not yet assured, they were badly needed.[3]

The dilemma the medical officials faced was certainly unfortunate, and the choice they made unquestionably caused harm. But it was undoubtedly the right choice in that situation because the alternative choice would have caused more harm. Giving the penicillin to the patients with gonorrhea served the greater good.

The second example is the U.S. decision to drop atomic bombs on Hiroshima and Nagasaki. At that time the war was still raging in the Pacific theater, and even though the Japanese offensive had been rolled back, surrender was not expected. One option considered by the United States was an invasion of mainland Japan; this idea was rejected because the invasion would likely have been followed by a protracted military campaign, and the combined cost in Japanese and American lives that would have resulted was conservatively estimated at several hundred thousand. The atomic bomb option was chosen because it would shorten the war by many months and would result in less death and destruction. Given just this information, we might conclude that the decision to use the atomic bomb represented, at the very least, the lesser evil. But the consequences were considerably more complex.

Whereas most of the individuals who would have been killed in an invasion would have been combatants, the overwhelming majority of the victims of the bombing were noncombatants. Nor was this an accidental matter—Hiroshima and Nagasaki were selected precisely because they were not military targets and their destruction would therefore have a greater demoralizing effect on the Japanese people. (Incidentally, the bombing of civilian population centers violated a centuries-old prohibition.) The combined total killed in the two cities was more than 200,000; tens of thousands of others suffered harmful exposure to radiation that caused them searing pain and disfigurement and could affect their children and grandchildren.

Other options existed that would have diminished the harmful effects. A single bomb could have been dropped on an uninhabited island as a demonstration of the destructive force of the bomb; the United States then could have demanded that the Japanese surrender or face similar devastation. (Because the number of bombs was limited and an extended period of time was necessary to create more, this plan was rejected.) Or the first bomb could have been dropped on an exclusively military target and more time allowed for surrender terms to be met, in the hope that a second bombing would not be necessary. That this option was available suggests that the decision to bomb Hiroshima and Nagasaki did not represent the lesser evil.

The question of the greater good/lesser evil arises, of course, not just in dramatic situations but in many everyday situations like the following one: For the first time in his twenty years as a high school football coach, Barney Bloom is looking forward with confidence to a winning season. His running back, Phil Blaster, is an athletic phenomenon. He has speed, power, and cunning. Then, with practice scheduled to begin in three days, Bloom's bubble bursts. In examining Phil, the team doctor has detected a serious knee condition. His report, backed by a specialist who has studied the X-rays, is that there will be great risk in Phil's playing this season. If the knee sustains a hard jolt from a certain angle, Phil may never be able to play football again. Both doctors advise Phil to undergo surgery at once, but they leave the decision to him and his parents. Coach Bloom, determined to have Phil in his lineup, attempts to persuade Phil to wait until the football season is over to have the operation. Is Coach Bloom behaving morally? Let's examine the consequences and decide.

If Phil plays football without further injury to his knee, the team will undoubtedly have a winning season, the coach and all the players will achieve satisfaction, and the student body will experience the feeling of pride that accompanies having a winning team. Phil himself may benefit greatly by arousing the interest of college coaches and paving the way for an athletic scholarship to college. On the other hand, if Phil plays and gets injured, he may have no chance at a college career. Thus the possible good effects to the coach, the team, the school, and even to Phil himself must be weighed against the possible harmful effect to Phil.

The balance certainly seems to tip in favor of the coach's attempting to persuade Phil to postpone the operation. A greater number of people will benefit if Phil plays. But does benefiting the greater number constitute serving the greater good in this case? Further reflection raises serious questions about whether it does. Both the team doctor and a specialist decided that there was great risk in Phil's playing. One hard jolt from the right angle might finish Phil's career. If the sport were tennis or baseball, such a jolt might be considered unlikely to occur. But in football it is more than likely.

The fact that further injury to Phil's knee is probable if he decides to play, the fact that such an injury would end a promising career, and the fact that both doctors have recommended immediate surgery suggest that Coach Bloom's attempt to persuade Phil to play does not serve the greater good and is therefore immoral.

A CAUTION

As difficult as it is to deal with the observable good and evil consequences of already completed actions, it is even more difficult to consider the consequences of contemplated or hypothetical actions. Therefore, in dealing with such actions, it is wise to keep this caution in mind: However clear and logical our determination of consequences may be, it is a prediction of future events and not a certainty. The particular responses that occur and the changes in the thoughts, attitudes, and behavior of everyone affected by the action are intricate and sometimes, in some ways, unpredictable. Thus we are dealing with probabilities at best. For this reason, we must be thorough in accounting for all possible consequences and willing to modify our earlier judgments as actual consequences become available for our examination.

DEALING WITH DILEMMAS

Many of the cases we have considered in this and previous chapters have been frustrating to deal with. No solution seemed completely satisfying. No matter which we chose, we were left with the feeling that somehow there ought to be a better solution, even though we couldn't imagine what it might be. There is a formal name for this disquieting situation. It is called a *moral dilemma* and is defined as any predicament that arises from the impossibility of honoring all the moral values that deserve honoring. A moral dilemma exists whenever the conflicting obligations, ideals, and consequences are so very nearly equal in their importance that we feel we cannot choose among them, even though we must.

Moral dilemmas do not exist only in textbooks. They confront us in everyday life and thus are a reality we must be prepared to deal with. We can never be completely comfortable in dealing with such dilemmas, but it is a consolation and source of confidence to remind ourselves from time to time that the frustration we experience with them is not a sign of incapacity on our part but rather is a reflection of the complex nature of moral discourse.

In evaluating a moral dilemma, consider first whether it can be avoided altogether; in other words, whether it is a *true* dilemma or only an *apparent* one. In Chapter 9, inquiry 23, for example, the personnel officer had to decide which candidate to select for an interview—Tina, the more qualified applicant, or Frank, the more needy applicant. The personnel officer chose Frank. In this case, however, there was a way to avoid choosing—to recommend that the boss interview *both* candidates.

In a true moral dilemma, of course, you must choose between two alternatives; there is no third. Once you determine that you are dealing with a true dilemma, look for an indication that one of the two goods is (however slightly) greater than the other or that one of the evils is less evil. In Chapter 9, inquiry 21 is an example of a true dilemma. In choosing to cannibalize their dead fellow passengers rather than starve to death, they were choosing the lesser of the two evils.

▣ INQUIRIES

1. What are the probable consequences of each of the following actions? (Try to identify all the consequences: direct and indirect; immediate and delayed; physical and emotional. If you are uncertain what the consequences are, consult knowledgeable people.) In each case, decide whether the favorable consequences outweigh the unfavorable ones.

> **a.** A rap music group creates song lyrics that recommend assaulting women.
>
> **b.** A comedian specializes in material that ridicules blacks, Hispanics, and homosexuals.
>
> **c.** A parents' group announces it will boycott companies that sponsor television programming that offends their moral values.
>
> **d.** A movie studio produces pornographic films.
>
> **e.** A school district uses a merit pay system; in other words, it awards salary increases based on the quality of teaching performance, as measured by student and administrative evaluation.

f. Beer and liquor companies sponsor athletic contests. For example, Anheuser-Busch sponsors women's beach volleyball, Miller Brewing Company sponsors men's, and Southern Comfort sponsors a national "Finger Flick" tournament.

2. In each of the following cases, identify the consequences of the action taken and decide whether the action represented the greater good.

a. The mayor of a large city was given a free membership in an exclusive golf club by people who have received several city contracts. He also accepted gifts from organizations that have not done business with the city but might in the future. (The gifts ranged from $200 tickets to professional sports events to designer watches and jewelry.)

b. A college instructor is pursuing her doctorate in night school. To gain extra time for her own studies, she gives her students the same lectures, the same assignments, and the same examinations semester after semester, without the slightest effort to improve them.

c. A physician on the staff of an urban medical center is approached by a lawyer from a remote part of the state and asked to testify on behalf of his client, a rural doctor charged with criminal negligence in the care of a patient. The lawyer admits that his client is guilty of the charge. He goes on to explain that although the doctor is old and not well versed in the latest medical knowledge, she is nevertheless competent; the negligence she is charged with resulted from the strain of being the only doctor in a large mountain area with a number of tiny towns and a total population of two thousand people. The lawyer pleads with the medical center physician to testify that the negligent act was proper treatment. The physician does so.

d. John and Martha, both married and the parents of several children, are having an adulterous affair. One night, when they are meeting secretly, they witness a murder. They agree that they cannot report it without exposing their affair. The next day the body is found, and within a week a suspect is apprehended and charged with first-degree murder. When John and Martha see his picture in the newspaper, they realize that he is not the murderer. They meet again, discuss their dilemma, and decide that despite the new, dreadful development, they will not step forward as witnesses.

e. An English teacher in a two-year technical college has several students in his composition course whose ignorance of the English language has proved invincible. He has given them extra work and extra counseling from the first week of the semester. They have been diligent in their efforts to improve. Though they are in a construction technology program and will undoubtedly be employed in jobs that require little writing skill, the composition course is required for graduation. In the instructor's judgment, the students would not be able to pass the course legitimately if they took it three times, so he raises their F grades to Ds.

f. Regina is chairperson of her city's United Fund campaign. In her annual meeting with her staff of canvassers, she gives this advice: "Hit the business places first. Don't approach anyone who is walking alone in a hall or working alone in a closed office. Look for two or more people standing together or working side by side. Try to make them compete with each other in giving. Capitalize on their desire to show off and outdo the other person."

g. A senator has a bill before the Senate that promises to correct tax inequities that affect thousands of workers. However, the bill is being held up in committee. The committee chairperson is responsible. The senator, however, has learned of a secret scandal in the chairperson's personal life. He visits the chairperson and tells him that unless the bill is released from committee, he will divulge the scandal to the press.

h. By day Sylvester is a high-ranking executive in a leading lingerie company. By night he is a modern Robin Hood. He scales walls and creeps over rooftops to enter the homes of the wealthy and steal cash and valuables. Everything he takes he gives to the poor.

i. Jake runs a delicatessen in a high-crime section of a large city. After being robbed at gunpoint eight times in the past two years, Jake obtained a pistol permit and bought a pistol. Yesterday a man entered the store brandishing a knife and demanded all the money in the cash register. Jake moved to the cash register as if planning to open it. Then he quickly grabbed the gun hanging under it and, without warning, shot the man six times in the chest.

j. After a young college instructor submits her final grades, she receives a music CD from two students with whom she has become quite friendly outside of class. The note accompanying the gift explains that it is a token of their gratitude for the instructor's presenting such an interesting and meaningful course. She keeps the compact disc.

k. Todd and Edna have been married for three years. They have had serious personal problems: Edna is a heavy drinker, and Todd cannot keep a job. Also, they have bickered and fought constantly since their marriage. Deciding that the way to overcome their problems is to have a child, they stop practicing birth control, and Edna becomes pregnant.

l. A member of the House of Representatives is encouraged by a big-business lobbyist to vote for a bill that is against the interests of her constituents. The lobbyist implies that if the representative supports the bill, big business will support her campaign for reelection. The representative knows that she faces a tough campaign against an unprincipled opponent. Without the support or at least the neutrality of big business, she has virtually no chance of reelection. She decides to support the bill.

m. A company has a policy of strongly encouraging all workers over the age of 55 to retire in order to allow younger workers to be hired and to advance within the company. The company pension is modest, but a retiree can survive on it.

n. A fiberglass firm is the only major employer in a small community. Local governmental officials are aware that the firm's safety practices are lax and that assembly workers suffer a variety of respiratory problems due to fumes and exposure to toxic materials. However, no action is ever taken against the company.

o. A major aircraft manufacturer is dependent on government and private contracts. In good times it offers bonuses and recruits technical employees throughout the United States. In lean times the company engages in mass layoffs. Employees and technicians may be laid off within a year of moving their families across the country for a job.

p. A college receives reduced operating funds. It closes its on-campus day-care center to save money for funding academic and technical instruction. The center previously served many low-income families.

3. Compare the consequences of cheating in a class in which the professor grades on a curve with the consequences of cheating in a class in which the professor does not grade on a curve. Is one instance of cheating a greater moral offense, or are both equal? Explain.

4. Stock experts appearing on financial talk shows have on occasion engaged in the practice known as "pumping and dumping," which consists of giving favorable recommendations to stocks they personally hold, waiting until the show's listeners buy the stock, and then selling their shares at a profit. Some networks require guests to disclose their personal holdings in any stock they recommend on the air; other networks do not. Consider the obligations, moral ideals, and consequences involved in cases of pumping and dumping and decide whether broadcasters have a moral obligation to institute a disclosure requirement.

5. Reportedly, at least two companies specialize in buying the body parts of fetuses from abortion clinics and selling them to universities and medical institutes for use in research. One of these companies reportedly charges $999 for a human brain under eight weeks' gestation, $50 to $100 for eyes and ears, and $400 for an intact limbless trunk. Evaluate the morality of (a) abortionists selling fetal body parts to the companies, (b) the companies selling such parts to research institutions, and (c) the use of fetal body parts in research. In your evaluation discuss the relevant obligations, moral ideals, and consequences.

6. What consequences does divorce produce? Make your list as complete as possible. Then consider relevant obligations and ideals and decide whether divorce is ever morally justifiable. (If you decide that it is in certain circumstances but not in others, specify each set of circumstances and explain your reasoning.)

7. Several years ago a married couple, faced with the tragic fact that the husband had terminal cancer, made an important decision: His sperm would be frozen so that the wife could conceive their child after his death. Three months after his death, she was impregnated with his sperm and subsequently gave birth to a little girl. The Social Security Administration ruled that the child was not entitled to receive benefits as his heir. At first thought, you might be inclined to judge this ruling morally insupportable because the ideal of fairness requires that this child be treated as any other heir. Resist that judgment until you have used your imagination to identify the significant consequences that would likely follow (a) denying the child the status of heir and (b) granting the child the status of heir. Compare those consequences and make your decision.

8. In Chapter 4, inquiry 8c, we considered the case of a candidate for the local school board. She had heard the rumor that her opponent gave "wild parties." As she proceeded with her campaign, she visited the homes of many voters. She made it a point to tell everyone what she had heard about her opponent, always adding, "Of course, it's only a rumor that no one has yet proven to be true." Reexamine this case, focusing on the effects of her action.

9. In Chapter 3, inquiry 5, we considered the case of the Little League baseball coach who discovered a new boy in the neighborhood who was an excellent pitcher, though he was over the age limit for Little League participation. Because the family was not known in the area, the coach was sure he could use the boy without being discovered and ensure a winning season for his team. Reexamine this case, focusing on the effects of the action the coach planned.

CHAPTER ELEVEN

DETERMINING MORAL RESPONSIBILITY

*How do we determine whether a person is
responsible for her or his immoral actions?
Are there degrees of responsibility?*

The previous ten chapters focused on the ethical character of various kinds of behavior. This chapter examines a separate matter that is also of interest to ethicists—the issue of people's responsibility for their behavior. The distinction between the action and the person who performs it is not always a pleasant one to make. When someone commits a moral offense, particularly a grievous one like assault or murder, we understandably expect the person to be held accountable. At first thought, the idea that the person's state of mind or the circumstances surrounding the action might diminish his or her responsibility seems to mock the ideal of justice. However, as we will see, this thought is mistaken. The degree of responsibility can in fact vary from person to person and from situation to situation. Thus, to consider whether moral responsibility has been diminished in a particular situation is not to mock the ideal of justice but to *honor* it.

Because the idea of responsibility for behavior is closely related to the concept of free will, we will begin our discussion of moral responsibility by considering the practical implications of that concept.

HOW FREE ARE OUR CHOICES?

Moral situations, as we have seen, involve choice. For choice to be possible, however, we must be free to act. In other words, we must not be *compelled* to act by any irresistible force, whether outside or within ourselves. At this moment, for example, you are reading this book. Are you free to continue doing so? Suppose someone walked up to you and said,

"I've got an extra ticket to the ball game, but we've got to leave right now to be there for the start" or "Put down that silly book and join Susan and me—we're going out for a pizza." Would you be free to make a choice? Or would staying or going be completely outside your control? The question is not whether you would be strongly tempted one way or another—it's whether you have the power to *resist* temptation.

Chances are your answer is "Of course I am free to make my own choices. I do so hundreds of times a day, in matters great and small." Deterministic philosophers would dispute that answer. They claim that free will is an illusion, that forces *outside our control* determine what we think and say and do, if not all the time, then at least most of the time. Among the forces they cite are our genes, the social or economic conditions we grew up in, and the beliefs and values our parents instilled in us.

No doubt you have heard the argument that criminals who come from poor or dysfunctional families, or neighborhoods in which the main role models were drug dealers, are not responsible for their crimes. That is a deterministic argument. But however impressive it may seem, it does not withstand close examination. The same neighborhoods that produce criminals also produce law-abiding citizens. As often as not, the criminal's *own brothers and sisters* lead honest lives. These facts challenge the notion that troubled families or neighborhoods force people to commit crimes.

Most philosophers reject determinism, believing instead that, although a wide variety of factors—including our genes, socioeconomic background, degree of education, habits, and attitudes—may influence our free will and on occasion diminish it, they seldom take it away entirely. If reality were otherwise, the study of ethics would be pointless. As Henry Veatch explains, "If there is to be any such thing as ethics, there must be such a thing as personal responsibility. And if there is to be personal responsibility, then one must maintain the claims of something like free choice as a cause of human behavior."[1]

Note that the previous paragraph says that most philosophers believe free will may be "diminished" but "seldom" is taken away entirely. The implication is that in rare cases free will might not be present at all. Note, too, that Veatch describes free choice as "*a* cause," not "*the* cause." The clear implication here is that, in some cases, some other cause may be operative. Several questions arise: What circumstances diminish free will? What circumstances take it away entirely? What effect do such circumstances have on a person's moral responsibility? And, most important in the practical sense, how can the degree of moral responsibility be determined in specific situations? We turn now to these matters.

DETERMINING MORAL RESPONSIBILITY

Many ethicists prefer the term *culpability,* which is derived from the Latin word for "fault," to the term *moral responsibility.* For our purposes the two terms are interchangeable. The fundamental principle of culpability can be stated as follows:

> *If we are aware that an action is wrong and freely choose to do it anyway, we are fully culpable for the action.*

Consider the case of a neurotically insecure woman who constantly seeks reassurance that she is attractive and desirable and therefore is vulnerable to sexual misuse by men. Whenever a man uses her for his sexual gratification and then casts her aside, the rejection makes her all the more insecure, all the more anxious to prove her attractiveness, and all the more vulnerable. Eventually the woman seeks help from a psychologist in order to understand and overcome her problem, and the psychologist determines that she has been emotionally harmed by her sexual experiences. However, despite his understanding of her problem, despite the special relationship of trust he has with the woman, and despite his awareness that the code of ethics of his profession forbids sexual involvement with clients, the psychologist uses her for his own sexual gratification. The most reasonable conclusion would be that the psychologist's action is morally wrong and that he is fully culpable. (Moreover, because of his professional obligation and his knowledge of the special harm he is causing the woman, his culpability would be greater than, say, that of a man who had sex with her after meeting her in a bar.)

Several other principles complement the fundamental principle of culpability by expanding on and/or qualifying it. These complementary principles follow.

> *If through no fault of our own we are unaware that an action is wrong when we perform it, we are not morally culpable.*[*]

Suppose a young man was born into a family of "grifters"—that is, people who make swindling others a way of life. The young man has been instructed since infancy in techniques for cheating others and praised when he developed skill in doing so. Since families like his move about frequently and prevent their children from contact with social agencies that would expose them to traditional morality (in particular, schools), the young man has never considered that cheating others is morally wrong. As long as he remains in this state of ignorance, he is not culpable for his moral offenses.

> *If some person or circumstance forces us to do something wrong against our will, we are not morally culpable.*

*We may nevertheless be *legally* culpable because the general legal standard is that ignorance of the law is no excuse.

A prisoner of war who is tortured into revealing military secrets he swore to keep is not morally culpable for breaking his oath. Similarly, a person who is told that her family will be harmed if she does not commit an immoral act—for example, participating in a burglary—is not morally culpable for committing the act. In such cases, the action was performed under coercion, so the people cannot be said to have acted freely. In cases where we are not truly *forced* but only *influenced*, our culpability is diminished in proportion to the strength of the influence.

If we lack the mental capacity to determine that an action is wrong at the time we perform it, we are not morally culpable.

The young child who sees one person stab another on television and then, in imitation, picks up a kitchen knife and stabs his sister is not morally responsible at all. Nor is the severely retarded teenager who, while shopping with her mother, steals an expensive watch. They lack both an understanding of the nature of their behavior and the mental development to make an informed choice.

Traditionally, it has been thought that psychopaths suffer from a similarly diminished capacity for free choice, although the forces that influence them are internal rather than external. If this is so, then some of history's most infamous characters may not have been entirely responsible for their actions. Gilles de Rais, for example, the fifteenth-century marshal of France and patron of the arts who ritually murdered as many as 200 kidnapped children, may have been acting compulsively. Even Adolf Hitler, whose monstrous record of evil staggers the imagination—nearly 10 million human beings wantonly exterminated and the entire world plunged into strife, suffering, and destruction—may not have been fully responsible for his deeds. (There is evidence to suggest that he was emotionally disturbed.) Ironically, the moral responsibility of sane people who acted in his behalf was greater than his, even though the scale of their crimes was considerably smaller.

Not all evidence supports the traditional notion, however. Some authorities believe that psychopaths enjoy more freedom to choose than has been thought. One such authority is Stanton E. Samenow, a clinical psychologist specializing in criminal behavior. (Samenow and his colleague, Samuel Yochelson, authored the highly regarded three-volume study *The Criminal Personality*.) Samenow believes the extensive literature on psychopathology has drawn an inaccurate picture of the psychopath. He writes,

> To say that a psychopath or criminal is unable to profit from experience is misleading because there is no such *incapacity*. He does learn from the past, but he learns what interests him, not what society wants him to learn. To call him impulsive is to assert that he lacks self-control, whereas he actually has a rational, calculating mind that is very much in control. Conscience is present and the criminal has moral values, but he shuts off his conscience long enough to do what he wants.[2]

John Douglas, author of an investigative study of serial killers—including David Berkowitz, Ted Bundy, and others—has reached a similar conclusion. He discovered that most of the individuals he studied were abused as children, later read pornographic material, and fantasized about how they would abuse others, findings that could be interpreted as signs of compulsion. Yet he also found that most were bright—Ted Bundy's IQ was over 125, and Edmund Kemper's was 145—and that most could tell right from wrong. They committed their crimes not because of an irresistible impulse but because they simply didn't give a damn about others and enjoyed inflicting pain.[3]

The conflicting evidence concerning the psychopath's freedom of choice has complicated the *legal* approach to insanity cases. In the 1980s public concern over the wisdom of the insanity plea in American law reached a peak with the decision that John Hinckley, who had shot then President Ronald Reagan and three other men, was "not guilty by reason of insanity." The cries for legal reform generated by such notorious cases may result in change. (One possibility is the replacement of the present "not guilty by reason of insanity" plea with "guilty, but insane," which would prevent premature release from psychiatric detention.) The legal tradition of distinguishing the compulsive criminal from the noncompulsive is not likely to change, however. The distinction is too deeply rooted in the moral tradition, which deems it unjust to hold a person responsible for actions over which he or she had little or no control.

In situations where the evidence is insufficient to determine whether a particular person acted freely, prudence precludes judgment. Nevertheless, we can assert with conviction that if a person's freedom to act is diminished, then his or her culpability is diminished to the same extent. Keep in mind that diminished culpability does not lessen the wrongness of the act. A wrong act remains wrong even if the person has no moral responsibility for performing it.

Heroism Not Required

In considering the question of moral blame, we should keep in mind that we can be good men and women without being heroes. Naturally, it is desirable to aim for the highest and noblest actions, but there is no moral requirement to do so. The only requirement implied in the concept of morality is to do good and avoid doing evil.

A case in point occurred during World War II. Soon after the Nazis occupied Austria, they drafted Austrian men into their armed services. One citizen they called was Franz Jägerstatter, a simple, uneducated man in his mid-30s with a wife and young children. Because he believed that Hitler's cause "offended God," he was convinced that it would be morally wrong for him to serve, so he refused to be drafted. As a result, he was imprisoned. For months his friends, his parish priest, and even his bishop urged him to think of his family and reconsider his decision. They explained that in such a situation he was being forced to serve, not serving voluntarily, so he would not be guilty of any wrongdoing. Despite their pleading, Jägerstatter remained steadfast in his conviction. Finally, he was executed.

Jägerstatter was a hero. But does that fact mean that his friends were deserving of blame for not following his example? No, because they did not make a free choice to serve in the army; rather, they were coerced. We are justified in pitying them for lacking Jägerstatter's moral courage, but not in regarding them as culpable.

Conscience also complicates the determination of guilt and innocence in less dramatic circumstances. We observed earlier that people must follow their conscience and therefore cannot be condemned for doing what it bids them. Yet conscience is an imperfect guide, capable of directing one to wrong as well as right behavior. It would appear, then, that it is not fair to blame a person for doing any wrong act that his or her conscience supports. Most ethicists would accept this conclusion, provided two conditions were met: (a) the person did not neglect the job of developing his or her conscience in a responsible way and (b) the person did nothing to desensitize his or her conscience.

▣ INQUIRIES

1. Apply the understanding you have gained in this chapter to construct a reply to the following argument: *The view that people are not legally responsible for their behavior has resulted in lax law enforcement and absurd court decisions. In one widely reported case, a district attorney refused to prosecute three individuals who aided and abetted a man who abducted, raped, and murdered a young girl; in another, a judge decided not to send to jail a female teacher who had had sex with a young boy because she was "too pretty to go to jail"; in still another, a judge declared that a child molester was "too short" to serve prison time. The notion that some people are not morally responsible for their behavior is equally harmful, perhaps even more so because moral judgment is more fundamental than legal judgment.*

2. One reason determining culpability is difficult is that a person may have a basic understanding that an action is wrong yet this understanding may be so overlaid with self-deception and rationalization—"I had no alternative . . . honor demanded it . . . he deserved it . . . no one was really hurt by what I did"—that the person's understanding becomes inoperative. Moreover, the process of self-deception and rationalization may be so habitual that the person performs it mindlessly, without giving thought to what he or she is doing. Is it reasonable to regard self-deception, rationalization, and the habit of mindless behavior as *moral failings*? Why or why not?

3. On the same day during the same war, three soldiers performed an identical act—killing an unarmed, unthreatening civilian. However, the circumstances of the three cases differed. The first soldier was ordered directly by an officer to shoot the civilian or be shot himself. The second soldier received the same order indirectly but was not in a position to be observed, and therefore he could have ignored it without any threat to his own life. The third soldier received no order at all but shot the civilian out of anger over the support that many civilians gave to terrorists. Were the three soldiers equally culpable for their actions? State and explain your view.

4. Is it morally wrong to read literature or listen to speeches sponsored by groups that promote hatred of racial, ethnic, or religious groups? Are there any special circumstances in which you would modify your view? Explain.

5. A husband and wife are walking across a railroad track. She stumbles, and her foot gets caught in the switching mechanism. He tries to free her. Then a train comes roaring around the corner. Realizing he cannot free her before the train reaches them, the man leaps to safety. She is struck and killed instantly. Has the man behaved immorally? Why or why not?

6. In 1913 Leo M. Frank was found guilty of the murder of a 13-year-old girl in the pencil factory in which they both worked. He was sentenced to death. When his sentence was commuted to life imprisonment in 1915, an enraged mob hanged him. Sixty-seven years later, a witness to the crime came forward and testified that, as a 14-year-old boy, he had seen another man carrying the girl's body. He explained that he had not spoken out because the real murderer had threatened to kill him if he testified. Was that witness' silence morally justified? Comment on his culpability.

7. A man is falsely accused of a crime and spends fourteen years in jail. Finally, his accuser is overcome with remorse and admits having lied. When the man is released, he sues the state for wrongful imprisonment and seeks monetary compensation. The courts rule that the state has no *legal* responsibility. But does it have *moral* responsibility? Why or why not?

8. In the 1950s and 1960s, Navajo Indians and others worked in the uranium mines in New Mexico, Arizona, Utah, and Colorado. The Atomic Energy Commission (AEC) and the Public Health Service (PHS) allegedly knew that such work was hazardous. In the 1920s European studies had linked radioactivity to cancer and determined that ventilation of shafts could reduce the hazard. U.S. research in the late 1940s revealed that cancer was also caused by inhaling radon gas. Yet neither agency pressured the mine owners to install safety devices, and neither warned the workers. Moreover, the PHS monitored the health of a test group of miners; in the words of Stewart Udall, "The PHS used the miners as guinea pigs to study the effects of radiation." Today those workers develop lung cancer at a rate five times higher than that of other people. Do the AEC and the PHS have any moral responsibility for these consequences?

9. When suit was brought against the U.S. government in the case detailed in inquiry 8, an appeals court ruled that the federal government was protected by sovereign immunity, meaning that the government can decide when and if it can be sued. Discuss the morality of sovereign immunity in this case.

10. For a group of people to stand by without intervening as a man beats a woman into unconsciousness and then kicks her brutally would surely be immoral. However, the moral responsibility of the crowd would depend on a number of considerations. Determine the degree of the crowd's culpability in each of the following variations.

   a. The crowd is composed of very old men and women. The assailant is young, strong, and armed with an iron pipe.

   b. The crowd is composed of women 20 to 30 years of age. The assailant is unarmed.

   c. The crowd is a group of construction workers. The man is spindly, middle-aged, and unarmed.

11. A 7-year-old Virginia boy set fire to a building. As a result of the blaze, a 66-year-old woman died. The boy was charged with second-degree murder.[4] Could the boy be morally responsible for the crime of murder? If so, what circumstances might increase or diminish his responsibility?

12. A prominent Houston attorney, William Chanslor Jr., was charged with solicitation of murder and conspiracy to commit murder after he negotiated a contract with a professional assassin to murder his wife. At his trial, Chanslor testified that his wife, having suffered a stroke that caused brain damage and paralyzed one side of her body, begged him repeatedly to help her commit suicide. He explained that he had initially tried to talk her out of the idea of suicide and changed his mind only after her constant begging for help.[5] Assuming the circumstances were as the attorney described them, to what extent do they lessen Chanslor's moral responsibility?

13. Five New Jersey teenagers were drinking beer by the railroad tracks near their home when they heard a train approaching. They decided to throw a track switch and sent the train careening off the tracks, down a siding, and through the brick wall of a building. The crash killed the engineer, critically injured one passenger, and caused an estimated $5.5 million in property damage.[6] Discuss the teenagers' moral responsibility for their act in light of the circumstances in which it took place.

14. A college basketball team is heavily favored to win the forthcoming end-of-season tournament. Then the star player signs a professional contract and is no longer eligible to play with his team. Was his signing unethical? If so, what circumstances would lessen his responsibility?

15. The evidence that smoking is harmful to one's health continues to grow. Now smoking is linked not only to lung cancer, emphysema, and certain heart and artery conditions, but also to cancers of the bladder and pancreas. In addition, smoking by pregnant women has been linked to such fetal defects as low birth weight and poor general health. With these facts in mind, decide whether the following people commit any moral wrong and, if so, identify the circumstances in which each would be morally responsible.

   a. The heavy cigarette smoker

   b. The pregnant woman who smokes

   c. The smoker who encourages a nonsmoker to start smoking

    d. The farmer who grows tobacco

    e. The cigarette distributor

    f. The advertising person who creates ads to entice people to buy cigarettes.

    g. The well-known personality who lends her name to cigarette advertising

16. Is pushing heroin a moral offense? If so, is the moral responsibility of the heroin-using pusher any different from that of the nonusing pusher?

17. Louise is an investigator for the Internal Revenue Service. Her job consists of closely examining the tax returns of individuals selected at random by a computer. When she finds significant errors in the returns, she assigns penalties. Because the majority of the cases she handles involve middle-income families and because it is her strong conviction that the tax law discriminates against such people, Louise has begun to feel guilty for doing her job. Nevertheless, she refuses to quit. Is she doing wrong? If so, what is the degree of her moral responsibility?

18. A high school girl accuses a boy in her class of putting his hand up her dress. The boy is reported to the principal. The principal questions the boy and the girl. She must base her decision on these facts: There were no witnesses; the boy denies having touched the girl; the girl has made similar unsupported charges about other boys in the past. The principal is reasonably sure the boy is innocent. Nevertheless, she suspends him from school. Clearly, the principal has acted dishonestly. Speculate on the circumstances that might have been present that diminish her moral responsibility for her action.

19. A major pipeline is under construction. Federal inspectors discover that hundreds of improperly welded joints have been certified by state inspectors. To what degree is each of the following individuals responsible?

    a. The owner of the construction company who paid the state inspector to certify the welding jobs

    b. The state inspector who certified the welding

    c. The supervisor of the job who carried out the boss' orders to have the work done by unqualified (and lower-paid) workers

    d. The union steward who failed to make the situation known to authorities

20. All of the mechanics at a certain garage are expected to look for mechanical problems in addition to those presented by their customers. It is understood, but not discussed openly, that the mechanic will recommend unnecessary repairs if he can get away with it. To what degree is each of the following responsible for the continuation of this practice?

    a. The garage owner who encourages these practices

    b. The mechanic who does the work

    c. The customer who, through mental laziness, continues to be ignorant of mechanical matters

III

THE TRADITION

CHAPTER TWELVE

A PERSPECTIVE ON HISTORY

When did the study of ethics begin? Who were
the great thinkers in the history of ethics?
What contributions did they make?

This chapter is as much a beginning as a conclusion. It opens the way for you to deepen your understanding of the subject of ethics, to become acquainted with some of the great ethical thinkers and thoughts of the past, even as you continue to apply your evaluative skills to the ethical problems of today. You will probably appreciate its contents more now than you would have if you had read it at the outset, for now you have struggled with numerous ethical issues yourself, felt the pull of conflicting values, and wrestled with moral dilemmas to which no answer seems completely satisfactory. Now, too, you know the value of careful analysis and a systematic approach. This will enable you to appreciate the ideas advanced by the various ethicists as they attempted to construct an ethical system. Even when you do not share their philosophic perspective, you will understand their efforts and share their enthusiasm for the task.

Historians usually divide the history of ethics in Western thought into three broad periods: the *classical*, the *medieval*, and the *modern*. Any division, naturally, is arbitrary. There are no real breaks in time; the flow of moment to moment is constant. Nevertheless, the divisions are convenient. They help us grasp major developments more fully and see shifting focuses and changing perspectives more sharply.

THE CLASSICAL PERIOD

The classical period of ethical thought extends from 500 B.C. to A.D. 500. At the beginning of this period, a rapid change was taking place in Greek society. Once an agrarian monarchy, it was now becoming a commercial industrial democracy. These changes brought new challenges to old values and traditions. The ethics of the time reflected the central feature of the society, the city-state. Thus the moral focus was the duty of the individual as a citizen. Ethics was regarded as the spiritual counterpart of medicine, its function being to provide care of the soul as medicine provides care of the body.

With values in flux, a number of moral views arose to clash with the traditional view. The Sophists, a group of itinerant teachers, questioned to what extent morality was a matter of nature and to what extent a matter of custom or tradition. Their general view was that good and evil are matters of personal decision or social agreement. Some of the more liberal Sophists suggested that all morality was a matter of convenience only.

Socrates (469–399 B.C.) was the dominant figure of the classical period. Indeed, he is generally regarded as the father of Western philosophy. He left no writings, but many of his views were recorded in the writings of his pupil Plato. Like the Sophists, Socrates rejected the idea that tradition justifies conduct. But unlike them, he believed that morality is more than a matter of personal choice or convenience. It is possible, he believed, to develop a universal set of ethical principles to guide conduct, and the key to doing so is human reason, the careful examination of beliefs and actions and the logic that underlies them. His focus was on self-knowledge. "The unexamined life," he taught, "is not worth living."

Socrates is best known for his philosophic method. Rather than teach directly, he conversed with others, asking basic questions about important matters (for example, What is justice? What is virtue?) and then examining the answers people gave, exposing vagueness and inconsistency, clarifying problems, and pointing the way to further inquiry. He was also the first to probe the relationships between facts and values, an ethical issue that virtually all ethicists since his time have grappled with.

Plato (427–347 B.C.) built upon the teaching of Socrates. Plato's writings are in dialogue form, and Socrates is the main character in most of them. Plato's greatest work is the *Republic*. He shared Socrates' view that the life of reason is the happiest and best life. For both men, sense perception and bodily pleasure were less desirable than intellectual pursuits, but the two men differed somewhat in their emphases. Socrates apparently believed in enjoying himself at all levels of experience in a balanced way. He believed that nothing should be done to excess, that moderation should be the rule in everything. Plato's view was more extreme. His denial of bodily pleasure and sense perception made him a model for later religious and idealistic ethicists.

Plato's central notion was that the real world is not the world that our senses perceive, but the world of ideas. The concrete reality that surrounds us, in Plato's view, is merely an imperfect reflection of the world of abstract ideas or "forms," which are timeless and unchanging. The most important reality in this world of ideas is the idea of the Good. Goodness for Plato was a central fact about the universe. Thus the main goal of his ethical system is to gain a vision of the Good.

Aristotle (384–322 B.C.) was a student of Plato and followed his and Socrates' philosophical tradition. Nevertheless, Aristotle's emphasis was quite different from Plato's. Aristotle authored as many as four hundred works on a variety of subjects ranging from theoretical and practical science to politics, rhetoric, logic, and ethics. His *Nicomachean Ethics* is the first systematic treatment of ethics in Western civilization.

Aristotle disputed Plato's theory of forms. There is no world of separate, abstract forms corresponding to the concrete things we perceive, he reasoned. Form cannot exist apart from particular objects, or, as he put it, "No form without matter, no matter without form." Accordingly, Aristotle rejected the notion that the Good exists independent of daily experience and human personality. In his view, moral principles exist in the daily activities of human life and can be discovered by examining those activities. Happiness is to be attained by developing one's potential for a life of reason. The life of reason has two aims: the pursuit of truth through reflection and understanding and the pursuit of virtue through intelligent conduct. Virtue, for Aristotle, represented a midpoint between extremes of excess and defect. (Some actions, however, like murder or theft, he saw as bad in themselves and therefore having no midpoint.)

Not all thinkers of the classical period shared the philosophical tradition of Socrates, Plato, and Aristotle. The Cyrenaics, for example, and later the Epicureans emphasized human feelings and desires and taught that the measure of an action is the amount of *pleasure* it brings. (This view is known as *hedonism*.) Epicurus, however, made a sharp distinction between "natural" pleasures, such as peace of mind and the absence of hunger, and "unnatural" pleasures, such as greed and lust, approving only the natural. In contrast to the Cyrenaics and Epicureans were the Cynics and the Stoics. These groups stressed overcoming feelings and desires and serving the demands of *duty* as revealed by reason.

As we will see, many of the differences in viewpoint that existed during the classical period, such as the difference over pleasure and duty, have continued to divide thinkers through the centuries.

THE MEDIEVAL PERIOD

The second period in the history of ethics in the West is the medieval period, which extends from 500 to 1500. Its intellectual and social context was Christianity. As the belief system of Christianity (itself a product of

Judaic thought) expanded across Europe, the idea of the citizen's relation to the state was replaced by the idea of the individual's obligation to God as set forth in the Bible and interpreted by the Church. Medieval ethics combined the classical emphasis on human reason with the idea of obedience to God's will.

Two great thinkers dominated medieval thought. The first was Saint Augustine (354–430). In his numerous works, notable among them *Confessions* and *The City of God*, Augustine made Plato's philosophy the basis of Christian ethics. Augustine's system was two-sided. On one side, the life of reason leads to temporal well-being; on the other, faith leads to salvation and eternal happiness. (Because this life is only a preparation for the afterlife, Augustine taught, no real happiness is possible here.) The concept of Good for Augustine was similarly two-sided: the natural, earthly side and the supernatural, other-worldly side, with the supernatural dominating. Augustine viewed man as having fallen from God's grace through original sin but retaining free will and responsibility for his actions. Virtue is possible, he taught, but to have real value it must be prompted by faith.

The Platonic system of Augustine was so emphasized in the early Middle Ages that Aristotle was all but forgotten until the time of the second great medieval thinker, Saint Thomas Aquinas (1225–1274). Aquinas rediscovered Aristotle, Christianized his philosophy, and made it the basis of the philosophical outlook of the later Middle Ages. Aquinas' greatest works were *Summa Theologica* and *Summa Contra Gentes*.

Aquinas aimed at demonstrating the harmony between Aristotle and Christianity. He taught that ethics has two dimensions: the natural and the theological. Natural ethics, as detailed by Aristotle, consists of the development of reason and practice in living morally and leads to earthly happiness. Theological ethics consists of achieving the virtues of faith, hope, and charity through God's grace and leads to eternal life with God. Aquinas believed that the Natural Law—the divine law as written in the heart of man—can be discovered by reason and cultivated by conscience. By allowing people to turn to secular knowledge without guilt, Aquinas prepared the way for the emergence of a more scientific view of humanity and of ethics.

THE MODERN PERIOD

The third period in the history of ethics extends from 1500 to the present.* The sixteenth and seventeenth centuries were times of intellectual upheaval. The Protestant Reformation challenged the supremacy of the

---

*In some classifications, the contemporary period (twentieth and twenty-first centuries) is accorded a separate category.

Roman Catholic Church and introduced the idea of each person's inter-
preting the Bible for himself or herself. The impact of this idea increased
with the invention of the printing press and the shift from Latin to the
vernacular. Finally, and perhaps most important, the work of scientists
like Copernicus, Galileo, and Harvey turned the attention of philosophers from theological to scientific explanations.

Thomas Hobbes (1588–1679) was the first thinker to systematically
approach ethics from a scientific viewpoint. Hobbes, whose major philosophical work was *Leviathan*, argued that the notion of mechanistic mate-
rialism that was central to the physics of the time applied to ethics as
well. He attempted to demonstrate that in humanity's natural (primitive)
condition the rule of self-preservation produces a morality based on *self-
interest*. In that condition, Hobbes reasoned, the concepts of right and
wrong do not exist; they only begin to exist when civil society is formed.
The only way civil society can control the pursuit of individuals' self-
interest and the conflict that such pursuit inevitably generates is to have
everyone give allegiance to the sovereign. Hobbes believed in the Golden
Rule, but he also believed that people could not be trusted to practice it.
With too much at stake for each person to follow his or her conscience,
Hobbes argued, the sovereign power—whether "monarch or assembly"—
must ensure "the safety of the people."

There was strong reaction against Hobbes' ethical perspective. In
refutation of that perspective, a number of ethicists argued that human
beings are not at the mercy of their drive for self-preservation. They have
a moral faculty, a specific intellectual guide that enables them to tell right
from wrong. Several different ways of describing that moral faculty were
advanced. Some described it as *intuition*, others as a *moral sense* (a natural
affection for virtue), and still others as *conscience*.

In the early eighteenth century, David Hume (1711–1766) proposed
an ethical theory that was in some ways reminiscent of John Locke's theory in the previous century. Locke (1632–1704) had argued that pleasure
is the standard of moral judgment. Sensations of pleasure or pain, he reasoned, lead us to reflect and form views of justice and goodness and thus
develop a system of moral judgment. Hume believed that the standard of
moral judgment is two-sided. One side of it is objective—the consequences of the action in question. The other, dominant, side, in Hume's
view, is subjective—a feeling of pleasure. (Hume did not approve of
doing anything we wish. He believed that every human being possesses
a tendency to be more pleased by benefiting others than by being selfish
and self-indulgent.) In Hume's theory, *reason alone* cannot answer moral
questions. But a *moral sentiment* that chooses what is useful or pleasant
can and does do so.

THE ETHICS OF DUTY (DEONTOLOGY)

The writings of Immanuel Kant (1724–1804) represent a significant milestone in modern ethics. Kant's main work was *Critique of Pure Reason.* However, it was in *The Fundamental Principles of the Metaphysics of Morals* that he set forth his views of the foundation of morality. Kant took issue with Hume's view about feeling and with the general position of all hedonists. He argued that moral judgments are not expressions of feeling but *imperatives* (commands) and so can be dealt with by reasoning. To those skeptics who say that there is no certainty in moral judgment, Kant replied that it is incorrect to look for certainty in the *content of experience.* It can only be found in the *form of reason.* In other words, he believed that certainty does not come from observation, but is a product of mind.

Things that are usually called "good," such as intelligence, courage, and perseverance, are in Kant's terms only good if they are joined by the person's *goodwill* (that is, good character). It is goodwill that directs people to do what they *ought* to do rather than what they wish to do or what will benefit them. Although Kant acknowledged that happiness is desirable, he suggested that reason can never achieve happiness; it can only achieve goodwill.

According to Kant, the basis of moral action is *duty.* People's goodwill is what makes them act for duty, and acting for duty gives their action moral value. The central thesis of Kant's ethical system is that there is a *categorical imperative* (command) binding on all people because it is affirmed by reason, and every rational person accepts his or her obligation to follow reason. Kant expressed this categorical imperative as follows, the first formulation being the principal one:

> Act as if the maxim of your action were to become by your will a universal Law of Nature [to be obeyed by everyone].

> Always treat every human being, including yourself, as an end in himself and never merely as a means to an end.

THE ETHICS OF CONSEQUENCES (TELEOLOGY)

Another significant milestone in modern ethics is the work of John Stuart Mill (1806–1873). Unlike many of the ethicists we have discussed, Mill did not create a system of ethics himself. He clarified and defended a system created earlier by his father, James Mill, and by Jeremy Bentham. That system is called *utilitarianism,* and its central premise is that the rightness or wrongness of actions is determined by the goodness or badness of their consequences. John Stuart Mill's most famous work is his

System of Logic, but it is his essay *Utilitarianism* that deals specifically with ethics.

Mill's utilitarianism is a hedonistic ethics. (In other words, it makes pleasure or happiness the standard of moral judgment.) Specifically, utilitarianism states that "Utility, or the Greatest Happiness Principle" is the foundation of morals. Mill admitted that some pleasures are of a higher type than others, and he suggested that competent judges who have experienced both kinds of pleasure will be found to prefer the higher over the lower. He acknowledged, too, that some people choose to follow the principle of utility because they seek the favor of friends and neighbors or they fear the wrath of God. However, such external motivations are secondary to the ultimate, internal motivation: *an inner feeling for humanity.* This feeling expresses what has been termed a *generalized benevolence,* an attitude that everyone's happiness is equal and one's own happiness should not be pursued at others' expense.

Though Mill himself believed that the inner feeling for humanity is acquired rather than inborn, he did not consider it important to demonstrate the point. Whether it is acquired or inborn, he explained, makes little difference. The main point for him was that it does exist, that it is a powerful sentiment, and that in its focus on the happiness of all people it constitutes the most solid ethical standard.

Since the time of Mill, numerous ethical theories have been advanced. One important focus of this time has been on the logic of discourse; that is, on the language used to express moral judgments and the logical implications of that language. Notable among more recent theories has been the "Good Reasons" approach taken by contemporary philosophers such as Stephen Toulmin, Kurt Baier, Kai Nielsen, and John Rawls. The central focus of that approach has revolved around the question "When is a reason for a moral judgment a *good* reason?" These ethicists hold that the primary purpose of moral discourse is not to advance theories or to express individual perspectives, but to guide conduct.

GREAT ISSUES IN ETHICS

As even this brief survey makes clear, the history of ethics has been essentially the story of the search for a single satisfying standard against which to judge moral questions. That the search continues—even after almost 2,500 years—may seem to imply that it has been a failure. That is surely not the case. Each contributor has advanced the cause of knowledge. If the task that the great ethicists set for themselves remains unfinished, it is only because of its magnitude. They were pursuing nothing less than the ultimate basis of moral judgment, the perfect explanation of morality.

Is such a perfect explanation possible? Perhaps, but many contemporary thinkers doubt it. Still, the paradoxical truth may be that progress in ethical understanding demands that we believe in the possibility and strive to realize it. We must, like Socrates, keep speculating, keep examining, keep questioning. In that spirit we end this brief historical perspective with some of the most challenging questions that have occupied the attention of the great ethicists over the centuries.

Do human beings have a natural tendency to good, a natural tendency to evil, or some combination of tendencies? What are the implications of the answer for ethics?

What conditions must be present before we can say a person is truly happy? Which of these conditions are most important? What is the best expression of the relationship between ethics and happiness?

Is the preserving of one's dignity or the serving of a principle other than self-interest ever a higher good than personal happiness?

Is there any action that is good in itself, without reference to the consequences it brings about? Or does every good derive its value from its consequences?

Whose interests should be paramount in ethical judgment? One's own? Those of the people directly affected by the action? The interests of all humanity? Is the answer necessarily the same in all situations?

Are some acts morally obligatory regardless of the consequences for human benefit or harm?

How important is objectivity in moral judgment? To what extent can the process of moral judgment be objective?

Is there a single universal moral code that is binding on all people at all times and in all places? If so, how are the differences in moral perspective to be accounted for? If not, how can people with different moral perspectives be expected to live in harmony and how is the notion of progress in ethics to be understood?

▨ INQUIRY

Answer one or more of the preceding questions as your instructor directs. Be sure to consider all possible answers before choosing any one. Try to anticipate the objections to your answer that might be raised by those who disagree with you, and present an effective response to those objections.

IV

CONTEMPORARY ETHICAL CONTROVERSIES

This section presents numerous ethical issues for analysis, grouped under nine headings: Education, Media and the Arts, Sex, Government, Law, Business, Medicine, Science, and War. In addressing these issues, use the approach explained in the preceding chapters, as summarized here:

The Steps	How to Proceed
STEP 1: STUDY THE DETAILS OF THE CASE	If you have all the details, note what circumstances distinguish this case from similar ones. If you do not have all the details, obtain them. If they are unavailable, consider what they might be.
STEP 2: IDENTIFY THE RELEVANT CRITERIA	Consider any *obligations* that might exist among the individuals involved—for example, contractual obligations, obligations of friendship or citizenship, business or professional obligations.
	Consider relevant *ideals,* including prudence, justice, temperance, courage, loving kindness, honesty, compassion, forgiveness, repentance, reparation, gratitude, and beneficence.

Consider all significant *consequences*—direct and indirect; obvious and subtle; immediate and delayed; physical, emotional, and intellectual; intended and unintended—of the action on the person performing the act as well as on others.

STEP 3: DETERMINE POSSIBLE COURSES OF ACTION	Identify the various alternative responses to the situation. Note that this step may require you to use your imagination.
STEP 4: DECIDE WHICH ACTION IS MOST ETHICAL	In light of your consideration of the criteria, decide which response is ethically preferable. If two responses produce good or two produce harm, choose the one that produces the greater good or the lesser harm.

EDUCATION

1. Non–English-speaking students are swelling U.S. public schools. The situation has sparked a debate over how best to teach them. Some people favor a bilingual approach in which students would be taught in their native languages for a period of time—for example, until they had learned to read and write in that language—and then switched to English instruction. Opponents of that idea argue for instruction in English from the outset, with tutoring for students who require it. What are the moral considerations that should be considered in this debate?

2. In recent years a controversy has arisen over the use of library computers. Some citizens object to the fact that it is possible to access pornographic websites on the computers and are demanding that software filters be used to block such access. Others consider any such action a violation of constitutionally guaranteed freedom. In light of appropriate moral considerations, which view is more reasonable? Would the answer differ if the library in question were not a public library but rather a public school library?

3. Some colleges and universities weight their admissions policies heavily in favor of black and Hispanic applicants. The net effect is that white and Asian students with significantly higher high school grades and admissions test scores have a significantly lower chance of acceptance at the university. Examine this policy and decide whether it is ethical.

4. High schools around the country sometimes experience problems with censorship. In most cases, school boards respond to community complaints that some books are immoral or un-American by banning those books from the school library. Is the censorship of books in schools ever morally justifiable?

5. Many colleges prohibit the drinking of alcoholic beverages on campus. Is such a prohibition morally justifiable?

6. Under what circumstances, if any, is it morally justifiable for grade school or high school teachers to hit students?

7. A complaint from a California state senator sparked a review of the women's studies program at the California State University, Long Beach, campus. The senator charged that the instructor of a course titled "Women and Their Bodies" showed the students in her class slides of her genitals and suggested that they imagine "doing things" with other women in the class.[1] Is either of these acts morally objectionable?

8. In education, as in business, mistakes are sometimes made in promoting a person. For example, a respected high school teacher with twenty years of service may be made principal of his school. After serving for a year in this new capacity, the man may have demonstrated clearly that he is incompetent in administrative affairs. But, by that time, his former teaching position will have been filled. Consider the various ethical considerations involved both in retaining him and in firing him, and decide what course of action and what conditions would be the most ethical solution for the school board.

9. Once in a while, a case of a teacher who has taught for years with forged credentials comes to light. Once the deception is found out, of course, he or she is dismissed and may even be prosecuted. But consider the moral dilemma that must exist for the principal when he or she first learns of the lie. Suppose, for example, the principal learns that instead of having the master's degree the records indicate, the teacher dropped out of college after one year as an undergraduate. Further suppose that the teacher is by every measure one of the very best in the school. Should the principal expose the teacher or allow the deception to continue? Would your judgment change if the teacher were not outstanding but merely average?

10. Every academic subject has areas of controversy, questions that different schools of thought answer differently. For example, in psychology there are Freudian, Jungian, and Adlerian perspectives; in literature there are several approaches to interpretation, such as the esthetic and the psychological. Is it ethically acceptable for an instructor to teach only the school of thought he or she personally accepts? Would your answer be different in the case of an introductory course than in the case of an advanced course?

11. In determining students' final grades, some college instructors use as one factor their personal, subjective judgment of students' effort and contribution to class discussion. The factor may vary in its weighting from

10 to 20 percent or even higher. Is this practice ethical? Under what conditions, if any?

12. More than a few college professors today believe that the very idea of a grading system is punitive and archaic. Some of them, however, are in the minority at their institutions and therefore are required to submit grades in their courses. One way to do so and still serve their consciences is to give every student an A, regardless of the quality or quantity of the work he or she submits. Discuss the morality of this practice.

13. In most colleges, the chairperson of an academic department is responsible to the academic dean. If the dean should, for example, criticize the chairperson's department for submitting too many low grades in a particular semester and demand that the department review its grading policy so that it can begin assigning "more reasonable" grades, the chairperson would have to decide how to deal with the matter. Each of the following is a possible approach. Evaluate the ethical character of each.

a. The chairperson can call in each faculty member and review the member's grading policy with him or her in an attempt to determine whether the policy is too stringent.

b. The chairperson can issue a memorandum to the department members explaining the dean's concern and desire that the department grades improve in the next semester.

c. The chairperson can issue a demand that each department member's grades conform in the future to the normal distribution curve.

14. Few colleges today are without their experimental courses or curriculums. In their most sophisticated form, such courses or curriculums are run side by side with traditional ones so that their effectiveness can be compared. At the outset of such experiments, of course, it is impossible to be certain that the experiment will be even minimally effective. Are such experiments ethically permissible? If so, under what conditions?

15. A teacher is usually assigned to teach courses with specific content. He or she is expected to select or create lessons that will impart the knowledge and develop the skills that are associated with that content. To do other than that—for example, to teach economics instead of literature in a literature course—would clearly be to break his or her moral obligation to the students who enrolled for the advertised course. Yet in subtler cases, the answer is not so clear. Would it violate that obligation if a chemistry professor presented a filmstrip on chemical weapons as part of an antiwar lecture? Would it violate that obligation if a math instructor spent one class period talking about the importance of population control? Why or why not?

16. Term paper ghostwriting is surely not a new idea. But doing it on the scale of big business—with advertisements in college newspapers, branch offices, and a stable of writers—is. It is possible today to buy a term paper on virtually any subject, complete with footnotes and bibliography. Some companies even offer tailor-made papers. Is such a business ethical?

17. Some time ago a young man filed a $1 million lawsuit against the high school that graduated him, charging the school with legal responsibility for his inability to read and write adequately.[2] It seems unlikely that the courts would find the school legally responsible for his ignorance. But is it possible that the school is morally responsible? Under what conditions might it be?

18. Compulsory education, the required attendance of young people between certain ages (for example, between 5 and 16 in many states), has become a tradition in the United States. The idea that requiring young people to attend school is an infringement of their rights as citizens, a kind of slavery, is unthinkable to many Americans. Yet there are men and women, some of them respected educators, who are openly expressing that idea. They argue that children themselves, or at least their parents in their behalf, should decide whether they will attend school and, assuming they decide in the affirmative, where, what, and for how long the children will study. Consider the ethical side of the question. Are compulsory education laws morally wrong?

19. The age difference between teachers and students is sometimes relatively slight. A high school teacher could be 21 and a high school senior 17. A college instructor could be 25 and a college senior 22. Would it be unethical in any way for such teachers to date their students? Would it be different if the students were not in their classes?

20. Tenure is the permanent right to a position or an office. In teaching, tenure has traditionally been reserved for those who have proven themselves competent in the classroom. Once it is awarded, usually after a provisional term of from two to five or six years, the teacher may not be fired except for gross negligence of duty or some moral offense. The proponents of tenure have maintained that it frees teachers from fears of petty pressures inside or outside the school and enables them to function at their creative best. Recently, however, there seem to be a growing number of opponents of tenure. These people contend that it tempts even the best teachers to relax professionally and stifles creativity. What are the ethical considerations that any full discussion of tenure should address, and why are those considerations important?

21. When faced with the annual decision of how to distribute salary increases to faculty, many administrators elect wherever possible to divide the money among all teachers rather than single out the most deserving ones. (Having everyone a little happy is less troublesome than having a few thrilled and many angry and questioning.) Which action is more justifiable ethically? Be sure to consider all aspects, including the effects of each action on the quality of education.

22. Most teacher retirement programs calculate the individual's pension based on the average salary earned during his or her highest earning years. Realizing this, some college presidents routinely promote faculty members the year before their retirement (whether they meet the established requirements for the rank or not). Thus the faculty members can get a slightly higher pension. Is this practice of routine promotion ethical?

23. Is it ethical for students not to work to their capacity? Is it ethical for them to study so diligently that they strain the limits of their physical and emotional endurance? Discuss the various degrees of underwork and overwork that occur among college students and decide in what circumstances each becomes a moral issue.

24. The practice of cheating on homework and examinations is probably as old as education itself. Few would deny that it is an unethical practice in most cases. But what of the dilemma of students who do not cheat on their work but know other students who do? Discuss the moral considerations they should make in deciding whether to inform the teacher. Then decide when they should and when they should not do so.

MEDIA AND THE ARTS

1. Most talent shows of the past presented contestants of obvious talent; less talented contestants were screened out in preliminary phases of competition. But modern talent shows often reverse this pattern—from all appearances, many contestants are selected precisely because they are remarkably *untalented*. As a result, they are held up to ridicule by the judges. Is it unethical for such shows to be produced? Is it unethical to watch them?

2. Traditionally, journalists were taught to keep their personal opinions out of their reporting. The place for opinion, it was stressed, was on the editorial page or in an opinion column. Today, that view has changed. Many journalists, including Internet bloggers, have not learned the traditional rule; others simply ignore it. Is the mixing of opinion and fact in news reports ethical? What about reporters using their opinions to decide whom to interview—in other words, interviewing only people who share their views?

3. Over the past several decades, television programmers have used a number of devices to make their programs interesting and keep ratings high. Among those devices are frequent shifts of camera angle and frequent alternating between long shots and close-ups. Action scenes featuring car chases, explosions, and martial arts sequences have also increased. Exposure to such fast-paced entertainment obviously has an effect on people's attention span, causing, at the very least, impatience with slow-paced presentations, including those that typically occur in the classroom. Discuss the ethical considerations, if any, involved in this situation.

4. The scene is a large room at a political convention. The members of a state delegation are entering to caucus about an important issue. The meeting is closed to the public and press. However, one enterprising reporter has anticipated the caucus and is carrying forged credentials identifying her as a member of the delegation. Hoping for a news scoop, she flashes her false credentials at the door, moves inside the room, flips on a concealed tape recorder, and mingles with the crowd. Is she behaving ethically?

5. In 1990 the parents of two young men who committed suicide brought legal action against the rock group Judas Priest. The parents contended that hidden messages ("Do it" and "Let's be dead") in the group's album *Stained Class* caused the men to take their lives. The court held that the rock group bore no legal responsibility, but the moral question remains unanswered. Assuming the alleged messages were in fact hidden in the recording, are the individuals who put them there guilty of a moral offense?

6. In their book *The Early Window: Effects of Television on Children and Youth,* researchers Robert M. Liebert and Joyce Sprafkin cite three detailed reviews of the scholarly literature on violence: Andison's in 1977, Dorr and Kovaric's in 1980, and Hearold's in 1986. (Hearold's review covered 230 separate studies.) All three researchers agree that the effects of violence shown on television are substantial. Specific effects include direct instruction and imitation, lowering of inhibitions to aggression, and cultivation and shaping of values.

In addition, Liebert and Sprafkin say the following about a fourth study:

> In a large-scale study conducted for CBS, Belson (1978) collected information about television viewing, aggressive behavior, and other personal characteristics of more than 1,500 male adolescents in London. After equating for a variety of variables related to aggressive behavior, the extent of aggressive behavior of the heavy and light TV viewers was compared. Belson concluded that the evidence "is very strongly supportive of the hypothesis that high exposure to television violence increases the degree to which boys engage in serious violence" (p. 15). (The antisocial behaviors included deeds that were serious enough to be labeled juvenile delinquency such as inflicting bodily harm to others and damage to property.) CBS chose to view the findings as inconclusive, and the study did not receive much publicity. (Just as a note of interest, this study took 8 years to complete and cost CBS $300,000.)[1]

If the authors' assertions are accurate, what conclusions do you draw about the morality of showing violence on television? What action, if any, should be taken about violent shows, and by whom?

7. The essential purpose of advertising is to inform the public that certain goods and services are available. Modern advertising, of course, goes beyond informing and attempts to persuade the public that one product or service is better than all others. And the persuasive tactics that are used are sometimes morally questionable. Examine at least five print ads or commercials and evaluate what is said and implied. Then decide whether each is morally defensible. Detail your findings.

8. One device increasingly used in modern advertising is the testimonial. An athlete, former politician, or movie/TV star is paid hundreds of thousands of dollars to lend his or her name to a product and become its spokesperson. The celebrity recites someone else's words to praise something he or she may not even use in order to influence readers or viewers to use the product. Discuss the ethical issues this advertising practice raises.

9. In recent years Hollywood has produced a number of horror films that graphically depict violence. Many of these films force the audience to adopt the perspective of the psychotic killer by filming the action as the killer would see it. All the artistry of special effects departments and new technology, including filming in 3-D, combine to make the stabbings and decapitations more realistic than ever. Discuss the morality of producing and viewing horror films.

10. When advice columnists Ann Landers and Abigail Van Buren were discovered to have recycled old letters (some of them used in their columns fifteen years earlier) without notifying their publishers or so labeling the material for their readers, a minor controversy arose. Some readers and newspaper editors believed that the columnists had committed a moral offense, while others disputed that view. What do you think about the morality of such recycling of material?

11. Now that homosexuality is more open and more tolerated in our society, some advertisers are beginning to design advertisements that appeal to a homosexual audience—for example, ads for jeans, whiskey, and cologne. The appeal is often subtle to avoid offending straight consumers. Is there anything morally offensive about this advertising practice?

12. There have been reports that the staff of a popular TV show about the investigative work of a government agency is required to submit all scripts to the agency's director for his prior approval. Any scripts that show his agents making a mistake or using questionable tactics in conducting an investigation are allegedly rejected. If these charges are true, is the agency's action ethical? Is the TV staff ethically justified in cooperating?

13. The sponsors of TV shows also can exert influence over the subjects and treatment presented. In some cases, they may demand veto power over scripts, reasoning that since they are paying for the show and their product will be identified with it favorably or unfavorably, they should have the final say about its content. Is it morally right for them to demand this veto power?

14. It is common knowledge that most TV commercials have very little appeal to the mind. They aim for the emotions and use our hopes and desires and needs to condition us to buy the products they advertise. Do the writers of TV commercials commit any moral offense by these appeals and devices? Do the sponsors, by endorsing them? Do the networks, by permitting them to be aired?

15. For a number of years, it has been widely recognized that TV has the potential to be the greatest educational device in history. (This includes not just what is presently considered educational TV, but commercial TV as well.) Does the TV industry have any moral obligation to realize that potential? If so, explain the source of that obligation and the kinds of changes in present programming that would be necessary to honor it.

16. TV news reporting calls for careful editing. Thousands of feet of film must be trimmed to fit a tight time schedule. Events that could not be fully covered in hours must be presented in minutes. Without intending to do so, the people who prepare news broadcasts can distort the news and misinform the viewing public. Do TV networks have any special ethical obligation to ensure that such distortion does not occur? If you believe they do, explain why and what kinds of regulations and safeguards would fulfill the obligation.

17. In many newspapers, the letters-to-the-editor column is given more than token space and becomes a lively forum for a public discussion of timely issues. The number and relative quality of letters published for or against an issue, and even their arrangement on the page, can subtly influence public opinion. Does this power to influence carry with it any ethical responsibility? If so, what is it and how can it best be met?

18. Newspapers derive part of their income from taking advertisements for, among other things, movies. Occasionally, a paper will set standards that must be met by movie ads—for example, the stipulation that the ad contain no prurient appeal. Is it ethical for newspapers to exercise such censorship? If you believe it is, do you think that newspapers that do not censor their ads are behaving unethically?

19. Newspaper columnists very often are given information that amounts to news scoops. They may be given a copy of a letter or memorandum that incriminates a government official or a political aspirant. The dilemma they must face is to decide whether to publish it quickly so that the public can be informed or to delay publication until the information is verified. Do columnists have any ethical obligation in such cases? Explain.

20. Magazine editors are regularly faced with the difficult job of appraising manuscripts submitted by writers. Often, they must consider factors other than the quality of the writing. For example, a well-known writer and a relatively unknown one may submit articles about the same general topic. If the better-known writer's piece is chosen because it is superior, there is no moral issue. Yet sometimes it is chosen even though it is inferior. Under what conditions, if any, would such selection be ethically justifiable?

21. It is a psychological truism that everything we say and do, every experience we have, helps to shape us favorably or unfavorably. Children in their formative years are especially vulnerable. Yet certain films, because of their story line, require child actors to portray mentally disturbed, criminal, and even savage characters. Is the use of children in such roles ethically acceptable? If you believe that it sometimes is, be sure to specify the conditions that differentiate those situations from unacceptable ones.

22. Is it ethical for an actor or actress to accept a role in a film or TV show if he or she finds its theme morally objectionable?

23. Most colleges today employ media specialists, men and women who prepare audiovisual aids for teachers. Sometimes these people are given assignments that conflict with their principles. For example, they may be directed to produce for a psychology instructor slides and transparencies that mock their religious beliefs. Is it morally acceptable for the media specialists to accept such assignments?

24. Some companies pay movie producers to display their products in films. For example, a soft drink company may pay to have its soda prominently featured, an automobile manufacturer may donate a car with the provision that the hero be shown driving it, and so on. Is there anything morally objectionable about this practice?

SEX

1. In *A Return to Modesty,* author Wendy Shalit presents an interesting argument that challenges an entrenched notion of modern mass culture. She argues that modesty in dress and behavior is a good quality that exists naturally in women and helps them avoid being victimized by men. In many cases, she maintains, it also motivates men to exercise sexual restraint and develop a more respectful attitude toward women. If Shalit is right, then the half-naked look affected by many young actresses and singers and imitated by their admirers is harming them (and perhaps the rest of us). Is Shalit right? What, if any, are the moral implications of this issue?

2. Some states have laws designed to protect children from sexual offenders. A common provision is to require offenders who have served their sentences to register with the police, so that the police can notify the public of the offenders' presence in the community. Some civil rights supporters object to this provision, claiming it continues the sex offenders' punishment after they have paid for their crimes. Discuss the morality of this provision.

3. During the trial of two men who were eventually convicted of raping and murdering a 10-year-old boy, it was determined that one of the men had viewed the North American Man Boy Love Association (NAMBLA) website before the crime. The website allegedly contained instructions on how to find children for sex, gain their trust, and avoid law enforcement. The parents of the slain boy then brought a civil lawsuit against NAMBLA for inciting a crime. Soon thereafter, the American Civil Liberties Union (ACLU) announced that it would defend the convicted killers and argued that the information on the NAMBLA website was constitutionally protected speech. Evaluate the morality of the ACLU's argument.

4. In many states, the law now offers protection against sexual harassment. Moreover, behavior that formerly was considered playful teasing is now considered sexual harassing. For example, a man may make a verbal pass at a woman or merely offer what he considers a compliment about the shapeliness of her legs and be technically guilty of sexual harassment. Many men believe that a law that makes no distinction between "real offenses" and teasing is unethical. Are they correct?

5. In our culture, fornication (sexual intercourse between unmarried men and women) has traditionally been viewed as immoral. The reasons that have supported this judgment have ranged from religious prohibitions to practical considerations, such as the dangers of pregnancy and sexually transmitted disease. The liberalization of religious views, the improvement of birth control techniques, and the development of antibiotics have resulted in a softening of the traditional judgment. The question of the rightness or wrongness of fornication is seldom hotly debated anymore. Yet it remains a debatable issue. Evaluate the morality of fornication in each of the following situations: (a) between two pre-teenagers, (b) between a teenager and an adult, (c) between two adults. If your judgment differs among these situations, explain why.

6. Consider this special, though perhaps not altogether uncommon, case of fornication. A 28-year-old man is engaged. About a month before the wedding he meets an old sweetheart with whom he had been intimate. They have dinner together for old times' sake and recall their relationship. By the end of the evening, memory has rekindled passion. They spend the next three days and nights together. Is their fornication ethically justifiable?

7. Some degree of sexual experimentation appears to be a normal part of growing up in our culture. Many teenage boys and girls will indulge in necking and petting (and even intercourse) with partners toward whom they feel only a slight and passing affection. Some, in fact, will on occasion do so with partners they have no feeling for. The sexual activity in such cases is performed not to express love, but to gain experience or to satisfy a biological urge. Is there anything morally questionable about this practice?

8. Sexual promiscuity is frequent indulgence in intercourse with a variety of partners, indiscriminately selected. Is promiscuity immoral? Explain.

9. An unusual case occurred in England some years ago in which a man and his wife were arrested for having sexual intercourse in their yard. Because only a row of flowers separates their yard from their neighbors' and the neighbors' children observed them, the couple was charged with crimes—he with indecent exposure and she with aiding and abetting him. He was found guilty, but she was acquitted after promising not to use the yard for sexual activity again.[1] Was what they did immoral?

10. Like fornication, adultery (sexual intercourse between a man and a woman, either or both of whom are married to someone else) has traditionally been considered immoral. Evaluate the morality of adultery in each of the following cases. If your answer depends on certain conditions, state those conditions.

a. A married woman whose husband was left impotent after an automobile accident has intercourse two or three times a month with a bachelor who works in her office.

b. A man is married to a woman whom he loves but who doesn't meet his sexual needs. Because his job takes him out of town two or three times a month, he uses those occasions to find a woman to supplement his sexual activity.

c. A soldier is fighting overseas for a year. During that time both he and his wife, without telling each other, engage in sexual relations with others.

d. A "liberated" couple joins a mate-swapping club. They attend club parties together, engage in sexual activities with others, then go home together.

e. A married man enjoys a good sexual relationship with his wife but has affairs without her knowledge just to add variety and a sense of adventure to his life.

11. Is it ethically justifiable for a married person to become celibate (for, let us say, religious reasons) without consulting his or her spouse? Is it justifiable to do so if he or she consults the spouse and the spouse refuses to consent?

12. Dr. William Masters and Dr. Virginia Johnson are well known for their research into human sexuality. The method of treatment that they have found effective in treating couples with sexual problems is a two-week vacation "course." The couple checks into a hotel near the clinic and receives instruction in the therapy technique, which consists of proceeding very slowly from just gently embracing each other during the first few days to intercourse later. Though the explanations are provided in the clinic, all physical contact between the couple is reserved for their hotel room. The therapists do not observe the couple.[2] Are these clinics ethically acceptable?

13. The Masters and Johnson clinics have a number of imitators. One of these is a nude encounter group in which men and women with sexual problems meet and learn to perform sexually by experimenting with one another.[3] Is this group ethically acceptable?

14. A number of other sex clinics operate more along the lines of Masters and Johnson but differ in one respect: They use surrogate partners for single patients. That is, if a single man or woman enrolls in the program for treatment, they provide him or her with a sexually skilled partner. (Masters and Johnson used surrogates in their original clinic, but ceased to do so when their use became controversial.) These partners are paid for their services by the clinic.[4] Is the use of surrogate partners ethically acceptable?

15. The problem of crew members' sex drives is a factor in two-month nuclear submarine cruises. It is solved by providing pornography.[5] Is that solution morally acceptable?

16. Legend has it that prostitution is the "world's oldest profession." Some societies have approved it, others have tolerated it, and many have tried to eliminate it. Is prostitution immoral in all cases?

17. Our society has traditionally regarded homosexual behavior as a moral abomination. Is it? In answering, comment not only on situations involving consenting adults but also on those involving a consenting adult and a consenting minor. If your answer differs from your answer to the fornication question (inquiry 5), explain why.

18. What are the ethical considerations that arise in cases where people undergo sex-change operations? Are there any situations in which it would not be ethically justifiable to have such an operation? A University of Massachusetts professor has argued that a sexual relationship between a professor and a student can be "quite beautiful and genuinely transforming" and can "touch a student in a positive way." He specifies a situation in which a female college student who had "unnaturally" prolonged her virginity offered it to her professor and the professor accepted it.[6]

GOVERNMENT

1. The idea of *free trade* is to eliminate tariffs, quotas, embargoes and other barriers designed to protect certain industries and their workers against foreign competition. The *fair trade* movement aims to raise the wages and living standards of the people whose labor *produces* goods and services. To accomplish this, the movement seeks to make consumers aware of inequities and to set standards that will guide corporations. Free trade and fair trade are not incompatible but their goals and initiatives are not always in agreement. Evaluate the morality of each type of trade. (Helpful search terms: "free trade" and "fair trade.")

2. Since 2002 the federal government has had the legal authority to engage in wiretapping without a court order. Defenders of this practice claim that it is necessary to protect the country from terrorist attacks such as occurred on 9/11. Opponents argue that the practice infringes on citizens' right to privacy. Discuss the morality of such wiretapping. (Helpful search term: "ethics of wiretapping.")

3. Some civil rights advocates have proposed that the U.S. government pay reparations to all African American citizens as compensation for slavery and its harmful effects. Opponents agree that the institution of slavery was evil and had long-term effects but challenge the wisdom of reparations. Some of these opponents say that the blood spilled in the Civil War and the passage of civil rights legislation have been appropriate and sufficient signs of remorse and repentance. Other opponents claim that for African Americans to accept money for their ancestors' suffering is an insult to their ancestors. Evaluate the morality of the reparations proposal.

4. Many countries have outlawed the death penalty. The United States, as a country, has not, although many people believe it should. Evaluate the morality of the death penalty.

5. A number of groups have urged restrictions on child labor. For example, they believe that no one under age 16 should be permitted to work in the manufacturing, mining, agricultural, and construction industries; that hours of work should be limited in all jobs for workers under the age of 18; and that no one under 21 should be allowed to have any contact with pesticides. Discuss the moral considerations attending this proposal.

6. When President George W. Bush offered his tax reduction plan to Congress, a number of Democrats claimed it favored the wealthy. The president's spokespeople responded that the plan was fair because everyone who paid taxes would receive a proportionate reduction. The Democrats said that any plan that did not treat all citizens equally was unfair. After researching the question more thoroughly, decide which argument on tax reduction is more ethically sound.

7. Some senators threaten to block any candidates for superior courts who are not avowedly pro-choice on abortion. Critics say that such a requirement for prospective judges is a disservice to them and to the country because it refuses to allow what has traditionally been considered essential in judges—an open mind on all issues. Discuss the moral dimension of this issue.

8. Does the federal government have a moral obligation to cover the cost of health care for individuals who cannot afford health insurance or whose health insurance benefits have been exhausted? What about individuals who could have afforded health insurance but gambled that they would not suffer serious illness and now find themselves unable to afford health care?

9. A businessman has significant holdings in airline stock. He runs for Congress, is elected, and is about to serve on the House Government Activities and Transportation subcommittee, which holds hearings on airline industry issues, such as airline safety. Would it be ethical for him to continue to hold his airline stock?

10. The U.S. government continues to give subsidies to the agricultural industry. Most people have no moral objection to that practice in general. However, many people feel it is morally wrong for the government to give such subsidies to tobacco farmers, whose product is harmful to people's health. Is it morally wrong to subsidize the growing of tobacco?

11. Many people were shocked and angered to learn that the Small Business Administration had made federally guaranteed loans to a pornographic movie theater in Miami Beach and a Times Square sex emporium that features films, peep shows, sexual aids, and pornographic literature.[1] Is there anything morally wrong with a government agency's making loans to such businesses?

12. Just after World War II, when the Allies were prosecuting Nazi war criminals, the U.S. State Department secretly smuggled several hundred Nazi war criminals into the United States, offering them citizenship and jobs in exchange for Soviet intelligence information. The State Department's action contravened the orders of Presidents Franklin Roosevelt and Harry Truman. For decades after the illegal operation took place, relevant files were withheld from Congress, the courts, and the CIA. Only the FBI and military intelligence officers knew of the operation.[2] Is it possible that the smuggling and subsequent cover-up were ethical despite their illegality? Why or why not?

13. At present it is against the law for teachers to lead students in prayer in U.S. public schools. However, a growing number of citizens believe that the law should be changed. Discuss the ethical implications of this controversy.

14. Does the United States, as a democratic nation, have any moral obligation to accept immigrants from poor, less developed countries? Does it have any obligation to grant political asylum to defectors from totalitarian regimes?

15. Political campaigns frequently raise the dilemma of to what extent a person is justified in tolerating evil to achieve a good end. A senatorial candidate, for example, may find his staff attacking his opponent with slogans and emotional appeals unrelated to any campaign issue. Is there anything morally offensive in his allowing such methods to continue? If so, are there any special circumstances in which their use would be justified?

16. In order to gain information to help in the election campaign, members of a political party may infiltrate the opposing party. Pretending acceptance of the opposing party's philosophy and the desire to serve, they may attend the convention and try to get as close as possible to the decision makers, in person or with electronic devices, so that they can inform their own party leaders. Comment on the morality of this practice.

17. The ancient military saying "To the victor belong the spoils" is traditionally applied in politics. A large number of government jobs—at the local and state as well as the national level—are appointive. Every time one party is voted out and another voted in, the old appointees step aside and new ones are named, usually from among the ranks of the hardworking party faithful. Examine this practice in light of the principles you have learned.

18. Modern political campaigns are expensive, with costs frequently running into the millions of dollars. The contributions of individuals are seldom sufficient to meet this expense, so political action committees (PACs) representing special interest groups often make sizable donations to candidates for state and federal offices. If elected, candidates may feel obligated to endorse legislation that benefits groups that supported them and oppose legislation that does not benefit the groups. Discuss the reasonableness of this feeling in light of the principles you have learned.

19. Some states have rules forbidding all executive and legislative employees to have an interest in business activity that could conflict with their public service, to personally hold any investment in an enterprise about which they might be making decisions as government officials, and to communicate to others any confidential information that would help them gain a business or professional advantage. Are such rules ethically sound? Show how the principles we have been using support or challenge such rules.

20. Elected officials are sometimes offered special considerations. They may, for instance, be given preferential treatment in obtaining travel accommodations and reductions in fare. When they take a vacation, the hotels and restaurants they visit may discount their bills. Is it morally wrong for them to accept such considerations? Why or why not?

21. Lobbying is a political institution almost as old as government itself. It is the advocacy of a particular interest group's viewpoint, usually by paid employees. Such employees—lobbyists—are registered with the government. Their job is to bring the interests of their employers to the attention of the lawmakers by informing them of which bills have the support of their people and which do not, encouraging lawmakers to write special legislation, and even suggesting the specific details such legislation might include. Is it ethical to allow lobbying to take place? In what ways and to what extent, if any, is it ethically acceptable for legislators to be influenced by lobbyists?

22. Do rich nations have any obligation to help poor nations? If so, in what ways and to what extent?

23. Whether or not they have an obligation to help poor nations, rich nations often do help. But sometimes they attach conditions to their aid; that is, they demand the privilege of influencing the poor nation's government or they expect support for their international trade policies. Is it ethical for rich nations to attach such conditions to their aid?

24. Pollution is threatening our natural resources. Every responsible person wants to protect our planet for the future. Yet some irresponsible people care only for the profit or pleasure of the moment. Does the government have any moral obligation to eliminate pollution? If so, identify some ways in which it might fulfill that obligation. (Be sure not to gloss over any moral dilemmas that those ways would cause.)

25. Most countries that have tried to deal with the problem of over population have found that one of the most difficult tasks is to educate the poor to use birth control techniques according to directions (for example, to take birth control pills each day rather than skip several days). Some of these countries have found it much simpler and more effective to run campaigns urging men and women to submit to sterilization operations. At least one country gave a free radio to anyone who was sterilized. Are such campaigns ethical? Is it morally right for governments to become involved in population control at all?

26. According to the Anti-Slavery Society for the Protection of Human Rights, "slavery, serfdom, debt bondage, the sale of children, and servile forms of marriage" exist in many countries in Asia, Africa, and Latin America.[3] Presumably, the United States enjoys diplomatic relations and trade with some of these countries. Does the United States have any moral obligation to do something about these practices? If so, what?

27. The ideological differences that have existed among the major world powers for the past several decades have made spying among countries almost inevitable. Although the extent to which the United States practices spying is understandably not easy to ascertain, it seems certain that the Central Intelligence Agency is involved in such work in numerous countries around the world. In what circumstances, if any, and to what extent is its spying morally permissible?

28. In its efforts to maintain national security, the Federal Bureau of Investigation has used informants, men and women who make accusations against others or provide the information that supports such accusations. In some cases, informants step forward to assist the FBI in advance and are directed what to learn and how they might go about learning it. In such cases, this question often arises: How far is it ethically permissible for an investigative agency to go in contributing to illegal activities in order to gain evidence to prosecute lawbreakers? For example, would it be permissible for the agency to provide (through the informant) the guns, explosives, and vehicles needed to commit a crime? Would it be right for the agency to permit or encourage the informant to provoke the criminals to commit a more serious crime than they had intended?

29. Some years ago the tomb of an ancient Chinese noblewoman was discovered near the city of Changsha. The remarkable condition of the body, the clothes, and the ornaments of the tomb recalled the greatness of the dynasty to which she belonged—the Han dynasty, which ruled from about 200 B.C. to A.D. 200. Under these rulers, within a single generation wars among numerous territories were quelled; all of what is now China was united under one economic system, one political philosophy, and one legal system; roads were built and agricultural reforms introduced. As a result of these stabilizing social changes, the arts and crafts flourished as never before. Yet these reforms were not introduced democratically; they were forced on the people, often tyrannically. Dissent was not tolerated.[4] Did the positive consequences that resulted justify the methods used to achieve them? Would tyranny today be morally acceptable if there were a guarantee that it would achieve good?

30. The North American continent was "discovered," claimed for various countries, and later colonized and developed into the nations of Mexico, the United States, and Canada. However, at the time of the various discoveries, there were already people living on the continent. Discuss the morality of the process by which the continent was claimed and colonized.

31. In recent years there has been growing concern about the safety of nuclear power plants. At the same time, continuing energy shortages have increased pressure to build more of these plants. Should the government approve further building? Do present regulations and restrictions meet the moral demands of the situation? If not, how should present regulations and restrictions be modified?

32. Is the concept of private property ethically justifiable in a world where there is widespread proverty? Why or why not?

LAW

1. "Virtual child pornography" is the term given to video depictions of child–child or child–adult sexual activity in which the "participants" are not actual children but realistic computer-generated images of children.

The Federal Child Pornography Prevention Act banned this kind of pornography, but in April 2002 the U.S. Supreme Court declared the ban unconstitutional. (The Court upheld the section of the law that bans pornographic depictions of actual children, however.) Evaluate virtual child pornography from an ethical standpoint.

2. Many civil rights activists argue that the states and the federal government should provide all the rights and privileges of citizenship to individuals who are in the United States *illegally*. This would mean that these people would be able to have driver's licenses, health benefits, and education for their children, all at taxpayers' expense. Discuss the moral considerations related to this issue.

3. A number of prominent people have expressed the opinion that it is immoral to own a sport utility vehicle (SUV) because such vehicles use more fuel than cars, endanger other motorists, pollute more, and increase U.S. dependency on foreign oil. They have urged the outlawing of SUVs or, alternatively, the imposition of tax penalties on those who own them. Discuss the merits of this position from an ethical standpoint.

4. A California Superior Court judge ordered a Sacramento woman to stop smoking around her 5-year-old son. The decision came during a custody dispute. The boy's father claimed that breathing secondhand smoke could harm the boy's health. Do moral considerations support the judge's ruling?

5. Often the penalty for white-collar crime is considerably less than for street crime. Someone who makes millions of dollars in illegal insider trading in stocks, for example, will spend less time in jail than someone who steals a car. Moreover, he will serve his time in a comparatively comfortable facility. Is this difference in punishment morally justifiable?

6. Some years ago an American Indian group occupied some public land in the Black Hills National Forest in South Dakota. They claimed the area was a holy land to them: their birthplace, the graveyard of their ancestors, and the center of their universe. For this reason, they said the area should be turned into a permanent, religion-based Indian community. The government argued that the Indians have no legal right to the land; the Indians argued that they have both a legal and a moral right. Do you agree that the Indians have a moral right?

7. A number of law enforcement agencies are now using a handheld device called a Taser gun to deal with violent-crime suspects and unruly prison inmates. The flashlight-size device shoots darts connected to wires to deliver a 50,000-volt shock. (Reportedly, the device produces no after-effects.)[1] Discuss the conditions, if any, under which the Taser gun's use would be morally acceptable.

8. Alan Dershowitz, Harvard law professor and successful criminal lawyer, has written these words about his defense of people accused of violent crimes: "I do not apologize for (or feel guilty about) helping to let a murderer go free—even though I realize that someday one of my clients may go out and kill again. . . . I am proud to be regarded as overzealous on behalf of my clients."[2] Is this view ethically sound? Is it moral for a lawyer to offer a vigorous defense for those who admit (at least in private) that they are guilty of the crimes with which they are charged?

9. In recent years there have been numerous expressions of public outrage over the parole of people convicted of violent crimes. Discuss the ethical considerations in the issue of parole and decide what direction they suggest for lawmakers.

10. In many colleges across the nation, students are required to pay an activity fee that supports cultural, entertainment, and sports programs. Apparently, in most cases the student bodies of the colleges originally approved of the idea, and from all indications the majority of students do not object to paying the fee because the student government decides how the funds are to be used. However, in at least one state, legislators have challenged the idea. Presumably acting on behalf of the minority of students who oppose the fee, a group of New York state legislators introduced a bill some years ago that would forbid any college in the state university system to charge a student activity fee. (The bill was defeated.) Is it ethical for a university to require students to pay such a fee? Does a legislature have the moral right to forbid a university to do so?

11. Some states still have laws on the books that make fornication, sodomy, and even the practice of contraception by married couples a crime. These laws are seldom applied, and the climate of opinion today would surely support their repeal. Yet when they were written, it was taken for granted that the state had the moral right, and even the obligation, to make laws about such matters. Evaluate that view, applying the appropriate ethical principles.

12. Laws concerning statutory rape not only are still in existence but are often still applied. (Statutory rape, unlike rape, need not involve the element of force. Any act of intercourse between a minor and an adult is a statutory offense because a minor is held to be incapable of giving consent. The definition of minor, of course, varies from state to state.) Are such laws ethically sound?

13. The job of the police is to protect the health, safety, and welfare of the general public. To meet this responsibility, they obviously must not only prevent any activity that threatens the public but also anticipate such activity before it actually threatens. Many police officials believe that this latter responsibility is moral justification for maintaining close surveillance of political action groups and for dispersing large groups of people listening to inflammatory political speeches. Others disagree, claiming that this line of reasoning leads to the denial of the constitutional rights of free speech and free assembly and to the establishment of a police state. Which position is more in keeping with the ethical principles presented in this book? Explain your position.

14. Is it ever morally permissible for the state to take children away from their natural parents and place them in orphanages or with foster parents?

In answering, consider situations in which the parents are alcoholics or drug addicts or neglect or abuse their children.

15. Capital punishment is the taking of a criminal's life in punishment for his or her crimes. Throughout history it has been supported by most societies, often even for crimes we would consider minor. During this century, however, more and more people in Europe and America have come to regard it as morally intolerable, even in the case of heinous crimes. Do you agree? Explain.

16. Due to the increase in crime and the inability of the courts to process cases, a practice known as plea bargaining has developed in large metropolitan areas. It consists of the defense attorney's making a deal with the prosecution: If the prosecution agrees to reduce the charge against the defendant, the defendant will plead guilty and waive his or her right to a jury trial. Plea bargaining appeals to criminals because it allows them to be tried for a lesser crime than they committed. It appeals to prosecutors because it spares them the task of keeping track of witnesses for months and even years. It appeals to judges because it expedites their handling of cases. Evaluate the morality of plea bargaining.

17. In civil lawsuits, it is established practice for attorneys to charge contingency fees, in other words, to have their clients agree in advance to pay them a percentage of their settlement award. The percentage charged is commonly a third and sometimes even half of the total award. Evaluate the morality of contingency fees.

18. Is it ethical for attorneys to base their fees on their clients' ability to pay—that is, to charge a rich person much more than a poor person for the same services? Explain your position.

19. The ideal of justice demands that every person charged with a crime receive equal legal representation regardless of race, creed, nationality, or financial status. However, in practice, minority groups and the poor receive second-class representation at best. Does the legal profession have any moral obligation to strive to realize the ideal? If so, in what ways might it honor that obligation?

20. There is controversy today over what kinds of conditions society ought to provide in prisons. Advocates of improved conditions suggest that society has been vengeful in its practices, seeking more to punish than to rehabilitate. They call for more humane conditions consistent with the human dignity of the inmates. On the other hand, many criticize this thinking as too permissive. Prison should be a drab, monotonous, unpleasant experience, they reason, or it will not deter criminals from repeating their crimes. Discuss the ethical considerations that must be faced in any full discussion of prison conditions.

21. A young woman removed her bathing suit on a public beach. Many people gathered around her, some to take pictures, others to scold her. Then someone called the police. They arrested her and charged her with "public lewdness." The young woman believed the law violated her rights. Do you agree? Is a law that, in effect, forces people to wear clothes in public unethical?

22. Many urban police departments use undercover policewomen to arrest men who do business with prostitutes. The policewomen dress like prostitutes and walk up and down streets where prostitutes are known to work. When unsuspecting men approach the policewomen and proposition them, they are arrested. Is it ethically defensible for police to use such tactics?

23. The most controversial moral issue of our time may well be the issue of abortion. The Supreme Court's liberal ruling has not diminished the vigor of the debate. The very mention of the issue can trigger emotional outbursts. Most people tend to gravitate toward polar positions: "Anything less than abortion on demand is a denial of the most basic right of women" or "Any form of abortion at any stage of pregnancy is premeditated murder." In taking such positions, they close their minds to the complexities of the issue and miss the many distinctions that must be made. Any meaningful discussion of abortion must address at least these fundamental questions: Does a woman have absolute rights over her body or are there limitations on those rights? When does life begin? At what stage of prenatal development, if any, is the fetus properly regarded as a person? (This question is a crucial one in the law because at the moment a person is present, the issue of civil rights arises.) Are there sufficient differences among the various kinds of abortion cases to call for different moral judgments? For example, is the case of the 14-year-old victim of rape different from that of the wealthy, childless society matron? Are either of those cases different from that of the poor woman who already has ten children or from that of the young married working woman? Discuss the morality of abortion.

BUSINESS

1. In recent decades, it has been common for top executives in U.S. corporations to receive the kinds of contracts that used to be associated only with professional athletes. In addition to seven-figure annual salaries, they often receive signing bonuses, stock options, and retirement packages worth tens of millions of dollars. Moreover, their contracts usually contain clauses that require the terms to be met even if the company falls on hard times and lays off thousands of employees. This practice contrasts sharply with that in countries such as Japan, where top executives cannot earn more than six or seven times the salary of the average employee. Is the U.S. practice ethical?

2. A group of hemophiliacs who have contracted AIDS is charging that the manufacturer of the blood-clotting product that infected them knew there was a chance that some of the blood was contaminated with the hepatitis virus. The group further charges that the manufacturer had available a process that would have purified the product, yet chose for economic reasons not to use the process on the product or to discard the tainted supply already on hand. The AIDS virus had not been identified when the company made its alleged decision; however, it is now known that the purification process would have killed the AIDS virus as well as the hepatitis virus. Did the company behave morally? Discuss the degree, if any, of the company's culpability.[1]

3. Some years ago a soup company wanted to feature in advertisements a picture showing the solid ingredients in its soup. Unfortunately, the advertising group found that the solid ingredients sank to the bottom and were barely visible. All that could be seen was the broth. Then they hit on a solution—they put marbles in the bottom of the bowl before pouring in any soup. Thus the vegetables sat nicely on the top, giving the appearance of thick soup. Discuss the morality of this solution.

4. The idea of equal pay for equal work is generally accepted as morally sound. But are there situations in which the application of this idea would be immoral? Why or why not?

5. Because products tend to become obsolete much faster today than they did thirty or forty years ago, research and development are among the most important activities in modern business. However, it is an expensive activity. Some companies try to save money by paying people to conduct corporate espionage, that is, to spy on competitors' research and development operations. Is such espionage ever morally justifiable?

6. Is it ethical for companies to require employees to take a polygraph test before they are promoted? Would your answer be different in the case of a company whose products are made from a secret formula that competitors have so far been unsuccessful in imitating?

7. Is it ethical for liquor companies to create ads linking the consumption of liquor with friendship, popularity, love, and financial success? Would your answer change if the liquor company created an occasional public service ad that stressed the need for responsibility in drinking?

8. In the Middle Ages, the seller was considered responsible for defects in merchandise. Today, although the courts may give relief to a buyer if the defects are glaring, the basic rule is "Let the buyer beware." Is this rule more ethically defensible than the medieval rule?

9. Is it morally acceptable for employers to screen employees for HIV? For company health insurance carriers to drop the coverage of anyone who tests HIV-positive on a company AIDS test?

10. An evening news coanchor at WBZ-TV in Boston decided she wanted a child even though she was unmarried. When she became pregnant, several newspaper reporters and columnists criticized her. One said she and other single mothers "thumb their noses at the old social and moral conventions." Several local clergymen said her high visibility on TV would make her decision seem like an endorsement of unwed parenthood, an inappropriate message to send to young people. The station management disagreed and stood behind her decision. Were they on solid moral grounds in doing so?

11. The Reagan administration once proposed that an existing ban on the export of unapproved drugs and pharmaceuticals be repealed, thus permitting American drug companies to sell abroad drugs that have been banned (or have not yet been approved) by the Food and Drug Administration. The justification offered for the proposal was that it would help the U.S. balance of trade and be beneficial to individual companies.[2] Is such a proposal morally defensible?

12. Several decades ago, nineteen people, most of them employees of two Japanese electronics firms, were charged with scheming to steal computer secrets from IBM.[3] Such activity is a legal offense, but many businesspeople believe that there is nothing morally wrong with it, that it is necessary in today's fast-changing, competitive business world. Discuss the morality of this practice.

13. Sometimes a new invention is viewed as a threat by an industry. For example, if an efficient steam engine were developed for automobiles, the oil industry could anticipate a ruinous decline in gasoline sales. In such cases, the industry might be tempted to buy all rights to the invention in order to prevent it from being marketed. Would such a purchase be moral in any circumstances? Explain.

14. Drug manufacturers are required to conduct tests on new drugs for a full year to be sure that there are no dangerous side effects. One relatively small company has had a promising new antibiotic in testing for eight months. There have been no indications of any harmful effects. Now the company learns that a large competitor is about to market a similar drug. It concludes that with a four-month advantage, the competitor will control the market. The small company will be driven out of business. It decides to change the dates on its research and add four months of fake test results so that the antibiotic may be marketed immediately. Discuss the morality of this decision.

15. Barbiturate and amphetamine addiction continues to be cause for national concern. Each year hundreds of thousands of pills manage to slip into the black market and are sold illegally, often to young people. Some observers, including the head of a congressional crime committee that spent two years probing the problem of illegal drug trafficking,[4] believe that the drug manufacturers cannot be blamed if their products are put to illegitimate use. Do drug manufacturers have any moral responsibility to ensure that their products are not put to such use?

16. It is fairly common today to read of professional athletes refusing to sign contracts with their teams until they are given higher salaries. These demands, which can be for millions of dollars, are regarded by team owners as a form of blackmail. The players, however, believe that their skills are a salable commodity and that they are justified in getting as high a salary as they can bargain for. Are such demands justifiable? Are they so only in certain circumstances? Explain.

17. In the early days of the labor union movement, workers were often treated unfairly. Working hours and conditions were injurious to their health, wages were unfairly low, and fringe benefits were nonexistent. Today the situation is different. Some unions have achieved most of their reasonable demands. However, because of the pressure to keep winning new benefits, they make ever-more-extravagant demands and use the threat of strikes to gain them. Do union demands ever become an unethical use of power? If so, in what circumstances?

18. Investment brokers sometimes have a few clients who live hundreds of miles from their offices. For example, a Wall Street broker may provide investment counseling for his hometown relatives in upstate New York. By arranging to see them during his vacation visits home, he can claim his plane fare or car rental fees and perhaps even many of his meals as business expenses. In other words, he can deduct them on his tax return or, if he is employed by a company, claim them on his expense account. Is this practice ethical?

19. In some businesses—for example, advertising—executives are relatively mobile, changing jobs with unusual frequency. Executives planning such a change can increase their worth to their new employer by taking their clients with them, that is, by meeting with their clients before leaving the company and encouraging them to switch their business to the new company. Discuss the ethical considerations of this practice.

20. Certain hotels do a good share of their business in "hot-bed" rentals—the rental of rooms by the hour for purposes of prostitution. Such hotels do not employ the prostitutes or have any direct connection with their trade. They merely allow the prostitutes to check into a hotel room many times a night, each time with a different partner. Is it moral for hotels to permit this use of their premises? Is it moral for a hotel clerk to work in a hotel in which this practice is allowed?

21. Restaurateurs may be strongly tempted to increase their profits by buying old, chemically preserved meat at discount prices or by reheating the same food several days in a row. Discuss the morality of such practices.

22. Heavy-construction companies usually must engage in competitive bidding for their contracts. This practice demands that they anticipate every material and labor cost months and even years ahead and commit themselves to complete a project for a specified amount of money. A mistake in calculating or a failure to anticipate a significant increase in prices can bankrupt a company. Is it ever ethical for a construction company to use materials that are substandard in order to offset such errors or increased expenses and thereby remain solvent?

23. Employees' worth to their employers may diminish before they are eligible for retirement. In such cases, the employer is faced with the dilemma of choosing between retaining an old and trusted yet unproductive worker for five or ten more years and firing that worker and jeopardizing his or her retirement. Does an employer have a moral obligation to such employees? In discussing this, be sure to mention any special circumstances that would alter your judgment.

24. As the costs of running a business increase every year, efficiency is more and more the byword of the successful businessperson. The axioms of the efficiency expert are "Eliminate what need not be done; simplify what must be done; combine tasks wherever possible." Putting these axioms into practice means, of course, eliminating people's jobs. Under what circumstances is it moral to do so?

25. Book publishers are always in search of a best-seller. When they find a manuscript that they feel has the requisite qualities for success, they try to offer the author the most attractive contractual terms they can in order to induce him or her to sign with their company. Sometimes they will realize that a competitor is in a better position to market the book than they are and that the author therefore would do better to sign with the competitor. Is it ethical for them to withhold that information from the author?

26. Employers have expressed concern about job candidates' lying on résumés and job applications. Consequently, some companies are requiring all job applicants to take a lie detector test as part of the initial job-screening process. Is such a practice ever ethically justifiable? If so, under what conditions? Is a job applicant ethically responsible for truthfully answering all questions asked by a prospective employer?

27. A manufacturer received a multimillion-dollar contract to supply vehicles for a city transportation system. The vehicles proved to have a number of major defects that endangered the safety of the riders. When city officials sued the manufacturer, an investigation was started. An employee of the manufacturer voluntarily testified that his company deliberately used substandard workmanship, practices, and materials. The employee was fired for giving out confidential information. Was the action by the company justifiable?

28. To guard against the destruction of their crops by pests, farmers often spray their crops with pesticides that are or may be harmful to humans. Discuss the morality of this practice.

29. Careless mining and timber harvesting in tropical forests can destroy entire species of flora and fauna, create soil problems, and even threaten the existence of primitive people who rely on what the forests provide. Yet in a number of countries, business entrepreneurs are exploiting the rain forests for profit. Under what conditions, if any, is it ethical for a mining or lumber company to harvest the resources of a rain forest?

30. Doris, an art historian, spends much of her spare time browsing in old shops, hoping to find a valuable piece of art at a ridiculously low price. At last her perseverance has paid off. She just bought a painting worth at least $25,000 for $7.50. The shop owner obviously had no idea of its value. Was it morally acceptable for Doris to take advantage of his ignorance?

MEDICINE

1. There are always more people who need organ transplants than there are available organs, so people have to be placed on one or more waitlists.

Some would argue that the fairest approach is "first-come, first-served"—in other words, that no one should be allowed to jump above his/her place on the list. But others say that other factors should be considered. For example, that people who have taken care of their bodies should have a higher priority than those who have abused theirs in some way, such as substance abuse. Or that children should be given preference over senior citizens, or people whose work makes an important contribution to society over "ordinary" citizens. (No reasonable argument has been advanced, however, for wealth or celebrity warranting preferential treatment.) Create a set of organ allocation guidelines that ensure that the assignment of organs is conducted ethically. (Helpful search term: "organ allocation.")

2. In recent years, a new medical specialty called *clinical ethics* has arisen. Practitioners and their supporters believe the specialty relieves doctors of the burden of helping patients make difficult moral decisions concerning medical treatment. Opponents say it adds a middleman who has no medical knowledge and is, in many cases, ignorant of the moral and religious beliefs of the patient and his or her relatives. The result is often unwelcome, if not downright offensive, intrusion that does more harm than good. After acquainting yourself more fully with this specialty, address the ethical questions surrounding it.

3. Some bioethicists believe that the law should be revised to allow for the "harvesting" of organs from people who are in a state of irreversible coma. This would mean that a kidney or a cornea could be taken from the patient to benefit someone in need. Presumably, this would be done with the permission of the "donor's" relatives and possibly for a fee. Would such a revision of the law be ethical?

4. Partial-birth abortion is a late-term abortion in which part of the fetus' body is allowed to exit the mother's vagina but then, before the birth is complete, the physician pierces the fetal skull and suctions out the brain. Identify the various ethical considerations pertaining to partial-birth abortion and decide whether it is an ethical procedure.

5. A doctor allegedly took one couple's frozen embryo and gave it to another couple. The embryo was subsequently implanted, and in nine months the child was born. Then the donor couple learned what the doctor had done and filed a lawsuit. Did the doctor behave unethically? If so, exactly what offense was he guilty of?[1]

6. Dr. Jack Kevorkian (also called "Dr. Death") achieved notoriety and a prison sentence by assisting terminally ill people in committing suicide. He provided them with a specially designed machine that allowed them to push a button and release a fatal dose of anesthesia into their bloodstream. Kevorkian believes that what he did was not immoral. In fact, he speaks of the "goodness of planned death" and dismisses criticisms of him as "emotionalism." Discuss the ethical questions surrounding Kevorkian's medical "specialty."

7. In testing a patient's blood, a doctor learns that the patient has AIDS. He tells the patient, who says, "I don't want my wife to know I have the disease." Should the doctor honor the patient's request, or should he tell the wife?

8. Some years ago surgeons in Mexico City successfully grafted tissue from a miscarried fetus into the brains of two patients with Parkinson's disease, and they both showed dramatic improvement. Researchers speculate that people with Alzheimer's disease may be similarly treated. This breakthrough raises a question about the use of aborted fetuses. Is it morally acceptable to use fetal tissue in this way? Would it be morally acceptable for a woman to get pregnant just for the purpose of having an abortion and selling the fetus to medical research institutes?

9. John L. Lacey of Savannah, Georgia, accidentally spilled paint solvent on himself and it ignited, burning every part of his body except the top of his head and the soles of his feet. Despite his critical condition, about thirty medical centers around the country refused to treat him because he lacked medical insurance. (Baltimore City Hospital finally accepted him after the governor of Georgia promised financial aid.)[2] Discuss the morality of the hospitals' refusal to treat Lacey.

10. Some medical clinics participate in the testing of drugs that are still in the experimental stage. In such situations, the Food and Drug Administration stipulates that the physician must explain to the patient the nature of the drug, its possible benefits, and the element of risk in using it. In certain situations, however, physicians may decide not to provide these explanations. The number of their patients may be so large that they feel they cannot spare the time to do so, or their patients may be generally uneducated and therefore likely to be confused by details. Does either of these reasons justify a physician's withholding explanation? Can you think of any other reason that would?

11. Is it ever morally justifiable to use orphans for medical research? For example, would it be justifiable to catheterize the urinary tracts of infants in an orphanage for a study of bacteria present in healthy individuals? (Such an experiment would pose no danger to the infants.)

12. Though outlawed in some states, the practice of fee splitting is widespread in medicine. It consists of a physician, usually a doctor of internal medicine, referring patients to a particular surgeon and the surgeon sharing part of his or her fee with the referring physician. Is this practice ethically acceptable?

13. Some hospitals are publicly financed and controlled. Others are run by private individuals or corporations and operate on a profit-making basis. The latter, by their nature, are run with an emphasis on efficiency and with a profit margin calculated in the charges for room, medication, and surgical costs. Is it ethical for hospitals to be profit-making enterprises?

14. In some cases, expensive medical treatments are necessary to maintain life yet are out of the average person's financial reach. An example is the use of a dialysis machine. To pay for such treatment, people must wipe out their savings and even mortgage their homes and sell any valuables. To qualify for state aid, they must in effect be prepared to take a pauper's oath. Such a situation is obviously tragic. Is it also unethical in any way? Explain.

15. The choice of who should be given priority in the use of a rare and expensive machine like the dialysis machine can be an agonizing one. Very often it is a life-or-death decision for the many patients whose existence depends on the treatment. Make a list of the most important considerations in reaching such a decision, and comment on the relative importance of each.

16. Some countries, notably Great Britain, have initiated maintenance programs for drug addicts. Merely by signing up, an addict becomes entitled to free drugs in doses sufficient to stabilize and maintain his or her habit. Such programs reduce the incidence of drug-related crimes and facilitate research into the phenomenon of addiction. Some critics, however, claim that these programs are immoral because they approve and support physically and emotionally harmful behavior. Is this criticism ethically valid?

17. Members of the Jehovah's Witnesses religious sect believe that blood transfusion is sinful. If they or their children suffer a serious accident and lose enough blood to require transfusion, they must in conscience refuse it. This poses a dilemma for attending physicians. Consider the following cases and decide whether the physician should or should not administer the transfusion. (In each case, the patient is not likely to survive without transfusion.)

   a. The patient is an adult and, while conscious, demands that she not receive blood.

   b. The patient is an adult but is unconscious; his wife states that were he conscious he would not accept blood.

   c. The patient is a child; he is unconscious; his parents refuse to sign the permission form.

18. For a long time in Western civilization, autopsy was regarded as an immoral practice that profaned the dead. As a result of this view, there was no legal way for medical school professors and students to obtain corpses. Dedicated to their art, they frequently either dug up recently buried corpses or paid others to do so, without the consent of the dead person's relatives. Were it not for this ghoulish practice, medical science would surely not have developed nearly as extensively or rapidly as it has. Was the practice ethically justifiable?

19. Psychologists and psychiatrists often deal with cases of impotence. As part of their treatment of unmarried patients, they may prescribe a visit to a prostitute. This practice is illegal in most states. Is it also immoral?

20. About 1 baby out of every 600 born in the United States has Down syndrome. Such children have slanted eyes, broad noses, and IQs of about 30. Many are born with fatal physical defects: Parts of vital organs may be missing, the intestines may be blocked, or the heart may not function properly. Often, surgery is necessary if they are to survive beyond the first few days of life. The parents must face the question of whether to permit such surgery and save the child, which would mean spending thousands of dollars for special care and education (and, in some cases, for institutionalization), or to withhold permission and let the child die. Anthony Shaw, an associate professor of surgery and pediatrics at the University of Virginia Medical Center, cites the conflicting views of surgeons over the morality of withholding permission.[3] One is that, in any such situation, not operating would be tantamount to murder. Another is that operating would be wrong because "the emotional and financial costs involved are too great to justify the procedure." Shaw's own view is more flexible. He believes that the circumstances, which can be fully evaluated only by the parents, may make an operation right in one case but wrong in another. Which position is most ethically sound and why?

21. Serious accidents can leave people comatose for months and even years. The longer the coma lasts, the less chance the person has of regaining consciousness. There are people who live in that state, cared for at considerable expense in hospitals or nursing homes, unable to relate to their loved ones, and unaware that they are technically alive. Such cases inevitably raise the question of euthanasia (mercy killing). Merely by injecting a poisonous substance into a vein, a doctor or nurse could spare people a limbo of near-life and grant them a painless death. Would it be ethically justifiable to do so in such a situation? Would it be justifiable in any other situation?

22. The development of organ-transplant techniques has increased the need for donors. Because organs such as the heart can only be (ethically) removed from persons who have just died, the age-old question "When does death occur?" has taken on new importance. Some medical authorities say it occurs when the heart has stopped beating and fails to respond to massage or chemical stimulants. Others say death occurs when the central nervous system has ceased to function (that is, when reflexes cannot be aroused). One authority, Hans Jonas, however, reasons as follows: "*Since we do not know the exact borderline between life and death,* nothing less than the maximum definition of death will do—brain death plus heart death plus any other indication that may be pertinent—before final violence [for example, the taking of an organ for transplant purposes] is allowed to be done."[4] Keeping in mind that Jonas' conclusion would reduce the number of transplant donors, evaluate his reasoning in light of the principles discussed in this book.

23. According to at least one authority, a number of doctors around the country are prescribing amphetamines rather freely for their patients. Is this practice ethical? In answering, consider that amphetamines are habit-forming and can produce symptoms of schizophrenia and paranoia.[5]

24. Hospital workers in a large urban area feel that they are not being paid enough and that their fringe benefits are substandard. They decide to strike. Taking advantage of the special need for their services during holiday periods, they plan for the strike to take place ten days before a major holiday weekend. This timing, they expect, will pressure hospital management to meet their demands. Discuss the morality of this strike.

25. An Alzheimer's facility has some open rooms and the directors are concerned because they know that their financial success depends on full occupancy. Then they get a patient whom they quickly realize is more advanced than they can care for—they lack the advanced care license necessary for such cases and their staff are not adequately trained for them. Yet instead of admitting these facts to the patient's family, they accept the patient, keep her for a couple of months and then, when they find another patient to fill the room, get rid of her by sending her away for psychiatric evaluation. The psychiatrists find no psychosis but only the behavior problems typical of Alzheimer's patients, problems that they say can be solved by appropriate medication and care. Realizing that the original facility had failed to do its job, the woman's family finds another facility. They also ask the original facility to return the $2,500 "community fee" they were required to pay at the outset. The facility refuses, citing the admissions documents that explain that the fee is non-refundable. What moral questions could be raised about the facility's handling of the woman's case? How would you answer those questions?

SCIENCE

1. In the process known as in vitro fertilization, human embryos are created by combining sperm and eggs in a laboratory and then stored in freezers for later implantation. The process almost always results in a surplus of embryos. But a number of questions with moral implications arise from this fact. What should be done with the embryos that are not used? Can they be thrown away? Should they, instead, be buried? Who should decide? Consider the moral criteria that are involved in this issue and answer accordingly.

2. Medical research has proven that secondhand smoke—smoke that is inhaled by nonsmokers in the company of smokers—causes lung disease, including cancer. What are the moral implications of this finding for parents? What are they for businesspeople such as restaurant owners?

3. Some people believe that no warm-blooded animal should ever be used in laboratory experiments that cause them pain. Others say the use of animals is legitimate only in research to cure serious diseases. What is the most ethical response to this controversial issue?

4. The site of an old Cherokee Indian village in Tennessee was about to be flooded in the process of creating a new Tennessee Valley Authority dam. In an effort to find and preserve the artifacts of Indian civilization known to be buried in the area, archaeologists from a University of Tennessee museum undertook extensive digging. The Cherokee Indians objected to the dam because it represented "flooding a whole race of people's history and heritage off the map." They also objected to the digging because in their view it desecrated the graves of their ancestors.[1] Evaluate the morality both of the government's building the dam and of the archaeological team's digging the area.

5. Some years ago a study was made to determine the psychological effects of oral contraceptives. About four hundred poor women, who had sought family planning assistance, participated. Most of the women were Mexican Americans with large families. Some of the women were given oral contraceptives; others were given dummy pills with no birth control chemical. As a result, six of the women in the "dummy group" became pregnant.[2] Evaluate the ethical character of the study.

6. It is now possible for a woman whose husband is sterile to be artificially inseminated with the semen of a donor. Is this practice ethical? If it is in some circumstances but not in others, be sure to explain those circumstances carefully.

7. It is now possible for a woman whose ovaries cannot produce an ovum to receive one from a donor. Is this practice ethical? If so, under what conditions?

8. A businesswoman wants to have a baby but can't spare the nine months. She goes to a laboratory and, following a new scientific technique, "conceives" a baby from her ovum and her husband's sperm. Then she has the fertilized egg implanted in another woman's uterus. Nine months later, the baby safely delivered, she pays the woman for her "labor." Comment on the morality of this procedure.

9. Much of what we hear about the advent of test-tube babies still has the ring of science fiction to it. Yet, if it hasn't already, a successful technique for conceiving and nurturing a human fetus in an artificial uterus is certain to be developed. Naturally, such an achievement will be preceded by many fumbling, partially successful efforts. Many scientists, in other words, will be creating human embryos and sustaining them for a time—for a few days at first, and then as their techniques become refined for a few weeks, three months, seven months. Most, perhaps all, of these embryos and fetuses will be destroyed when they have served their scientific purpose. Is such creation of fetuses ethical? Is their destruction ethical?

10. A scientific organization wishes to conduct research on the effects of ultrasound on human beings. It secures the permission of a local hospital to bombard fetuses that are about to be legally aborted and then to autopsy them after abortion. Is such an experiment ethical?

11. A famous experiment by Yale University's Dr. Jose Delgado dramatized the effectiveness of electrical stimulation of the brain (ESB) as a means of controlling behavior. He "wired" the brain of a fighting bull and demonstrated that merely by pushing a button and sending an electrical current coursing into the animal's brain, he could stop it in the middle of an enraged charge. He also showed that repeated stimulation diminished the bull's natural aggressiveness. Similar experiments have shown that the same effects occur in humans. For example, people given to uncontrollable fits of rage can have their brains so wired that, when they feel a seizure coming on, they need only press a button to be instantly calmed. Is the wiring operation ethical if the patient consents to it? Are there any circumstances in which it would be ethical if the patient did not consent?

12. Another area of research that shows potential for control of behavior is chemical stimulation of the brain (CSB). Tiny tubes can be placed in strategic parts of the brain and chemicals secreted on a timed-release basis. Thus a given emotional state can be maintained in the patient independent of his or her control. Following are some of the uses to which CSB might be put. Examine the morality of each.

   a. Candidates for high public office or for appointive positions such as the president's cabinet could be required to submit to CSB so that the public could be assured no conscious or subconscious aggressiveness in U.S. officials would lead the country into war.

   b. Persons convicted of violent crimes could be treated to ensure that they would not act violently again.

   c. Students who have very short attention spans that hamper their learning or who have negative attitudes toward teachers and the learning process could be treated to increase their learning potential.

   d. Newborn children could be treated so that they would not be susceptible to propaganda or to the promptings of fanatics.

13. Throughout history it has been the practice in many countries to use convicts in scientific experiments. The practice continues today. If, for example, researchers develop a chemical that preliminary exploratory work indicates will cure a fatal disease, they may seek volunteers from prison populations, administer the chemical to them, and determine its effects on the human body. Or a psychologist studying the effects of extreme variations in climate on the human body may subject consenting prisoners to such variations and test their reactions. Although such experiments usually are very carefully designed to minimize the risk to participants, an element of risk always remains. The participants may become ill or even die of unexpected physical or emotional effects. Because of this danger, volunteers are usually promised special privileges during the course of the experiment and even a reduction of their prison sentences. In cases involving unusual risk, full pardons may be promised. Is it ethical to use prisoners for such experiments? Is it ethical to provide such inducements to volunteers?

14. Sometimes medical school professors encourage their students to volunteer for research experiments. (Student volunteers are used just as prisoner volunteers are, though without rewards—except, of course, the emotional satisfaction of having contributed to progress.) Is such encouragement ethically permissible?

15. Some geneticists, notably Nobel Prize–winner Dr. Herman J. Muller, have proposed that sperm banks solicit donations of sperm cells from carefully selected men whose lives had shown unusual mental, emotional, or physical gifts. Couples would then be able to select the genetic material of their choice and thereby produce a child endowed with the hereditary characteristics that matched their ideals. Evaluate the morality of this proposal.

16. Transplants of organs such as the heart and the kidneys have been shown to be possible. Before too long, scientists assure us, the transplant of the brain will also be a reality. Will such an operation ever be ethically justifiable? In answering, be sure to consider the various activities of the brain and their influence on personal identity.

17. *Cloning* is making carbon copies—genetically exact duplicates—of individual organisms. It was first developed in the early 1960s by Cornell University Professor F. C. Steward, who agitated carrot root cells, causing them to divide and multiply. Eventually, he was able to prompt a single cell to develop into a fully grown carrot plant. Later, similar results were achieved with animals. The possibilities of using this technique with humans are very real. There are, of course, technical difficulties that must be resolved. But no knowledgeable person doubts that they eventually will be. When this happens, it may be possible to scrape a cell from a person's hand and create an exact copy of that person, a flesh-and-blood replica with the same genetic traits. (The procedure would be to destroy the nucleus of an egg cell from a donor and insert in its place the nucleus of any cell of the person to be copied. After being nurtured in a nutrient medium for several days, the egg would then be implanted in the uterine wall of the mother.) Thus there could be an unlimited supply of Angelina Jolies, Leonardo DiCaprios, and Kobe Bryants. Because heredity is only part of the influence on people, their behavior and interests would not necessarily be the same. But their appearance and basic capacities would be. Discuss the morality of cloning.

18. Hans Jonas has suggested that in considering the ethical character of scientific experiments, we should distinguish between "averting a disaster" and "prompting a good."[3] In the former, where the goal is *saving* society, Jonas concedes that extraordinary means may be used. However, in the latter, where the goal—*improving* society—is less urgent, such means may not be tolerated. According to Jonas,

> Our descendants have a right to be left an unplundered planet. They do not have a right to miracle cures. We have sinned against them if by our doing we have destroyed their inheritance—which we are doing at full blast; we have not sinned against them if by the time they come around arthritis has not yet been conquered (unless by sheer neglect). And generally, in the matter of progress, as humanity had no claim on a Newton, a Michelangelo, or a St. Francis to appear, and no right to the blessings of their unscheduled deeds, so progress, with all our methodical labor for it, cannot be budgeted in advance and its fruits received as a due. Its coming about at all and its turning out for good (of which we can never be sure) must rather be regarded as something akin to grace.

Would Jonas' distinctions be helpful in evaluating any of the preceding controversies (1–17) in this section? Explain.

19. David D. Rutstein made the following assertions about the selection and design of scientific experiments. Do you agree with these assertions? Do they have special application to any of the preceding controversies (1–18)? Explain.

a. "In selecting a question for human experimentation, the expectation of benefit to the subject and to mankind must clearly far exceed the risk to the human subject."[4]

b. "It may be accepted as a maxim that a poorly or improperly designed study involving human subjects—one that could not possibly yield scientific facts (that is, reproducible observations) relevant to the question under study—is by definition unethical. . . . Any risk to the patient, however small, cannot be justified. In essence, the scientific validity of a study on human beings is in itself an ethical principle."[5]

20. Given the threat that nuclear weapons pose for humanity, is it ever morally acceptable for scientists to engage in research and development work on such weapons? Discuss the conditions, if any, under which it would be acceptable.

WAR

1. War has been with humankind since the beginning of recorded history and no doubt long before that as well. Up until fairly recently, the pattern of events in war was fairly constant: One country would declare war and attack (or attack without declaring), the attacked country would respond, and the destruction and killing would proceed until one side conceded. Traditionally, ethicists held that any nation unjustly attacked had a right to repel the aggression. However, in recent decades, a radically new form of aggression has largely displaced traditional warfare. One or more nations "sponsor" a group of terrorists to carry out a series of attacks on a target nation. This is done without any formal declaration, so the nation that is attacked may not know where to direct its response or (because the terrorists forgo uniforms) how to distinguish combatants from noncombatants. Ethicists are now grappling with these difficult questions: What kind and quality of evidence is necessary before it is ethical for the attacked nation to respond? What limits, if any, should there be to the response?

2. Do citizens have a moral obligation to serve their country when it is at war? Under what circumstances, if any, is it ethical for a person to refuse to serve?

3. A growing number of people today believe that war is always wrong, that no circumstances ever justify one nation's taking up arms against another. Is the view ethically sound? In answering, be sure to comment on the questions of a country's defending itself against aggression and of a strong country's coming to the aid of a weak country that has been attacked unjustly.

4. A soldier's thinking about war may change during his service. For example, after experiencing his first real battle and seeing human beings lying dead or in the agony of pain, a soldier might be prompted to embrace pacifism and request discharge or transfer to a noncombat unit. Such a request would not be looked on favorably by his superiors and usually would be denied. Because the man had accepted training as a combat soldier, they would reason, he would be obligated to finish his term of service. Is this reasoning morally sound? Would it be morally acceptable for the soldier to continue fighting, even though he objected to it on principle?

5. A career officer may not object to war in general but may, after much observation and evaluation, conclude that his or her country's involvement in the particular war of the moment is morally unjustifiable. Would any circumstances make it morally acceptable for the officer to continue to serve in that war? Explain.

6. In the United States, Congress alone has the power to declare or end a war. The president, as commander in chief of the armed forces, therefore has the legal obligation to keep Congress informed of his dealings with foreign powers, particularly during wartime. Are there any circumstances in which it would be ethically justifiable for the president to conduct secret talks with the enemy and with interested third parties in order to set up the conditions for peace? Would any circumstance justify the president's lying to Congress? Explain.

7. Over the centuries the experience of war has produced many *conventions,* humane rules to limit the devastation and suffering that conflict brings. One of the foremost of these rules is that only military targets will be attacked and that civilian population centers that contain no significant deposit of war supplies and machinery will be spared. However, during World War II the United States firebombed the German city of Dresden, dropping thousands of tons of TNT and killing more than a hundred thousand noncombatants. That target allegedly was selected precisely because it was a civilian target and its elimination would demoralize the enemy and, as a result, shorten the war. Discuss the morality of the bombing of Dresden.

8. During the Vietnam War, reports from North Vietnam claimed that the United States was engaging in the deliberate bombing of the 2,500-mile network of dikes that protect countless farms and villages from the flooding of the Red River. The U.S. government denied the charges, explaining that any such bombings that may have occurred were accidental. Had such bombing been done deliberately, it would have had several obvious consequences. It would have threatened the food supply, the homes and factories, and the lives of tens of thousands of civilians. It also would have hindered the North Vietnamese war effort, prompted them to be less demanding at the conference table, and perhaps hastened the end of the war. Would it have been a morally acceptable policy?

9. The argument that has underlain many of the wartime atrocities that people have perpetrated is "They started the war, so we're justified in using whatever means are necessary to finish it." A variation of this, which is used whenever it is not clear who "started it," is "They violated the humane warfare convention first, so we have a right to also." It was used in the Indian wars (although objective scholarship has shown that much of the savagery attributed to the Indians was done first by whites). It was used during World War I and World War II. It was used in Korea and Vietnam. Evaluate the argument from an ethical standpoint.

10. The practice of torturing prisoners to obtain military information is as old as the art of war. Captives are beaten, subjected to electric shock, made to go without sleep for days, "waterboarded," and given little or no food. Is such treatment ever justifiable? Be sure to consider unusual situations as well as more common ones—for example, the situation in which the captive is a terrorist who, there is reason to believe, may have poisoned a city's water supply or placed a timed nuclear device in a public area.

11. Anticipating the possibility that their soldiers may one day be captured by the enemy, some modern armies include in their basic training exposure to torture techniques. That is, they subject their own troops to mild forms of torture in order that they may learn how to resist it. Is this practice justifiable morally? If you believe it is justifiable only under certain conditions, specify the conditions.

12. Like every aspect of modern existence, the waging of war is largely technological. Among the weapons now available are bombs that seek out groups of people (presumably the enemy) through heat sensors and fragmentation bombs that burrow into the earth to await detonation when someone (presumably an enemy soldier) steps on them. Are such weapons morally legitimate in war? Explain.

13. The Pentagon has spent millions of dollars for research into "electro-optical warfare." The device that was the subject of much of this research is the versatile laser beam. It has the potential for use as an ICBM interceptor. Traveling at the speed of light, it can catch and explode the most sophisticated missiles an enemy might launch. It can ignite wooden targets miles away and can instantly burn out the eyes of anyone who looks directly into it. When aimed at an enemy soldier, it can unerringly burn a fatal hole in his body.[1] Is research into the use of such weapons ethically justifiable? Is the use of such weapons any less moral than the use of guns?

14. If weapons such as those discussed in the preceding case become a reality, would it be morally wrong to work for a company that makes them? To hold stock in such a company?

15. Another avenue of potential for warfare is meteorology. Scientists agree that we presently have or will soon have the technological ability to change the earth's temperature, cause tidal waves, create holes in the atmosphere that would permit harmful solar radiation to shower selected geographical areas, and create precipitation where we wish. (There have been reports that the last potential was actually realized by the United States in the Vietnam War to impede travel along the Ho Chi Minh trail.) Comment on such practices from an ethical standpoint.

A SUGGESTION FOR FURTHER STUDY

Many times students will complete an enjoyable college course with a firm resolution to continue studying the subject on their own. Yet somehow, despite their good intentions and their genuine interest in the subject, they never get around to keeping their resolution. The reason is usually that they think of further study in terms of buying or borrowing a book. But which book? They don't know and they don't know how to find out because they are not sure whether they want a general history of the subject, a discussion of one particular aspect of it, a treatment of contemporary issues, or a biography of a famous contributor to the subject.

If you are now making such a resolution about the subject of ethics, here is how to be sure you keep that resolution. Make it very modest. Instead of resolving to buy or borrow a book, resolve to read a single *article* the next time you visit the library and have a few spare minutes. To find the article you want, you needn't search through the magazine index or browse through current periodicals. All you have to do is consult one of the following works.

The Great Ideas: A Lexicon of Western Thought, by Mortimer Adler (New York: Macmillan)

Adler, the author of dozens of scholarly books, is one of the foremost authorities on the history of Western philosophy. Unlike most of his works, *The Great Ideas* does not argue for any particular perspective but recounts, in a nonpartisan manner, what significant thinkers have said about 102 subjects from "Angel" to "World." The essays cover most major topics related to ethics, including "Courage," "Desire," "Duty," "Good and Evil," "Justice," "Prudence," "Temperance," and "Virtue and Vice."

If this book is not available in your library, look for the larger companion work, *Great Books of the Western World* (of which *The Great Ideas* was originally a part). The Great Books collection includes selections from 434 works by 73 authors. An unusually thorough indexing system, called the *Syntopicon,* enables the reader to find what any of these authors had to say about the most specific aspect of a subject—for example, what thinkers from Plato to Freud had to say about "the relation between love and friendship."

Encyclopedia of Philosophy, eight volumes (New York: Macmillan)

This resource contains numerous authoritative articles on all aspects of ethics (as well as articles on other philosophical disciplines). You may want to begin with an article about one of the great issues in ethics—for example, "Conscience" or "The Good" or "Happiness." Or perhaps you would rather learn more about the schools of ethical thought. In that case, you would choose an article like "Deontological Ethics," "Teleological Ethics," "Hedonism," or "Utilitarianism." You will also find individual articles on all the great ethicists from Socrates to the present. Finally, you might choose to read one or both of the two detailed survey articles "Ethics, History of" and "Ethics, Problems of."

At the end of each article is a bibliography of works that provide even more specific and detailed information on the subject of the article. Most of these books will be either on the shelves of your college library or obtainable through interlibrary loan. If you have the time to read one or more books, you can pick them up or order them while you are in the library. If your schedule does not afford you that kind of time, you can at least return again and again to the *Encyclopedia of Philosophy,* thereby ensuring that your knowledge of ethics will continue to grow long after your formal course in ethics has ended.

WRITING ABOUT MORAL ISSUES

The principles that apply to writing about moral issues are the same ones that apply to all expository writing. However, because moral discourse often involves the expression of ideas that readers may be inclined to disagree with, sometimes vigorously, there is a special reason to apply the principles thoroughly and thoughtfully. In this kind of writing, where persuasion is the main intention, there is no margin for carelessness.

The fundamental principles can be stated briefly: The main idea must be clear, the relationships between sentences and paragraphs must be coherent, the space assigned to each part of the presentation must match the relative importance of that part (in relation to other parts), all interpretations and judgments must be sufficiently explained and supported to satisfy the critical reader, and the overall style must be at least readable (and, preferably, *pleasurable* to read).

Let's examine these principles closely, concentrating on the strategies that will help you achieve each one in your writing.

HOW TO MAKE THE MAIN IDEA CLEAR (CLAR)

In most papers about ethics, the main idea will be the writer's judgment of the morality of the action that is being considered. Lack of clarity in expressing the main idea usually occurs because the writer began without knowing exactly what he or she wanted to say, hoping to discover the idea in the process of writing. Sadly, the writer will often reach the end of the piece without having made that discovery. Even when the writer is lucky enough to do so, perhaps midway through the piece, by that point he or she usually has confused the reader and made one or more statements that are inconsistent with the main idea. In such cases, the reader is apt to dismiss the writer as confused or uninformed. You can prevent this development in your own efforts by scrupulously following two simple strategies:

Begin writing only after you have determined exactly what you are going to say; that is, after you have done your research, considered various viewpoints, and decided what your judgment is and what basis you have for making it. This strategy does not rule out brainstorming and freewriting.* In fact, it is perfectly compatible with them, as long as they are used as *preliminaries* to formal writing and not as formal writing itself. If you use brainstorming and freewriting—and they are well worth using—be sure to resist the temptation to deceive yourself by saying, "These notes look good enough to submit as they are; I'll just copy them over to make them neater and the job will be done." Instead, when you have finished producing your ideas, review the ideas and ask yourself what you really want to say.

Experiment with different ways of expressing your main idea and select the best one. Don't settle for your first way of expressing the idea. That way may lack the qualifications and the exactness that reasonableness demands. As you try different ways of expressing the idea, look at the related ideas and evidence that your preliminary work produced. Ask which way of expressing the thought is most reasonable and best reflects the relevant moral principles that are involved. Ask, too, what your readers' reactions are likely to be, particularly what objections they might have. Refine your statement of the idea in light of these considerations.

How to Keep Sentences and Paragraphs Coherent (COH)

You will already have taken one step toward achieving coherence when you determine your main idea. The very fact that you have that idea before beginning will provide a center for your piece of writing, something to relate the other parts to. Yet there are specific strategies you can use to increase the coherence of your writing even more.

Plan the piece before you write it. The easiest way to plan is to develop an outline. This does not necessarily mean using Roman numerals,

---

*These techniques consist of letting your mind range over the subject (or forcing it to do so), without evaluating the ideas that occur, screening any out, attempting to organize them in any way, or correcting your errors. The aim of such techniques is to produce a large body of ideas from which you can *later* select the best ones, the ones you wish to include in your final piece of writing. The principle that underlies brainstorming and freewriting is that ideas and associations flow best when they are uninterrupted by analysis and judgment.

capital letters, and so on. (Of course, if you feel comfortable using them, then by all means do so.) It means arranging the ideas that will appear in your paper, deciding which will come first, which second, and so on. The easiest way to do this is to study the ideas you have on your rough-idea sheet and *number them in the most effective order.* The following guidelines will help you decide what that order is:

> The introduction to your paper should identify the essential features of the issue and present a careful statement of your judgment.*
> If possible, this should be done in an imaginative way that arouses reader interest and creates a positive impression as it informs.
>
> The body of your paper should develop and support your judgment, presenting the various considerations that underlie that judgment and discussing the various questions and objections that might occur to critical readers. Useful patterns of organization for the body of the paper include *time order* (you might, for example, discuss the effects of an action in the order in which they would occur in time), *order of complexity* (simpler considerations first, followed by more complex ones), and *order of importance* (less important considerations first, followed by more important ones).
>
> The conclusion of your paper should reinforce the main idea—that is, your judgment. This reinforcement is usually not accomplished by direct repetition (except in rather long treatments—say, more than 3,000 words). Instead, you should use a more subtle method, such as the use of an apt quotation or a statement of your own that recalls the main idea without using the same words.

Decide what connecting words or phrases will make clear the relationships between your ideas, and add them to the numbers on your rough-idea sheet. The basic relationships among ideas in persuasive writing are *and* relationships, *but* relationships, and *therefore* relationships. These relationships exist whether or not they are expressed. By expressing them, you make it possible for your readers to move from one idea to another without confusion and help them understand your reasoning more easily. To indicate the basic relationships, you may use the words *and, but,* and *therefore* themselves or substitute words. Some common substitutes for *and* are *also, first, second, in addition, next, another,* and *finally.* For *but,* you can use *however, nevertheless, yet, in contrast,* and *on the other hand.* For *therefore,* you can use *so, consequently, accordingly, thus, as a result,* and *in conclusion.* Other relationship words that are helpful in making your writing more coherent are *for example* (to illustrate a point), *now* and *then* (to signal a time change), and *similarly* (to compare). At times, a single word or phrase will not do, and you will have to add a complete sentence to make the connection clear.

---

*Skilled writers often withhold the complete statement of the judgment until later in the paper, sometimes at the very end, but this approach is not recommended for beginning writers.

How to Achieve Emphasis (EMPH)

Emphasis is stress or prominence. A word, sentence, or paragraph has emphasis if it stands out from other words, sentences, or paragraphs in a piece of writing. Not every part is deserving of the same emphasis, so the careful writer controls the placement of emphasis. The following guidelines will help you exercise such control in your writing:

Assign an important idea more space than other ideas. If you discuss three considerations in a moral issue and give each consideration the same amount of space (say, a couple of sentences or a paragraph apiece), the subtle implication to your readers will be that all considerations are of equal importance. On the other hand, if you give one consideration more detailed treatment, that consideration will seem more important than the others. The space given to the development of each consideration should not be left to chance; it should be consciously chosen.

Assign an important idea better space than other ideas. Not every place in a piece of writing carries the same emphasis. Generally speaking, the end has the greatest emphasis because whatever is read last will usually be remembered longest. "End" in this context does not mean conclusion only. It means the final position of any sentence, any paragraph, or any section of a piece of writing (the body, for example). The construction of individual sentences that observe the principle of emphasis may be a little difficult for the beginning writer, but you should be able to make the final sentences of your paragraphs, the final paragraph of your body, and your conclusion more emphatic. The place of second greatest emphasis is the beginning, because first impressions tend to last. Accordingly, the beginnings of sentences, of paragraphs, or of any section of a piece of writing (the body, for example) are important places. If you have a number of considerations to discuss in the body of your paper, it will usually be possible to use both the beginning and the end positions to achieve maximum emphasis. For example, begin with the second most important consideration, then turn to the lesser considerations, and end with the most important one.

Use repetition, echo words, and underlining judiciously. (Echo words are words that do not repeat what was said but are so close in meaning that they recall it; *courage,* for example, might be used as an echo word for *bravery.*) The key word here is *judiciously.* To use any of these devices carelessly, particularly repetition, will distract and even offend the critical reader.

How to Develop Your Ideas (DEV)

Developing your ideas means adding more words, lengthening your treatment of the case or issue. However, unlike padding, developing is not adding words simply for the sake of adding them. It is *purposeful* enlargement of your treatment that enhances its persuasiveness by removing any confusion or misunderstanding your readers might experience, fulfilling their desire to know more about your judgment and the reasoning that underlies it, and answering any doubts or objections they might have. There are two steps to follow in the development of your ideas:

Look at your rough-idea sheet and determine which of your ideas might be misunderstood or disputed by your readers. To perform this step effectively, you must get beyond your own perspective. (From that perspective, every one of your ideas will seem unquestionable simply because it is your idea.) You must adopt a critical perspective and see your ideas as your readers, who are unfamiliar with them and uncommitted to them, will see them.

Decide which techniques of development will best overcome confusion or answer objections. The following techniques are especially helpful in a variety of situations:

Detailed description. This consists of a more specific presentation of the considerations in the case. For example, instead of merely stating that a certain consequence is likely to result, you would show why it is likely and exactly how it would happen, step-by-step.

Brief or extended illustration. This consists of offering examples, scenarios, or cases in point to support your assertions. Instead of saying that the effects of a certain action would be harmful to the people involved, you would give examples of the harm that would (or might) be done. Illustrations may be actual examples that occurred in similar situations or hypothetical examples (plausible speculations).

Definition. This technique is helpful whenever you are using a term in a special sense or in a way that might be misunderstood.

Comparison. This consists of evaluating the relative strengths and weaknesses of two or more different lines of reasoning about a case.

Explanation. This technique is useful for answering those questions that you anticipate your readers will ask. Common questions are why you consider a particular illustration typical, why you choose one interpretation over other possible ones, and why you believe that one consideration in a case (an obligation, for example) outweighs all others.

Tracing and summarizing. These techniques are more commonly used in advanced ethical analyses, but you may find them appropriate to some of your treatments. *Tracing* consists of briefly presenting the historical development of an idea or a perspective. *Summarizing* consists of presenting a capsule version of some material that is too long to use in its original form. One of the most common uses of it in ethical analysis is to present the reasoning of ethicists to reinforce your analysis of a particular case.

HOW TO WRITE READABLE PROSE (STYLE)

Readable prose is prose that people find interesting, even pleasurable, to read. To some extent, interest lies in the taste of the individual reader. What one person finds interesting will put another to sleep. Nevertheless, there are at least three qualities that tend to generate or at least increase enthusiasm among readers, qualities associated with energy and vitality rather than with dullness and monotony. Those qualities are *exactness, economy,* and *liveliness.* Here are some guidelines to help you achieve them in your writing.

TO ACHIEVE EXACTNESS

Avoid empty or overworked expressions. It is easy to acquire the habit of expressing your thoughts in clichés or in currently fashionable phrasing. To break that habit, take note of your language. If you find it filled with the kind of phrasing you hear many times each day, make an effort to substitute less predictable phrasing.

Prefer concrete, specific terms to abstract, general terms. It is not always possible in ethical analysis to avoid abstraction or generality, but it is important to do so whenever you can. Keep in mind that the purpose of writing in ethics, like the purpose of any writing, is to make your thoughts clear to your readers, not to befuddle them.

TO ACHIEVE ECONOMY

Choose words to communicate your thoughts, not to impress your readers. Many people have the notion that fancy language and jargon will make them seem knowledgeable. The truth is quite the opposite; such language only makes them seem foolish. The right approach was best summed up by the distinguished essayist and novelist George Orwell when he said, "Never use a long word where a short word will do."

Wherever possible without sacrificing meaning, reduce a sentence to a clause, a clause to a phrase, a phrase to a word. (This does not prevent you from developing your ideas. Development is adding content, not multiplying words unnecessarily.)

TO ACHIEVE LIVELINESS

Control the rhythm and pace of your phrasing. Rhythm refers to the melodiousness of your writing, pace to the relative speed at which it moves. By reading your writing *aloud,* you can get a good idea of whether it is lively to read, whether it not only looks good but sounds good as well. If your writing does not sound good when read aloud, try changing the phrasing of rough passages (to improve the rhythm) and moderating the sentence and paragraph length (to improve the pace).

Use vivid language in place of bland, colorless language. This guideline must be used with care, of course. Vividness can add a dramatic quality to your writing that will increase its liveliness, but if you use it carelessly, it will undermine exactness. To use it effectively, be sure the vivid expression does not convey an idea you cannot defend.

Vary your sentence style and your paragraph length. The essential ingredient in boredom is *sameness*. By reducing the degree of sameness in your writing, you overcome monotony and increase liveliness. Examine your sentences and paragraphs whenever you write. If the sentence length is unvaried, change it; make some sentences longer, some shorter. If all your *sentences* begin in much the same way, change the order of phrases or clauses or move an adverb around. Similarly, if your *paragraphs* are all the same length, and especially if they are all long, your paper will appear monotonous even before it is read. With a little skillful adjusting, you can usually achieve some variety in paragraph length without awkwardly separating related ideas. (A good average length for your paragraphs is ten lines, with variations from perhaps five to fifteen lines.)

One final note: Throughout this section we have been discussing rhetorical principles but have not mentioned grammar and usage. The reason for this is not that those concerns are unimportant, but that they cannot be treated adequately in a brief appendix. Critical readers may overlook an occasional lapse in grammar and usage. However, numerous errors will create a formidable distraction and suggest to readers that you are a careless person. Such a suggestion will hardly help your efforts to persuade readers of the soundness of your views. To make the best impression on your readers, see that you correct any errors in grammar and spelling before you complete your final draft. Word-processing tools that check for such errors, though helpful, are sometimes mistaken. A good dictionary and a composition handbook are indispensable tools for this task.

⌈ NOTES ⌉

CHAPTER ONE

1. Both cases are cited in John Leo, "On Society," *U.S. News and World Report,* July 21, 1997, p. 14.

2. G. K. Chesterton, *Orthodoxy* (Wheaton, IL: Harold Shaw, 1994; first published in 1908), 70.

3. Greg Brown, "Mutilated Voodoo Dolls Found in Delaware," *Oneonta* (New York) *Star,* July 23, 1982, p. 1.

4. "Couple Who Let Baby Die Guilty," *Binghamton* (New York) *Press,* May 18, 1982, p. A5.

5. The section "Making Discussion Meaningful" is copyrighted by MindPower, Inc., and used with permission.

6. The section "Avoiding Plagiarism" is copyrighted by MindPower, Inc., and used with permission.

7. *Binghamton Press,* August 7, 1982, p. A4.

8. James Brooke of the *New York Times,* "Canada Wants Cigarette Packs to Bear Photos . . . ," *Tampa Tribune,* January 23, 2000, Nation/World, p. 11.

9. *Burden of Proof,* CNN-TV, November 30, 1995.

10. "Zoo Kills Two Bears for Lack of a Home," *Oneonta Star,* May 15, 1982, p. 1.

11. "Right to Liberty," *New York Times,* April 25, 1982, p. 49.

CHAPTER TWO

1. http://www.gallup.com/poll/1681/moral-issues.aspx; accessed May 11, 2010.

2. *Research on the Effects of Television Advertising on Children: A Review of the Literature and Recommendations for Further Research.* National Science Foundation, 1977, pp. i–ii.

3. *Facts on File: 1971,* Vol. XXXI, No. 1588, p. 248.

4. *Facts on File: 1956,* Vol. XVI, No. 800, p. 68.

CHAPTER THREE

1. Among the books that set forth the assumptions and approaches of values clarification are S. B. Simon et al., *Values Clarification,* rev. edition (New York: Hart, 1978); also L. E. Raths et al., *Values and Teaching,* 2nd edition (Columbus, OH: Merrill, 1978).

2. Carl R. Rogers, *On Becoming a Person: A Therapist's View of Psychotherapy* (Boston: Houghton Mifflin, 1961), 22.

3. Ibid., 60–61.

4. Ibid., 119.

5. Allan Bloom, *The Closing of the American Mind* (New York: Simon & Schuster, 1987), 175, 228.

6. William J. Doherty, *Soul Searching: Why Psychotherapy Must Promote Moral Responsibility* (New York: Basic Books, 1995), 40–41.

7. *Today Show,* NBC-TV, November 14, 1995.

8. "White Slavery, 1972," *Time,* June 5, 1972, p. 24.

9. Lucy Morgan, "A Funeral Leaves a Town Torn," *St. Petersburg Times,* July 27, 1991, p. B1.

10. "Mummy Removed from Public View," *New York Times,* September 10, 1972, p. 42.

11. "He's Cashing in on the Jobless Trend," *Los Angeles Times,* April 21, 1982, Part V, p. 1.

12. "Nassau Officer Pleads Guilty . . . ," *New York Times,* April 18, 1982, p. 45.

13. "Two Accused of Selling Unborn Babe," *Oneonta Star,* July 23, 1982, p. 20.

CHAPTER FOUR

1. Andrew P. Morrison, *The Culture of Shame* (New York: Ballantine, 1996).

2. John Grisham, *The Testament* (New York: Dell, 1999), 480.

3. T. W. Adorno et al., *The Authoritarian Personality* (New York: Harper & Brothers, 1950), 147–48.

4. Else Frenkel-Brunswik, "Prejudice in Children," in *Psychology in Action,* edited by Fred McKinney (New York: Macmillan, 1967), 276–90.

5. Samuel Johnson, quoted in *The Quotable Johnson: A Topical Compilation of His Wit and Moral Wisdom,* edited by Stephen C. Danckert (San Francisco: Ignatius Press, 1992), 39.

6. Elizabeth Loftus and Katherine Ketcham, *Witness for the Defense* (New York: St. Martin's Press, 1991), 57.

7. "Thompson Lauds Grant for Lewdness," *Denver Post,* September 4, 1995, p. A2.

8. See "Letters," *U.S. News and World Report,* December 27, 1999, p. 5.

9. David L. Wheeler, "Researchers Debate Ethics of Payments for Human Subjects," *Chronicle of Higher Education,* August 14, 1991, p. A7.

10. Douglas Pasternak and Peter Cary, "Tales from the Crypt," *U.S. News and World Report,* September 18, 1995, pp. 70–82.

11. "Priest Picketed for Drowning Cats," *Oneonta Star,* February 19, 1982, p. 2.

CHAPTER FIVE

1. Clyde Kluckhohn, *Mirror for Man* (New York: McGraw-Hill, 1949), 18–19.

2. May and Abraham Edel, *Anthropology and Ethics* (Springfield, IL: Thomas, 1959), 88–89.

3. Ruth Benedict, *Patterns of Culture* (Cambridge, MA: Riverside Press; and Boston: Houghton Mifflin, 1934), 45–46.

4. Ibid., 210, 216.

5. Ibid., 130–72.

6. Colin M. Turnbull, *The Mountain People* (New York: Simon & Schuster, 1972).

7. Kluckhohn, *Mirror for Man,* 41.

8. Edel and Edel, *Anthropology and Ethics,* 88–89.

9. Mortimer J. Adler, *Desires, Right and Wrong: The Ethics of Enough* (New York: Macmillan, 1991), 193–94.

10. Mortimer J. Adler, *Truth in Religion: The Plurality of Religions and the Unity of Truth* (Macmillan, 1990), 156.

11. Cited in Hadley Arkes, "German Judges & Undue Burdens," *Crisis,* July–August, 1994, p. 16.

12. Debbie Taylor, "China Dolls," *Caracas* (Venezuela) *Guardian Weekly,* November 27, 1994.

CHAPTER SIX

1. These examples are taken from the Tao (the "way") in C. S. Lewis, *The Abolition of Man*, softcover edition (New York: Macmillan, 1965), 97–121.

2. "Statements on Standards of Professional Conduct," as amended in January 2002. http://www.theaha.org/pubs/standard.htm#Introduction.

3. Mortimer J. Adler, *Ten Philosophical Mistakes* (New York: Macmillan, 1985), 126.

4. Stephen Burd, "U.S. Won't Back Creation of Human Embryos for Research," *Chronicle of Higher Education*, December 14, 1994, p. A32.

5. "The Inhuman Use of Human Beings: A Statement on Embryo Research by the Ramsey Colloquium," *First Things*, January 1995, pp. 17–21.

6. Joseph Fletcher, *Situation Ethics: The New Morality* (Philadelphia: Westminster Press, 1966), 44, 39.

7. Norman L. Geisler, "The Collapse of Modern Atheism," in Roy Abraham Varghese, editor, *The Intellectuals Speak Out About God* (Dallas: Lewis & Stanley, 1984), 149.

CHAPTER SEVEN

1. Errol E. Harris, "Respect for Persons," *Daedalus*, Spring 1969, p. 113.

2. Geoffrey Edsall, "A Positive Approach to the Problem of Human Experimentation," *Daedalus*, Spring 1969, pp. 470–71.

3. Yahlin Chang, "Was It Virtually Good for You?" *Newsweek*, January 1, 2000, p. 71.

4. "Selling to School Kids," *Consumer Reports*, May 1995, pp. 327–33.

5. Jack Anderson, "Army Scientists Move Closer to Orwell's 1984," *Oneonta Star*, August 5, 1972, p. 5.

CHAPTER EIGHT

1. Nancy Mathis, "On Behalf of Nation, an Apology," *Houston Chronicle*, May 16, 1997.

2. Cited by American Center for Law and Justice (www.aclj.org), January 13, 2000.

3. James Q. Wilson, *The Moral Sense* (New York: Free Press, 1993), as excerpted in *Education Week*, September 8, 1993, p. 41.

CHAPTER NINE

1. Mortimer J. Adler, *The Great Ideas: A Lexicon of Western Thought* (New York: Macmillan, 1992), 838–39.

2. Ibid., 110.

3. W. D. Ross, *The Right and the Good* (Indianapolis: Hackett, 1988; first published in 1930), 20–23.

4. "Hollow Holiness," *Time*, August 14, 1972, p. 45.

5. Deborah Lutterbeck, "No Sacred Cows," *Common Cause*, Spring 1995, pp. 4–5.

6. "Cop Suspended for Nude Photos," *Oneonta Star*, July 31, 1982, p. 9.

7. "Hundreds Reply to Pregnancy Cost Ad," *New York Times*, August 13, 1972, p. 67.

8. *Parade*, September 21, 1997, p. 16.

CHAPTER TEN

1. Douglas Pasternak and Peter Cary, "Tales from the Crypt," *U.S. News and World Report*, September 18, 1995, pp. 70–82.

2. *60 Minutes,* CBS-TV, August 28, 1993.

3. Henry K. Beecher, "Scarce Resources and Medical Advancement," *Daedalus,* Spring 1969, pp. 280–81.

CHAPTER ELEVEN

1. Henry B. Veatch, *Rational Man: A Modern Interpretation of Aristotelian Ethics* (Bloomington: Indiana University Press, 1962), 160.

2. Stanton E. Samenow, *Inside the Criminal Mind* (New York: Times Books, 1984), 180–81.

3. "Mind Hunter," *Dateline NBC,* November 1, 1995.

4. "Seven-Year-Old Boy Charged . . . ," *Oneonta Star,* July 22, 1982, p. 2.

5. "Husband Says Wife Begged for Death," *Oneonta Star,* July 31, 1982, p. 2.

6. "Five Teens Charged in Fatal Derailment," *Oneonta Star,* July 9, 1982, p. 1.

CONTEMPORARY ETHICAL CONTROVERSIES

EDUCATION

1. "'Lesbianism' Charges Prompt Course Review," *Oneonta Star,* July 19, 1982, p. 2.

2. *New York Times,* November 26, 1972, p. 41.

MEDIA AND THE ARTS

1. Robert M. Liebert and Joyce Sprafkin, *The Early Window: Effects of Television on Children and Youth* (New York: Pergamon Press, 1988), 147.

SEX

1. "Under the Yum-Yum Tree?" *Binghamton Press,* December 12, 1972, p. 1.

2. Boyce Rensberger, "Clinics for Sex Therapy Proliferate over Nation," *New York Times,* October 29, 1972, p. 1.

3. Ibid., p. 66.

4. Ibid.

5. "1986: A Space Odyssey to Mars," *Time,* December 11, 1972, p. 47.

6. Quoted in *Chronicle of Higher Education,* September 22, 1993, p. B3, from an article in *Harper's,* September 1993.

GOVERNMENT

1. "SBA Sex Palace Loan Irks Reformers," *Oneonta Star,* June 10, 1982, p. 2.

2. "U.S. Recruited Nazis in Spy Network," *Oneonta Star,* May 17, 1982, p. 1.

3. http://www.antislavery.org/homepage/antislavery/modern.htm; accessed December 3, 2006.

4. Walter Sullivan, "The Lady Was 2,000 Years Old," *New York Times,* August 6, 1972, Section 4, p. 9.

LAW

1. "Taser Gun 'Wilts' Feisty Prisoners," *Oneonta Star,* June 26, 1982, p. 1.

2. "The Lawyer of Last Resort," *Time,* May 17, 1982, p. 64.

BUSINESS

1. *Today Show,* NBC-TV, December 2, 1995.
2. "Products Unsafe at Home Are Still Unloaded Abroad," *New York Times,* August 22, 1982, Section 4, p. 9.
3. "U.S. Charges Nineteen . . . ," *Oneonta Star,* June 23, 1982, p. 1.
4. Jack Anderson, "Double Suicide," *Oneonta Star,* November 24, 1972, p. 4.

MEDICINE

1. *Dateline,* NBC-TV, November 1, 1995.
2. "Burn Victim Shuffled for Lack of Insurance," *Oneonta Star,* May 10, 1982, p. 12.
3. "'Doctor, Do We Have a Choice?'" *New York Times Magazine,* January 30, 1972, p. 24.
4. "Philosophical Reflections on Human Experimentation," *Daedalus,* Spring 1969, p. 244.
5. "Society Speed," *Time,* December 18, 1972, pp. 76–77.

SCIENCE

1. Rick Scott, "Indians Charge Heritage Plundered, Flooded Out," *Oneonta Star,* October 2, 1972, p. 1.
2. Jane Brody, "All in the Name of Science," *New York Times,* July 30, 1972, Section 4, p. 6.
3. "Philosophical Reflections on Human Experimentation," *Daedalus,* Spring 1969, p. 229f.
4. "The Ethical Design of Human Experiments," *Daedalus,* Spring 1969, p. 529.
5. Ibid., p. 524.

WAR

1. "Now, the Death Ray?" *Time,* September 4, 1972, p. 46.

⌐ INDEX ⌐